THE TURBULENT QUAKER OF SHAFTESBURY

Oil painting of John Rutter (1796–1851) by Monsieur Jacqueline, reproduced by kind permission of Rutters Solicitors and members of the Rutter family.

THE TURBULENT QUAKER OF SHAFTESBURY

John Rutter (1796–1851)

Author, Printer, Publisher, Social and Political Reformer,
Public Servant, Philanthropist and Lawyer

JOHN STUTTARD

HOBNOB PRESS
for the
SHAFTESBURY & DISTRICT
HISTORICAL SOCIETY

This book is dedicated to Raymond Simpson, Librarian & Archivist of The Gold Hill Museum, Shaftesbury & District Historical Society, who assisted with the research of material and information about the life of John Rutter.

First published in the United Kingdom in 2018
on behalf of the Shaftesbury & District Historical Society CIO
by The Hobnob Press,
8 Lock Warehouse, Severn Road, Gloucester GL1 2GA
www.hobnobpress.co.uk

British Library Cataloguing in Publication Data
A catalogue record for this book is available from the British Library

ISBN 978-1-906978-63-1 (hardback)
978-1-906978-64-8 (paperback)

Typeset in Scala.
Typesetting and origination by John Chandler

Printed by Lightning Source

Contents

THE SHAFTESBURY & DISTRICT HISTORICAL SOCIETY CIO
Registered charity No. 1156273

THE OBJECT OF The Shaftesbury & District Historical Society charitable incorporated organisation is to encourage the appreciation, study and enjoyment of history, especially that local to Shaftesbury, Dorset and its environs, and thereby to advance the education of members of the Society and of the public of all ages and backgrounds.

The Society owns, maintains and operates Gold Hill Museum, which comprises a collection of artefacts reflecting the history and life of the area; an archives centre and library of books and documents of local historical interest; and a seminar room for lectures and other events.

Entry to the museum is free. In addition to the regular displays, there are at least two temporary exhibitions each year. The archives centre and library are open to members of the public for research purposes. Lectures are held throughout the year and, for both adults and children, there is a learning and outreach education programme, some elements of which are conducted with the Shaftesbury Abbey Museum and Gardens.

The museum and its activities are managed by volunteers, who organise a programme of lifelong learning, cooperating with other groups in the area and with the local community.

The Shaftesbury & District Historical Society owns manuscripts, letters, publications and other material relating to John Rutter. Some of these are held at Gold Hill Museum. Many boxes of material, also owned by the Shaftesbury & District Historical Society, are stored in Dorchester at the Dorset History Centre which has the proper environmental conditions to look after historical material in a secure building staffed by professionally trained staff. During the preparation of this book, with the agreement of the Archivist of the Dorset History Centre, these boxes have been brought to the Gold Hill Museum in Shaftesbury to facilitate the research and the preparation of this biography.

Acknowledgements and Thanks

I AM GRATEFUL to members of the extended Rutter family for their help and support in this project. I am particularly grateful to Simon Rutter for his pump-priming with the loan of four books and booklets: *The Rutter Family*, edited and typed by Elizabeth Beaven Rutter, John Rutter's granddaughter, from notes made by her father, John Farley Rutter, who was John Rutter's eldest surviving son; *The Family of Le Roter or Rutter*, compiled and edited by W. Huggins Wingate in 1966, published privately for the family; *Descendants of John Farley Rutter* by Francis Rutter, published in 2004 privately for the family; and *Corruption and Reform: Municipal Government in the Borough of Shaftesbury (1750–1835)* by F.C. Hopton, published by Shaftesbury & District Historical Society in 1975. I am also grateful to Anne Rutter and to her four sons, John, Paul, Michael and George, for stimulating my interest in John Rutter through their kind donation of *Delineations of Fonthill & Its Abbey*.

I could not have completed this work without the tireless and enthusiastic involvement of Raymond Simpson, Librarian & Archivist of The Gold Hill Museum, Shaftesbury & District Historical Society, who spent very many hours searching the internet for references to John Rutter, the Rutter family and the various subject areas. Ray also visited Dorset History Centre with me and provided information and illustrations from Gold Hill Museum and elsewhere. He further improved the quality of illustrations for the purpose of reproduction in this book. The research was a joint effort and I am grateful to him for the significant time he spent and the good humour that we enjoyed while undertaking this work. He deserves a very special mention for his contribution to the compilation of the John Rutter story and its successful completion. The finished work is dedicated to him.

I am indebted to many others who assisted with this research: Sidney Blackmore, Secretary of The Beckford Society; Dr Mark Forrest, Archivist of the Dorset History Centre, Dorchester; staff at the Shaftesbury Library; Dr Jenny Wilding, Hon Curator, Mere Museum; Steven Hobbs, Archivist, and Tom Plant of the Wiltshire and Swindon History Centre; The Curator, Lisa Brown, and Heather Ault, Sandy Haynes and James Kay of The Wiltshire Museum, The Wiltshire Archaeological and Natural History Society (WANHS), Devizes; Melissa Atkinson, Special Collections Curator, Library

& Archive of the Society of Friends, London; Louise Benson, Archivist of the Grosvenor Estate; Gary Best, Warden, and Kate Rogers, Collections Manager, of the New Room (John Wesley's Chapel), Bristol; Bella Hoare (and her husband Johnnie Gallop) for allowing me access to an original copy of volume IV Part I of *The Modern History of South Wiltshire*, written by James Everard, Baron Arundell and Sir Richard Colt Hoare, Bt., the brother of one of her ancestors; historian, researcher and author, Lawrence Clark; historian, author and journalist Richard Thomas; and The Law Society, London (via Stephen Levinson). In the Library of Stourhead, now owned by the National Trust, facilitated by the Operations Manager Emily Blanshard and under the watchful eye of Conservation Assistant John Hayward, I was able to inspect an original copy of Sir Richard Colt Hoare's *The History of Modern Wiltshire. Hundred of Dunworth and Vale of Noddre* (1829). Shaftesbury architect, Philip Proctor, shared his thoughts with me on the cause of the collapse of the main tower of Fonthill Abbey, bringing a new perspective to this calamitous occurrence. Samuel Rutter kindly sent me a copy of his dissertation submitted in 2014 to the University of Gloucestershire entitled *Shaftesbury: Problem Politics and the Impact of Municipal Corporations Act, 1775–1845*; Ben Rutter allowed me sight of his late father Jo's collection of personal letters written by John and Anne Rutter to and from their children. All this provided interesting material and a very helpful check on key facts and information. The image of the oil painting of John Rutter has been used on the front cover of the book with the permission of Rutters Solicitors and members of the Rutter family. Rutters Solicitors generously paid for the photography, by Pete Jenkins of PDMS Photography, of the oil painting and other images owned by the Shaftesbury & District Historical Society and Dorset History Centre. I am grateful to Charles Rutter, senior partner of Rutter & Rutter, solicitors in Wincanton, for his comments on the text and for allowing Pete Jenkins to photograph the sketches of the portraits of John and Anne Rutter and the photograph of their son John Farley Rutter. I am also grateful to Pete Jenkins for photographing many of the illustrations in this book and for enhancing the quality of many others. Thanks also to Audrey Hart-Roy (nee Rutter) for the advertisement of John Rutter's shop in Wincanton and to Jenny Lord for information about Shaftesbury's first Quaker Meeting House, in St. James. Finally, I am grateful to the following for reading drafts of the text and for their editorial comments: Jon Millington, author of *William Beckford: A Bibliography* and founding Editor of the *Beckford Journal*; members of the Rutter family; Ray Simpson; and my wife, Lesley.

This book has been written as part of research into the history of Shaftesbury and its interesting inhabitants among whom John Rutter made a very special contribution. Net sales proceeds from the sale of this book will be donated to The Shaftesbury & District Historical Society, the registered charity which owns Gold Hill Museum, maintains an archive of historical information about the town of Shaftesbury and the surrounding area, and advances the education of members of the Society and of the public of all ages and backgrounds.

Sir John Stuttard, Shaftesbury
October 2018

Live Adventurously
When choices arise, do you take the way that offers the fullest opportunity for the use of your gifts in the service of God and the community?

Let your life speak.

From Advices & Queries, The Yearly Meeting of the Religious Society of Friends (Quakers) in Britain, 1995

John Rutter's book plate with a design of three garbs (wheatsheaves) taken from the coat of arms of the 12th century Earl of Chester from whom the family's arms were derived and from whom he is believed to have been descended

Detail of Ordnance Survey large-scale mapping of Shaftesbury, 1901 edition. Key places mentioned in the text are as follows:

1 The Benedictine Abbey, founded 888
2 Grosvenor Arms Hotel, formerly the Red Lion
3 John Rutter's stationery and chemists' businesses and Subscription Library, shown on the map as 'P.O.'
4 The Town Hall, built 1827
5 Layton House, formerly Layton Cottage
6 Friends Meeting House, built 1746
7 The Shaftesbury Sunday and Infant School, built 1839, shown on the map as 'Meth. Chap. (Prim.)'

Alderman William Beckford, (1709-1770) by John Dixon, printed for Carington Bowles, mezzotint, published 1770, NPG D19348, © National Portrait Gallery, London

William Beckford, of Fonthill Abbey, (1760–1844) by T. A. Dean after the portrait by Joshua Reynolds which forms the frontispiece to Beckford's Recollections of an Excursion to the Monasteries of Alcobaca and Batalha (1835) (Sidney Blackmore)

I
Introduction

IN THE EYES of the establishment – the political clique that ruled Shaftesbury: the magistrates, the judges, Earl Grosvenor's agents and the Church of England – John Rutter was *turbulent*. He sought to initiate change at a time in the 1820s and 1830s when change was in the air but was not universally recognised or accepted. He could be very difficult and abrasive. He stuck to his guns and rarely sought compromise. Even his Quaker Friends in Shaftesbury discontinued his membership of the Society.

Yet his character was far removed from the dictionary description of the word *turbulent:* 'tempestuous, stormy, unstable, unsettled, tumultuous, explosive, in turmoil, full of upheavals, full of conflict, full of ups and downs, roller-coaster, chaotic, full of confusion'. He was, actually, quite the opposite in his dealings with family, friends and the causes he espoused. He was, to them, reflective, a clear thinker, dedicated, meticulous, steady and caring. He was avaricious for knowledge. He had strong beliefs, unwavering moral principles and a great ability to communicate and to relate to people. He was public spirited and possessed boundless energy.

But to those who were corrupt or nepotistic or who abused their power, he was a fierce and determined opponent. To them he was *The Turbulent Quaker*.

I first came across John Rutter when Lesley and I purchased Layton House in Shaftesbury, Dorset in 2011 from the Rutter family. John Rutter was their ancestor who coincidentally had rented Layton House in the 1830s and 1840s, from Robert Grosvenor, the 1st Marquess of Westminster. John Rutter had moved from Bristol to Shaftesbury in 1811, exactly 200 years before we acquired our Shaftesbury home.

Anne Rutter and her four sons, John, Paul, Michael and George, kindly gave us a limited first edition copy of John Rutter's classic work *Delineations of Fonthill & Its Abbey*. This magnificent book is a wonderfully illustrated history and description of the grandiose, cathedral-like mansion created by the controversial author and art collector, William Beckford, at the turn of the 19th century. Our copy of *Delineations* was special as it was inscribed 'John Rutter to his son John Farley Rutter'. This copy is a precious legacy of Shaftesbury's Quaker printer, author and publisher, who was also a political and social reformer, public servant, philanthropist and an accomplished lawyer.

My interest in William Beckford had been stimulated by the sight of the statue of his father, also named William, in the Great Hall of Guildhall in the City of London. The father, known as *The Alderman*, was, allegedly, the wealthiest Commoner in England. In the statue he is depicted as Lord Mayor, with one hand in the air, gesturing while speaking. Underneath is the text of the impromptu address that *The Alderman* gave in 1770 to George III when seeking Parliamentary reform. The stunned monarch was shocked at the impudence of this unplanned speech and did not know how to respond. In earlier times, the Lord Mayor might well have been taken to the Tower. But in the Age of Enlightenment, Beckford returned to the City and was given a hero's welcome. A few weeks later, having caught a chill while visiting his country estate at Fonthill, some 10 miles from Shaftesbury, *The Alderman* died. As a mark of enormous respect, the City's Court of Common Council voted £1,000 (a staggering £174,000 in 2018 prices) for a statue of Beckford to be placed in Guildhall. His is the only statue of a past Lord Mayor in Guildhall and, possibly, it was the first statue to be erected in the City's Great Hall. Today, *The Alderman* is surrounded by England's most distinguished political and military heroes: William Pitt the Elder (later Earl Chatham), William Pitt the Younger, Wellington, Nelson and Churchill. When Beckford died he bequeathed his Fonthill property, his sugar estates in Jamaica and £1 million (about £174 million in 2018 prices) in investments and cash to his ten year old son, William.

The younger William Beckford was an aesthete, educated in a love of music, literature, the fine arts and architecture. He knew how to spend money – on a luxurious lifestyle and on beautiful objects. His collection of paintings, furniture and objets d'art is now scattered among the world's great museums and galleries and some stately homes. Bisexual, William Beckford is a controversial character, spending many years in voluntary exile on the continent after revelations of an alleged affair with a young boy, William 'Kitty' Courtenay, later the 9th Earl of Devon. William Beckford is also known as an author and the builder of the extraordinary neo-Gothic Fonthill Abbey where he lived for almost 20 years at the beginning of the 19th century, having demolished his father's attractive Palladian mansion, Fonthill Splendens, in 1807. As a result of his extravagant lifestyle and declining sugar revenues, Beckford was obliged to sell the Abbey in 1822. Three years later, in December 1825, the huge central tower collapsed, destroying most of the building. But, prior to this, the grandeur and splendour of the Abbey, with its ornately decorated interior, had been captured in John Rutter's *Delineations of Fonthill & Its Abbey*, which was published in 1823.

I began reading about and researching the very different, but both fascinating, lives of the two Beckfords. This resulted in my presenting a paper on *The Alderman* to the Guildhall Historical Association in the City of London in October 2016. I subsequently gave lectures on both Beckfords to the Shaftesbury & District Historical Society and to other organisations.

But my attention drifted to John Rutter, the author, publisher and printer of *Delineations*. The more I read about him and the more I researched, the more interested I became in his life and his achievements. Orphaned at the age of ten, he was brought up in the Christian Quaker tradition by his older sisters in Bristol. Aged fifteen, he moved to Shaftesbury and, after serving an apprenticeship, he struck out on his own, initially as a stationer. Rutter was something of a polymath: printer, bookseller, author, publisher, political and social reformer, public servant, philanthropist and lawyer. Apart from publishing some extraordinarily high quality and collectable publications, of which *Delineations of Fonthill Abbey* is the most well-known, he was a great political and social reformer. He fought the corrupt and nepotistic political clique in Shaftesbury with its pocket borough which returned two MPs to Parliament under the patrimony of Earl Grosvenor. He was a devout Christian, a total abstainer, an abolitionist and a practising Quaker, who was later disowned by the Shaftesbury Friends for holding Bible readings outside the Meeting House. Yet, he continued to attend their Meetings for Worship. He was also an accomplished lawyer bearing the name of two firms of solicitors which still practise today in Shaftesbury, Gillingham and Wincanton. His life was cut short, aged just 54, as a result of being thrown from his carriage. He was interred in the Quaker burial ground in St James, Shaftesbury, next to the Friends Meeting House which had been erected in 1746 and which later became a private house. Interestingly, his death was recorded in the Friends' Burial Notes as 'not a member'.

I concluded that this fascinating life merited further research and a biography.

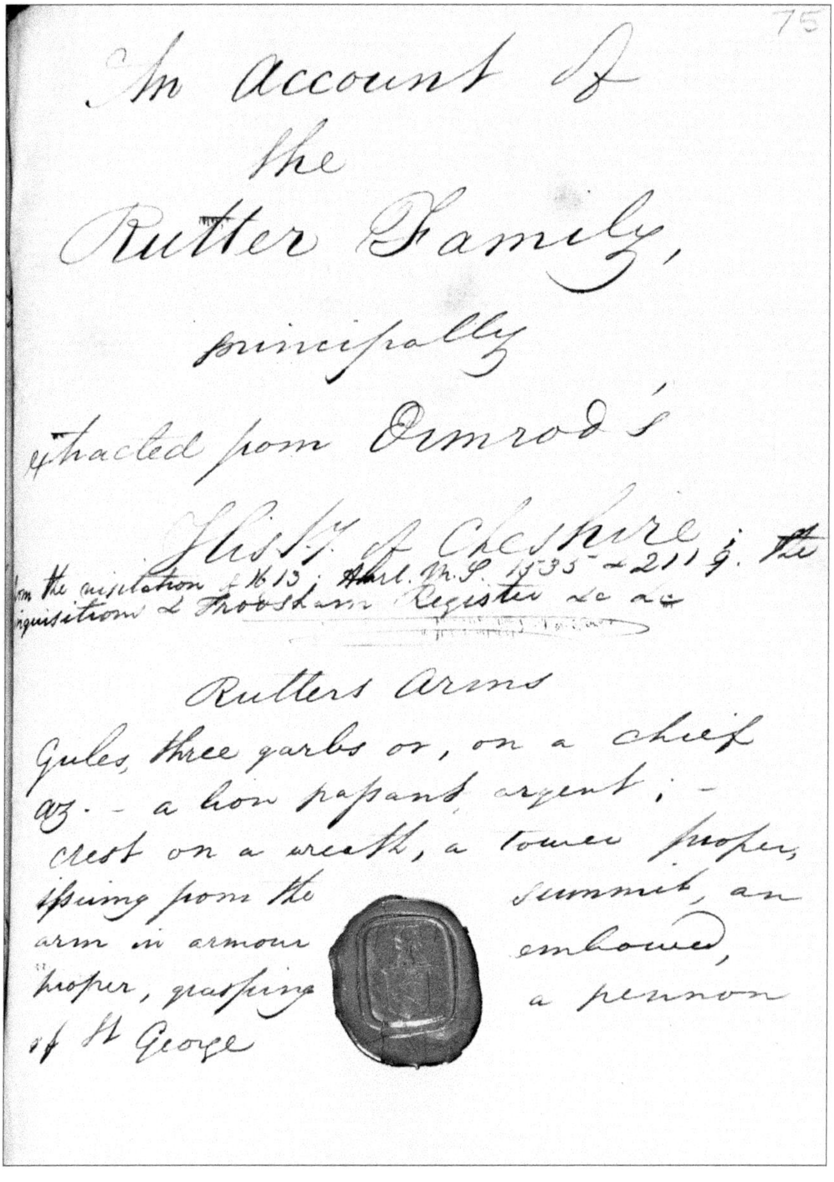

75

An Account of
the
Rutter Family,
principally
extracted from Ormrod's
Hist.y of Cheshire; from the visitation of 1613; Harl. M.S. 1535 & 2119; the
inquisitions & Frodsham Register &c &c

Rutters Arms
Gules, three garbs or, on a chief
az. – a lion passant argent; –
crest on a wreath, a tower proper,
issuing from the summit, an
arm in armour embowed,
proper, grasping a pennon
of St George

An Account of the Rutter Family (S&DHS, D.H.C., D-SHS/Box 41.3387)

2

Family Background and Early Days

FOR 350 YEARS, members of the Rutter family have been Quakers. Strongly held religious beliefs have evidenced themselves through the generations in simple values, known as 'testimonies'. These testimonies include equality and justice, peace, truth and integrity, simplicity and sustainability.[1]

For those not familiar with the ways of the Religious Society of Friends, Quakers believe in the Holy Bible, that God is in everyone and that each human being is of unique worth. They place great reliance on conscience as a basis for morality. Thus, over the years, honesty, integrity, moderation, care for the poor, equality of opportunity, education for all, political reform, opposition to war, liberal thinking and dissent have all been found in some measure in Quaker households.

The subject of this book, John Rutter, possessed these attributes in abundance. He was inspired and driven by a belief in God, by truth, by diligence and by purpose.

The precise origin and meaning of the name 'Rutter' remains obscure. An account of the family's history, *The Family of Le Roter or Rutter,* was published privately in 1966. This was based largely on a manuscript book, *An Account of the Rutter Family,* written by John Farley Rutter (1824–99), which was edited and produced in typed form as *The Rutter Family* by his daughter, Elizabeth Beaven Rutter (1857–1942).[2]

It describes the derivation of Rutter from Peter le Clerc (alias Pyers le Roter). Although not proven, he is referred to as a descendant of Hugh d'Avranches who was made Earl of Chester[3] after William the Conqueror's horrendous harrying of the North in the winter of 1069/70.

It is recorded that Pyers le Roter became secretary to the Palatine Earl of Chester from whom, in about 1200, he obtained the township of Thornton en le Mores in Cheshire. The seal which was affixed to the relevant charter has three garbs (wheat sheaves). This is the origin of the Rutter coat of arms in which 'a lion passant in chief, Argent'[4] (a silver lion walking, occupying the top third of the shield) was added.

The name Rutter replaced le Roter in the late 14th century.[5] For several centuries, from the reign of Edward I[6], the family lived in Cheshire where they owned land, including the manor of Kingsley Hall, Frodsham, not far from Thornton-le-Moors. Successive generations of Rutters were baptised and buried at Frodsham parish church.[7] In 1660, one Samuel Rutter became Bishop of Sodor & Man[8].

The family's involvement with the Quaker movement began soon after the Society of Friends grew in number in Cheshire in the mid-1660s. This was not an easy time for Quakers, who were persecuted for their beliefs and for nonconformity.

Born in 1661 and the heir to Kingsley Hall, young Thomas Rutter (the great grandfather of John Rutter) rebelled against the established Church of England. Although he had been baptized at Frodsham church in 1670, he joined the Friends and was disinherited by his father, Richard.[9] This show of defiance and rejection of the establishment are expressions of rebellious traits that seem prevalent in the Rutter genes. It has been recorded that, five generations earlier, Thomas Rutter (1540–1594) was estranged from the church after becoming connected with dissenters.[10] And, as will become apparent in due course, these traits were also very prominent in the character of John Rutter, who lived some 150 years later. Richard Rutter sold Kingsley Hall in November 1700.[11]

Thomas's fourth child, Benjamin (1699–1768), moved to Bristol in 1720 and made a comfortable living as a bellows and brush maker, based in Little Wine Street.[12] One might speculate as to the reasons for his leaving Cheshire. Benjamin was not the eldest son and, perhaps therefore, not the most advantaged when it came to inheriting family property, if there was any to be passed down by his parents, following Thomas's disinheritance. In addition, the second and third generations of Quakers were being encouraged to move away from agriculture towards trade. The burden of tithes and subsequent distraints, together with imprisonment for non-payment of them, were all tied up with the land. It was easier to levy tithe directly on land than on trade. Then, if a Friend was imprisoned in the late summer, the consequences of not being able to harvest the crop were much greater than absence from a shop where the wife and children could come to the rescue.[13]

At that time, the economy and the population of Bristol were expanding, buoyed by the growing triangular trade with Africa and the Americas in slaves, sugar and tobacco, with resultant employment and prosperity. By 1700, Bristol had become the second largest town in England and the second largest port in the British Isles. In 1687, 240 ships discharged cargo in Bristol; by 1717, some 30 years later, the number had increased to 375. These totals understate the growth in the local economy as, during this time, the average size of ships also increased.[14]

Thus, in the early 18th century, there were considerable career prospects in the city. Benjamin was 21 years of age in 1720 and, reaching the age of majority, with no ties, like so many young men over the centuries, he was free to leave home to take advantage of opportunities elsewhere. Still further, he would have been welcomed by the Bristol Quaker community which, at that time, was one of the largest in England, estimated in 1715 at between 1,720 and 2,000 Friends.[15] In Bristol, as he settled down and as his business thrived, Benjamin Rutter followed his father's beliefs as a Quaker. But this was not without a minor hiccup. Adopting the growing familiar family expression of nonconformity, in 1727 he married another Quaker, Jane Rutty (1708–1749), in a church ceremony rather than in the Monthly Meeting of Friends. Benjamin was summoned to attend the next Friends Meeting, where the minutes record that 'he acknowledged the rashness of his proceeding and that it has troubled him very much, and in general he hoped to be more careful of his conduct in all respects, desiring the advice and help of his friends if they observed him to act contrary to this resolution, in which we hope he is sincere'.[16]

Then, in 1739, a whirlwind hit Bristol and the Rutter family. John Wesley came to the city preaching for the first time on 2 April. This caused such a sensation that Jane Rutter was inspired to hear him speak.[17] Wesley was asked to create a 'New Room' for the religious societies which met in Bristol and,

Wesley's New Room Chapel at Bristol (The New Room)

after a foundation stone was laid on 12 May, a fund-raising began. A plot in the Horsefair was purchased and work commenced on altering the building on it. This house was rented by a strong-minded Quaker called Sarah Perrin, who became very involved with John and Charles Wesley and who, one suspects, had links with the Rutters. This building is, today, the oldest Methodist Chapel in the world. Above the chapel are rooms where Wesley and other preachers stayed. These rooms now house an attractive and informative museum.

The New Room opened in the autumn of 1739. Sarah Perrin became its housekeeper in 1743 and, although not officially recognised, a Methodist preacher. She was heavily involved in working with both John and Charles. In 1752 she married their right-hand man, John Jones, who was the first chief master of Kingswood School, of which more below.[18]

Being unmarried, Wesley was often entertained at private homes for lunch, tea or supper and this hospitality was usually accompanied by religious conversations and prayers.[19] Jane Rutter invited Wesley to her house and it is reported that he 'frequently visited her'.[20] An entry in Wesley's Journal of 2 July 1739 records 'Mrs Rutter, supper, conversed, singing: 11.15'.[21] A further entry of 11 July 1739 records 'G. Whitefield baptised Jane Rutter'[22], an act which cannot have pleased Benjamin as baptism is not part of the Quaker custom.

George Whitefield was one of the greatest preachers of the 18th century and he was the first to preach in the open air in Bristol in 1739. He had been a student in the so-called 'Holy Club' run by the Wesleys in Oxford and whose members were nicknamed 'Methodists' (partly because of their methodical religious lifestyle, which involved setting aside regular times for prayer, Bible study and public worship). It was Whitefield's constant references to his time as 'an Oxford Methodist' that led to him and John Wesley's followers being called Methodists. This was not a name they welcomed because they were not seeking to create a new denomination but rather a revival in the Church of England. Whitefield revisited Bristol in July 1739 to see how John was getting on. Hence he was present in the city to baptise Jane.[23]

Jane Rutter made her house available not just to Wesley but to any poor Methodist converts, even lending them her husband's clothes. This was very much in line with what John Wesley was doing at the New Room because he turned it into a food bank for the starving and also encouraged his followers to give clothing.[24] John Farley Rutter records that, up to this point in time, Jane was

> A very good and affectionate wife to her husband and attended to her family and domestic matters very satisfactorily. Her conduct however after Wesley had lodged in his house a few times was so different to

what it had been that he was obliged to shut the door against him. Her mind seemed completely wrapped up in Wesley and Methodism and in attending their meetings, and she would travel some miles to attend them. She left her husband and children, did not attend to her ordinary duties, and was continually away from home.[25]

John Wesley preaching ouside a church (Wellcome Collection)

On one occasion, Benjamin found that he did not have a single shirt to wear 'for want of mending and buttons'. It is related that he took a tattered shirt from his closet and stormed into a Methodist meeting where Wesley was preaching. In the midst of the meeting Benjamin produced the shirt and told Wesley that its sorry state was the result of his preaching. He berated Wesley, advising him to 'teach his converts their duty to man, their country and connexions (sic) as well as to God'. Although he tried to interrupt, Wesley couldn't stop Benjamin and he afterwards denounced Rutter as a mad man.[26] Whenever they subsequently met, Benjamin 'freely told John Wesley his mind', which did not amuse Wesley who was annoyed at Rutter's 'pertinacity'.[27] As Wesley records in his Journal in an entry of 29 July 1742, while staying in Bristol,

'I was desired to visit one in Newgate'[28], the city's jail. 'As I was coming out, poor Benjamin Rutter stood in my way, and poured out such a flood of cursing and bitterness, as I scarce thought was to be found out of hell'.[29]

Benjamin's unfortunate domestic concerns so affected him that he took to drink. Wesley's brother Charles referred to Benjamin in his Journal entry of 28 August 1739 'in the evening I accompanied my brother to the preaching-room, in the Horsefair, Bristol. A drunken Quaker (Benjamin Rutter) made a great disturbance by bawling out for his wife. Some of the brethren hardly saved him from the mob'.[30] Benjamin's business suffered and, in 1742, he was declared bankrupt.[31] Jane's affair with Methodism and her regard for Wesley had caused a rift between her and Benjamin who left Bristol (and his young family), to stay with his parents in Cheshire. After Jane died in 1749, Benjamin returned to Bristol to care for his children.[32]

Throughout his life John Wesley was naturally attracted to women and, in turn, he attracted a wide range of ladies to himself. For Wesley, women were a special class of beings with spiritual sensitivity and with gifts for elevated conversation and correspondence. He especially cherished contact with faithful women.[33] Jane Rutter was one of those ladies with whom Wesley would have enjoyed a special, spiritual relationship, much to the annoyance of her husband. It would be fair to say that other people often saw John's manner as being flirtatious.[34]

Benjamin and Jane had three sons and three daughters but only one son, Thomas, who was born on 22 July 1741, survived to maturity with children of his own. Thomas became 'heir to the Kingsley estate' but 'he did not think it right to interfere with or try to dispossess the then owners'.[35] It remains unclear as to whether Thomas had a legitimate claim to any property at Kingsley but this was not pursued. As a boy, young Thomas was close to his mother, Jane, who was 'extremely fond of me, and very indulgent'.[36] He was educated at a new school, Kingswood, founded in 1748 by John Wesley in Kingswood near Bristol. There the emphasis was on a strict Christian upbringing and 'the discipline was severe'.[37] Perhaps because of this and after his mother's death, Thomas did not follow her Wesleyan leanings. The School eventually outgrew its original site in Kingswood and moved to its present, attractive location in Lansdown, Bath in 1851.

Founded as a school for the children of Wesley's friends, Kingswood was designed to accommodate 50 boys who boarded there. Its location was in the midst of the Kingswood coal fields. Thomas is mentioned in the school history as being there in about 1750 when John Jones was chief master. The school's regime was dictated by John Wesley and it was very strict - basic food, simple beds, no playtime and no holidays - but it was also designed to be a

Kingswood School, Bristol (The New Room)

school where the teachers took a genuine interest in their pupils and ensured there was no bullying. There were problems in its early years, not helped by Jones' first wife being very unhappy there and then being taken seriously ill. She died in 1751. Many of the early teaching staff were chosen so they could also educate lay preachers and only one had experience of teaching children. Wesley sacked quite a few of the first masters. The school almost closed in 1752 after the death of a pupil who was accidentally drowned in the big cistern that supplied water to the school. It was kept going by the appointment of James Rouquet to be its chief master. According to a contemporary report he was a man 'compassionate almost to excess' and he believed in guiding children 'by the persuasive influence of love rather than by the rod of iron'. Rouquet rewrote the curriculum and entirely filled the school, but then he left in February 1754 as he wanted to enter the church. Thomas Rutter must have left at about that time as the school only catered for boys up to the age of 12. If they stayed on beyond that, it was to train to become a preacher.[38]

In 1754, Thomas joined his father's business as a maker of large bellows and brushes for use by blacksmiths. Thomas was sharp and clever such that the business recovered. But, as a teenager he was quite rebellious and he did not think much of the Quaker meetings, writing about them in scathing terms. However, in 1758, aged seventeen, he became an ardent Quaker after hearing the following words uttered from the Bible at a meeting 'And if the righteous scarcely be saved, where shall the ungodly and the sinner appear?'[39]

In time he became a Minister and, it is reported, he gave powerful and fluent addresses, travelling widely throughout England and in Ireland, preaching the word of God.[40] He encouraged the growth of the Society of Friends and enjoyed their company wherever he went. Despite his service in the church, his business in Bristol did not suffer but gradually increased until he became quite prosperous.[41] When his warehouse and workshops in Castle Street burned down in 1793[42], Thomas had them rebuilt out of the following year's profits from his business.[43]

Thomas's first wife, Ruth Waring, died in 1778 without issue and he married again, in 1780.[44] His second wife, Hester (nee Farley), brought the trade of printing and journalism to the Rutter line. Hester's grandfather, Samuel Farley, came from Exeter and settled in Bristol as a printer. He started *Sam Farley's Bristol Post Man: or Weekly Intelligence from Holland, France, Spain &c*, in 1715, renaming it *Farley's Bristol Newspaper* in 1725 and then *Sam. Farley's Bristol Newspaper* in 1733. After his death in 1738, his sons Felix and Samuel carried on in partnership, publishing weekly papers under variations of the same name (*S. Farley's Bristol Journal, F. Farley's Bristol Advertiser, Farley's Bristol Journal* and *The Bristol Journal*).[45] The Farley family of printers and publishers played an important role in the introduction and development of

FELIX FARLEY's BRISTOL JOUR
Printed and Published by J. M. GUTCH, at his PRINTING-OFFICE, 15, SMALL-STREET.
'. LXVII. SATURDAY, December 28, 1816. No 3536.—Price 7d.

Felix Farley's Bristol Journal (Allen, L., Jane Austen's London, Shire Publications)

printing and newspaper publication in Exeter, Bristol, Salisbury and Bath. For a period of 30 years they held the monopoly of newspaper printing in Bristol.[46] But, in 1751, the two sons appear to have quarrelled violently and split up.[47] It transpired that Felix and his family, including his daughter Hester, had become Methodists while Samuel's family remained Quakers.[48]

Felix was a committed Methodist and a friend of the brothers John and Charles Wesley. Together they collaborated in the publication of a large number of books and he employed their nephew in the family business. Of the 114 items in the 18th century Short Title Catalogue listed as printed by Felix Farley, or by F. and S. Farley, some 85 were written, abridged, edited or translated by John or Charles Wesley. Most are of a general evangelical or religious nature.[49] Three-quarters of all publications in Bristol came from Methodist sources in the 1740s and this turned the city into the second biggest publishing centre in the country.[50]

For some, the schisms that appeared in the nonconformist Christian faiths in the 18th and 19th centuries appear puzzling. Quakers and other nonconformists, particularly those influenced by John Wesley who founded Methodism, share a number of key convictions. Salvation is available to all; people can change their lives to reflect this; war and slavery are both evil; social justice and acts of mercy are the result of faith; there should be toleration in belief and conscience. Both believe that creation is good and that God loves all creatures. Quakers were generally very much prepared to treat women

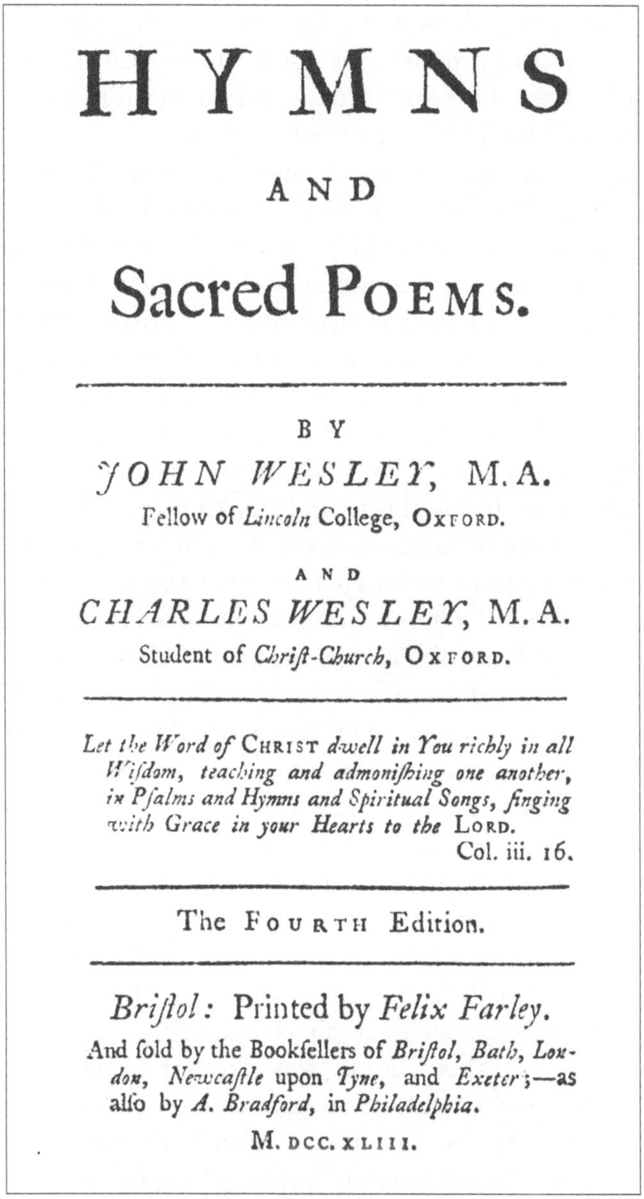

HYMNS

AND

Sacred POEMS.

BY

JOHN WESLEY, M.A.

Fellow of *Lincoln* College, OXFORD.

AND

CHARLES WESLEY, M.A.

Student of *Chriſt-Church*, OXFORD.

Let the Word of CHRIST *dwell in You richly in all Wiſdom, teaching and admoniſhing one another, in Pſalms and Hymns and Spiritual Songs, ſinging with Grace in your Hearts to the* LORD.
Col. iii. 16.

The FOURTH Edition.

Briſtol: Printed by *Felix Farley*.

And ſold by the Bookſellers of *Briſtol, Bath, London, Newcaſtle* upon *Tyne*, and *Exeter*;—as alſo by *A. Bradford*, in *Philadelphia*.

M.DCC.XLIII.

Felix Farley, publisher to the Wesleys, 1743

equally and so was John Wesley. Two thirds of the early Methodist members were women.

However, Quakers are distinguished from other nonconformist Christian communities in a number of significant ways. In the Society of Friends, there are no ordained clergy, no programmed worship and there are no outward sacraments. Scripture is not the primary religious authority and the ecumenical creeds are of less importance. They do not practise baptism with water but 'internal' baptism. Quakers believe they have a personal communion with and experience of God, through an 'Inner Light' or the 'Light Within'.[51] These have emerged as fundamental differences, which Felix and Samuel clearly found irreconcilable.

In March 1752, after the partnership was dissolved, Felix started a new paper, *Felix Farley's Bristol Journal*, which his widow, Elizabeth, with help from his daughter Hester, continued to print and circulate after Felix's death in 1753.[52] The title of the Journal continued well into the 19th century.

These Farley journals comprised content normally found in local and regional newspapers of their day – local news, political elections and scandals, sales of property and other advertisements, obituaries, details of ships leaving and arriving, as well as news from abroad. But, with a liberal reformist bent, the Farley journals also carried lurid stories of the conditions on board ship for both crew and slaves during the second leg, known as 'the Middle Passage', of the triangular trade from Africa to the West Indies or the Americas. They included articles in favour of the abolition of slavery and about the plight of the poor. They published letters drawing attention to electoral corruption and, in one case, complaining about the Corporation of Bristol's elected leaders feasting at the expense of the poor.[53] This trait of representing the poor and of highlighting injustice is very evident among Quakers and, as is shown later, in the character and behaviour of John Rutter.

The Rutter family was prosperous as a result of their successful businesses in manufacturing brushes and bellows and then in printing and publishing. In 1795, Thomas and Hester acquired a house in the country, Moorend Farm, Hambrook, on the outskirts of Bristol.[54] Thomas also felt it his duty to repay the old debts which his father had incurred before being declared bankrupt, thus removing the stigma on the family.

They became respectable members of the Bristol business community and, despite being a Quaker, Thomas was made a Freeman of the City.

Thomas and Hester Rutter had eight children, the eldest of which was a daughter, Rachel, born in 1782, who married Zephaniah Fry (1777–1845) in 1803 in the Quaker Bristol Monthly Meeting.[55] Zephaniah's brother, Joseph Fry, a London Quaker merchant, married Elizabeth Gurney (1780–1845) of the rich Quaker Norfolk banking family. Elizabeth Fry, as she became after her marriage, is well known as a great prison reformer and, in 1810, she became a preacher for the Society of Friends. She visited Newgate Prison for women in 1813 and found many women, with their children, huddled together in appalling conditions. This prompted her to devote her life to prison reform. Although this was her main concern, she was shocked by the images of homeless children in London during the winter months. She was especially seized by the plight of a poor boy who was found frozen to death on a doorstep. She established hostels and night shelters for the homeless. Her husband's bankruptcy in 1828 set her back but she received grants to enable her work to continue. She is buried in the Friends' burial ground at Barking and was commemorated on a £5 note issued in 2002, as well as by a statue at the City of London's Central Criminal Court, the Old Bailey.[56]

It may be worth noting that John and Charles Wesley were strong advocates of prison reform, because their own father had spent time in a debtors' prison in Lincoln when they were young. Newgate Prison in Bristol was largely reformed through the work of the school master James Rouquet after his ordination.[57]

Meanwhile Hester Rutter had much on her hands, looking after her large family and also helping her mother Elizabeth manage the weekly issues of *Felix Farley's Bristol Journal*. In those days, it was quite common for women to be found working in 'chapels' as the jobbing print shops were known. Typesetting had to be undertaken manually and required great care as well as nimble hands. Hester also knew how to manage a printing and publishing business. In 1774–75 she briefly edited and printed a competing newspaper, *The Bristol Journal*, which she (a Methodist) had been bequeathed by her late Uncle Samuel's niece, Sarah (a Quaker). Relationships within the extended Rutter/Farley families must have been quite complicated with a split along sectarian lines.[58] Hester was a strong-minded woman and a Christian of deep conviction. It is said that she spent whole nights in prayer and communion with God. She sometimes mentioned to her children, at the breakfast table, that 'she had been praying for them, specially, since four o'clock that morning'. With her knowledge and experience of the publishing industry and of journalism, reading would have been a regular activity in the Rutter household. One imagines Hester's children sitting, in turn, on her knee, before a fire in the kitchen, as a story was read to them. They would have learnt to understand the power of communication and the dissemination of ideas through the written word. They would also have learnt the practice of noting down and recording facts which could be later recalled when writing an article or a book.

After Thomas died in 1800, Hester carried on the bellows and brush trade with her husband's former business partner, Thomas Harding, under the name of Thomas Rutter and Co.[59] This business was continued by her children after her death in May 1806.[60]

The subject of this book, John Rutter, was the eighth and youngest child of Thomas and Hester. Although the family's main house was Moorend Farm, Thomas always arranged for his children to be born within the city boundaries so that each, in turn, could become a Freeman of the City of Bristol. Thus, John Rutter was born in Castle Street, Bristol - on 10 April 1796.[61] John lost his Quaker father when he was just four years old and his Methodist mother when he was ten, after which he was brought up by his older sisters, Rachel and Elizabeth.[62] They too would have passed on to the young orphan their parents' profound Christian beliefs, as well as some knowledge of journalism, printing and book production, each of which John was later to follow in Shaftesbury when he came of age.

According to his son, John Farley Rutter

> My father was sent to a school kept by a friend named John Naish at Hertford Place, near Bath. I know but little of his school life but one incident shews the character of the future man. On one occasion he was charged with a fault he had not committed, though his master thought he had. John asserted his innocence, but was disbelieved and told that unless he confessed he would be flogged. He refused and was accordingly flogged. A second time he was told to confess, again he refused and was flogged, yet a third time, the same command and refusal, followed by a third flogging after which the master gave up, saying 'if a boy would not confess after three floggings he never would', and John maintained his integrity and determination.[63]

In the late 18th and early 19th centuries, Quaker schools were under the care of the local Monthly Meetings. Primers and elementary grammars were commonly used in Friends' schools. These were combined with instruction in religious and moral precepts. Textbooks were available for the classical languages, illustrated with Biblical stories. Artistic subjects such as music, drama, fiction and dance were seen as 'vain customs of the world' and were therefore not typically part of the curriculum. There was a strong desire to create an environment in which a child would be secluded from evil influences and be subject to a 'guarded education'.[64] John Rutter would have received a thorough grounding in the classics, literature, some sciences and the scriptures, as well as a strong appreciation of silent prayer and of Quaker *Advices and Queries*, which are explained further in chapter five.

Towards the end of the 18th century, Bristol's dominance as a port began to wane. With their larger dock facilities and better access to the sea, Glasgow and Liverpool developed trade with overseas countries, particularly North America and the West Indies, in tobacco and sugar and, in the case of Liverpool, cotton and slaves. It was not so much that Bristol did not continue to expand but that the others took advantage of the opportunities presented to them and grew faster. From Glasgow, the sailing time to North America could be reduced by some two weeks by taking a route north of Ireland rather than journeying south to the African coast before catching the trade winds to travel west. This reduction in time had obvious commercial advantages for Glasgow. Liverpool grew significantly as it supported the expanding textile industry in Lancashire and Yorkshire.

Perhaps not surprisingly, statistics show that the volume of Bristol's trade suffered in time of war. The French Revolutionary Wars which lasted from 1792 to 1802 created a problem for Bristol's economy.[65] The abolition of the Atlantic slave trade in 1807 also contributed to Bristol's failure to keep pace with the newer manufacturing centres in the Midlands and the North of England.

Perhaps for these reasons it was time for another young Rutter to move away from home and to seek a livelihood elsewhere. An opportunity arose for an apprenticeship in Shaftesbury, in north Dorset, where there was a thriving Quaker community. Introductions were made via the Bristol & Somerset Quarterly Meeting of Friends. In 1811, aged fifteen, John Rutter travelled the 45 miles from Bristol to Shaftesbury, where he became apprenticed to a linen draper, another Quaker, by the name of John Shipley.[66]

The Shaftesbury dynasty of Rutters and their contribution to this ancient Saxon hill top town had begun.

Gold Hill, Shaftesbury, showing the rear of the 1827 Town Hall, St Peter's Church and, top right, the second of Shaftesbury's Quaker Meeting Houses from 1904, with a working men's club and replacing the old poor house (formerly the Lamb Inn). It is now St Peter's Parish Hall, with an antique shop and church office on the ground floor

3
Life in Shaftesbury

IN 1811, WHEN John Rutter moved from Bristol to Shaftesbury, or Shaston as it was colloquially known, the town was not exactly thriving. It had seen better days.

After its foundation as a Saxon burh, a settlement fortified by Alfred the Great in his defence against the Vikings, Shaftesbury was the site of the wealthiest monastic institution in the country. In 888, following his defeat of the Vikings at the Battle of Edington in 878 and the partition treaty of 886, Alfred gave extensive tracts of land and money to found a nunnery for his daughter, Aethelgifu. The abbey prospered and was much enhanced by the reburial in its precincts of the body of King Edward the Martyr who had been murdered at Corfe in 979 on the instructions of his step mother. It became a place of pilgrimage and benefited from the revenues from accommodation, hospitality and indulgences that accompanied such a religious site. King Canute's death, from a heart attack, in 1035 in the town, while paying homage to the Saxon King Edward's tomb as an early (Viking/Saxon) public relations exercise, only served to enhance Shaftesbury's attractions. But, being staunchly and so obviously Saxon, the town suffered after the Norman Conquest.

Shaftesbury recovered during the Middle Ages. Indeed the Lay Subsidy of 1332 suggested that it was the wealthiest town in Dorset in the early 14th century.[67] There was a popular medieval saying that 'if the Abbot of Glastonbury might marry the Abbess of Shaftesbury, their heir would have more land than the King of England'.[68] Shaftesbury's economic success was based in no small part on its location on a major road (between Salisbury, Sherborne and Exeter) and as a place of pilgrimage.

But in the 16th century, being on a hill-top, with sparse water supplies, Shaftesbury lost out to neighbouring towns with rivers which provided the water needed for the various trades based around the production of leather goods and clothing. The dissolution, in 1539, of Shaftesbury Abbey, which had been the largest Benedictine nunnery in the country, dealt a savage blow to the local economy with the loss of pilgrims and employment, resulting in empty properties. Despite this, the local agricultural market continued to thrive, attracting produce from farms within a ten mile radius, and it was a place of trade. However, by the early 18th century, Daniel Defoe (1660–1731) described Shaftesbury as 'now a sorry town upon the top of a high hill'.[69] His views were not shared by local attorney, artist and poet, Samuel Marsh Oram (1765–1791), who later painted a more inviting picture, writing from 'St John's Church Yard, Shaftesbury', with its views over the Blackmore Vale to the south and west[70]

> What ample scenes and prospects lie around,
> That rich with nature's vivid beauties glow ! .
> The eye delighted views the vale below,
> Whose wide extent the azure mountains bound.[71]

In the late 18th century, while attracting some admirers, the town was suffering economically and also politically. Shaftesbury had become a corrupt 'pocket' borough, where the two Parliamentary seats were in the hands of the landowning aristocracy and could be used by the patron or bought from him by prospective candidates. In turn they obtained votes through large handouts of beer and cash. With only 350 voters at a General Election, the seats were in the 'pockets' of these favoured candidates.[72] The town itself was also administered by a self-perpetuating oligarchy of ruling 'capital burgesses'.[73] There were a number of almshouses and a large proportion of the population was defined as poor. Perhaps for all these reasons, there was a strong nonconformist presence in Shaftesbury, including a Society of Friends dating from 1699, with its own Meeting House built in 1746.[74]

In the first two decades of the 19th century, when John Rutter arrived from Bristol, the town was known for its button making. But this industry and others such as tanning, glove making and shoe making had suffered in the face of competition from nearby Gillingham. Shaftesbury cannot have been described as prosperous.[75]

The town's decline and yet its mystical character were captured by Dorset's greatest novelist, Thomas Hardy, in *Jude the Obscure* which he wrote in 1895. Referring to Shaftesbury as Shaston, the ancient British Palladour,

> From whose foundation first such strange reports arise, (as Drayton sang it), was, and is, in itself the city of a dream. Vague imaginings of its castle, its three mints, its magnificent apsidal Abbey, the chief glory of South Wessex, its twelve churches, its shrines, chantries, hospitals, its gabled freestone mansions – all now ruthlessly swept away – throw the visitor, even against his will, into a pensive melancholy, which

the stimulating atmosphere and limitless landscape around him can scarcely dispel. The spot was the burial-place of a king and a queen, of abbots and abbesses, saints and bishops, knights and squires. The bones of King Edward 'the Martyr', carefully removed hither for holy preservation, brought Shaston a renown which made it the resort of pilgrims from every part of Europe, and enabled it to maintain a reputation extending far beyond English shores. To this fair creation of the great Middle-Age the Dissolution was, as historians tell us, the death-knell. With the destruction of the enormous abbey the whole place collapsed in a general ruin: the Martyr's bones met with the fate of the sacred pile that held them, and not a stone is now left to tell where they lie. The natural picturesqueness and singularity of the town still remain; but strange to say these qualities, which were noted by many writers in ages when scenic beauty is said to have been unappreciated, are passed over in this, and one of the queerest and quaintest spots in England stands virtually unvisited to-day.[76]

Shaftesbury High Street, 1840, published by Clarence Rutter (Gold Hill)

So, why did young John leave Bristol, which was faring economically much better than Shaftesbury, albeit being left behind by the growth of Liverpool, Glasgow, Birmingham and Manchester? The answer was connections, through the network of Quaker families living and working in the south west of England, and a job opportunity.

When he arrived in Shaftesbury in 1811, Rutter was apprenticed to John Shipley, a linen draper, who was also a Quaker.[77] He would have felt immediately at home with a support group akin to an extended family. The concept of apprenticeships had always been encouraged by Quakers who were requested to advise the Quaker Quarterly Meetings when opportunities arose. Shipley was a leading member of the Shaftesbury Monthly Meeting of the Society of Friends and informed the Bristol & Somerset Quarterly Meeting, held in Bristol, of a vacancy. A certificate from the Bristol Monthly Meeting dated 30 July 1811, relating to John Rutter's apprenticeship to John Shipley, is recorded in the minutes of the Shaftesbury and Sherborne Monthly meeting of 11 September 1811.[78] Added to this, the Farley family had been active in Wiltshire and Dorset trying to establish a newspaper in Salisbury, the *Salisbury Journal,* in the 18th century.[79] Perhaps this was another, historical, connection via his mother, Hester (nee Farley).

As part of being accepted as a draper's apprentice, John Rutter's family paid a premium of £100 (around £7,500 in 2018 prices) for the privilege. Following the deaths of his father and mother, young John's share of inheritance was held in trust until he reached the age of 21 but could be drawn on to fund education and an apprenticeship. Board and lodging would have been provided by John Shipley. In those days, it was normal for apprentices to work without remuneration, or for a pittance, and to pay a premium for being taught a trade or profession. This practice continued in England in many trades and especially in some professions, such as accountancy and the law, well into the 20th century and even after the Second World War. By all accounts, as an apprentice, he was very sharp, diligent and active. He soon acquired a good knowledge of the business and, before long, he took a prominent part in its management.[80]

But Rutter later declared that the draper's trade was only fit for women and he sought another occupation. Following in his mother's family's footsteps, he became a printer and stationer.[81] Rutter was aware of the power of the press and the ability of publishers to communicate facts, ideas and the word of the Lord. Perhaps he also harboured ambitions to bring about political and social change as well as earning a living.

As John Farley Rutter, relates

> He had been kept in the dark regarding his father's Will from which he expected to receive between £1,500 and £2,000 on attaining 21 years: when he realised that this was not so he was much disappointed and disheartened. However, he felt that a printing press was a power required at Shaftesbury and determined to have one; he accordingly

went to London and purchased the needful presses and type and a stock of stationery and began business in 1817.

The presses and type cost £700 (£65,000 in 2018 prices)[82], which made a large dent in his inheritance, already reduced by professional fees. It had taken seven years, after the death of Hester, for Thomas Rutter's will to receive probate, in 1807. Drawn up by a local Bristol solicitor, the will was not straightforward. In parts it was complicated and obscure and, as his grandson, John Farley Rutter, observed 'It would have been better if he had drawn up his own will'. In the process of sorting it out and obtaining probate, the fees of Bristol's Town Clerk and a local accountant, Mr Cossham, amounted to over £2,000 (a staggering £186,000 in 2018 prices), thus reducing the size of the inheritance to John Rutter and his siblings.[83]

In June 1817 John Rutter opened a shop in the High Street advertising himself as a 'Stationer, Bookseller, Binder, Letter-press and Copper-plate Printer'. He sold stocks of writing and other papers, account books, pens, quills and other drawing materials and 'new and standard Works, in plain and elegant bindings, School and Children's Books, Portable Writing Desks, Travelling Cases, Globes and Atlasses; and also a valuable assortment of Tunbridge Ware, Dutch and other Toys, Juvenile Games, genuine Patent

John Rutter's shop in the Commons, High Street, Shaftesbury (Gold Hill)

Medicines, and Perfumery'.[84] Aged 21, Rutter had started a business and had become one of the nation's shopkeepers.

But there was a more literary and cerebral side to his new found career. In addition to printing notices, minutes, reports, accounts and pamphlets, Rutter began selling books and is also recorded as printing and publishing books as well as writing himself.[85] John Rutter was a consummate reader who was avaricious for knowledge across a very wide range of subjects. He wrote notes about what he read and one of these notebooks survives and is kept at Gold Hill Museum by the Shaftesbury & District Historical Society. The topics cover the husbandry of animals, the culling of deer, poaching on manorial land, the Poor Laws, statistics on farm production and markets, the English economy and European politics. These facts were all being stored up for later use in a booklet or a book, which he would write and then publish. As an example, while researching the subject matter of his first publication about Cranborne Chase, he recorded a rhyme, which amused him, taken from a pamphlet about the illegal enclosure of common land in Epping and Hainault forests

To steal a goose, from off a common
Is surely wrong, in man or woman
But what shall plead that man's excuse
Who steals the common from the goose.[86]

In 1818 he wrote, published and printed a booklet *The History of Cranborn Chace* (sic) *and of the Dispute concerning its Boundaries.*[87] Cranborne Chase, as it is spelled today, with the neighbouring West Wiltshire Downs, is designated as an Area of Outstanding Natural Beauty covering some 380 square miles. The landscape of the Chase is quite diverse, with rolling fields, ancient woodlands, steep chalk escarpments and chalk river valleys. From before the Norman Conquest and then for many centuries, until its disenfranchisement in 1829, Cranborne Chase was owned by various members of the nobility (Salisbury, Shaftesbury and Rivers) as well as by the Monarch. On the Chase the land could not be cultivated. Deer roamed freely and were hunted by the proprietor. Over the years, there were periodic disputes as to ownership of the land outside the boundary and these became more serious as enclosure and agricultural cultivation increased. With its Neolithic earthworks, Bronze Age burial mounds and Roman settlements, Cranborne Chase was later subject to numerous archaeological excavations in the 19th century under Lieutenant General Henry Augustus Lane-Fox Pitt Rivers, who inherited the Rushmore Estate. It is an area of beautiful countryside.

Living in Shaftesbury, on the western edge of the Chase, in his first book Rutter related its history. He explained that the word Chace was 'derived from the French word Chacer, or Chasseur (sic), which signifies to hunt, drive, or pursue'. At the time of his writing, the disputes about the Chase focused more on the rights to kill deer outside the boundary, prompting him to research the history, husbandry and hunting of deer in England. In 1816 a legal action had been brought against a respectable landholder for driving deer from his land at Alvediston, in Wiltshire. At the landholder's trial in Salisbury, a verdict was given in the defendant's favour. Rutter described the history of the Chase and the current disputes in an objective manner, demonstrating the traits of a professional, unprejudiced, investigative journalist and historian. His descriptions of, and empathy with, his subject matter are attractive. This booklet and his later guides to the countryside and towns in south west England have led to him being described by many commentators and historians as a topographer.[88]

The label of Rutter as a topographer was perhaps further enhanced by his interest in fossils. In 1818, on Win Green hill, the highest point on the Cranborne Chase and five miles east of Shaftesbury, fossils were found of a huge marine lizard which was named a mosasaurus. Mosasaurs were large marine reptiles that flourished when the chalk deposits were laid down between 75 and 65 million years ago. An unpublished memorandum was written by Rutter consisting of extracts from geological texts by other authors, notes of various excavations and a number of pencil drawings of local fossils. He left a large collection of fossils which the Department of Geology at Southampton University later acquired.[89] The Gold Hill Museum in Shaftesbury also has some fossils from Rutter's collection.

In July 1818, aged 22, John Rutter married Anne Burchett Clarance (1791–1879) in the Quaker Meeting House in Houndsditch, London.[90] She was the daughter of Richard Clarance, a linen and woollen draper and, later, an upholsterer of Number 94, The Minories, London.[91] For a Quaker, Richard had an interesting way of advertising his 'printed cotton bed furnitures'. It was reported that

> R.C. has endeavoured many years to improve the Stile (sic) of Furnitures in General, and for which purpose, he has patronized that national and celebrated work, 'Dr. Thornton's new Illustration of the Sexual System of Linnaeus, or Temple of Flora,' from which many of his Patterns are taken. – It will be a pleasure to R.C. to gratify any of his friends, with a sight of that beautiful publication.[92]

Richard Clarance was not without funds following a legacy from Charles', his brother's, estate which included two small farms (Lodge Hall and Lee Tye) in south Essex.[93] Charles' wealth appears to have emanated from a generous marriage settlement, dated 25 August 1788, of £1,700 (£255,000 in 2018 prices) made by Earl Grosvenor on Miss Louisa Richardson whom Charles Clarance married in that year. On Charles' death in 1807, Richard was an executor as well as a beneficiary, sharing in the proceeds of the estate together with four others.[94]

In the record of John Rutter's marriage to Anne Clarance 'in a public Assembly of the people called Quakers, in Houndsditch'[95], her surname is spelled as above but is shown in later books and other documents as 'Clarence'. Similarly in his Burial Note of 3 April 1826 her father Richard's surname is also spelt 'Clarence'.[96] In the marriage certificate, her Christian name is spelt 'Ann'. The spelling of names at that time was not consistent.

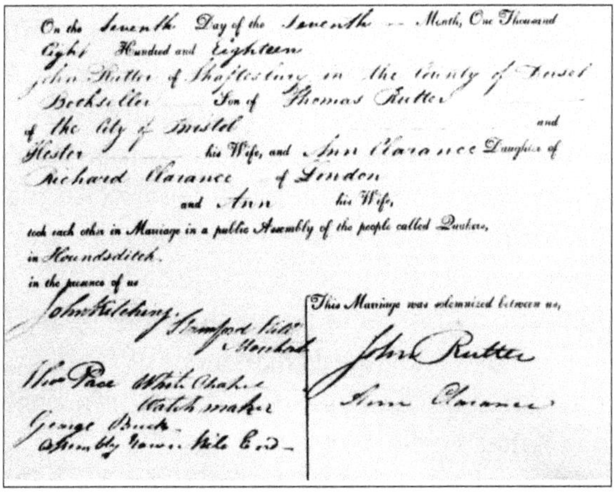
On the Seventh Day of the Seventh Month, One Thousand Eight Hundred and Eighteen
John Rutter of Shaftesbury in the County of Dorset Bookseller Son of Thomas Rutter of the City of Bristol and Hester his Wife, and Ann Clarance Daughter of Richard Clarance of London and Ann his Wife, took each other in Marriage in a public Assembly of the people called Quakers, in Houndsditch.
in the presence of us
This Marriage was solemnized between us,
John Rutter
Ann Clarance

Marriage certificate of John Rutter and Ann Clarance, 7 July 1818 (BMD)

Anne had been educated at the Friends' school in York and had served as a governess in the Shaftesbury family of John Shipley, through whom they met.

John Farley Rutter remembers her with affection:

> My mother, like my father, was no ordinary woman; she had an extremely clear, active mind which was remarkably balanced. Her judgement was clear and sound and she was able to help her husband in all his varied pursuits and engagements. She deeply sympathised with him in his political strife and in his religious activities and I attribute to her loving support and counsel that my father was able to overcome so many

difficulties and attain success in so many branches of business and in his public engagements.[97]

John and Anne started a family and, as was the norm in the early 19th century, not all the children survived to maturity. Those that did were[98]

Clarence, born 8 November 1820. Took over his father's business as a printer, stationer and chemist. Died without issue on 3 July 1855

John Farley, born 1 January 1824. Qualified as a solicitor, worked in practice with his father, based in Mere, reared a large family of eleven children, six of whom went on to marry and have families of their own. Died on 26 December 1899

Ann Elizabeth, born 4 March 1829. Died without issue in 1915

Llewellyn, born 26 June 1832. Also qualified as a solicitor, in practice with his father, based in Shaftesbury. Died without issue in 1857

John Rutter, drawn by Samuel Pearce, Bath, 1829, reproduced by kind permission of Rutter & Rutter, Wincanton

Anne Rutter, drawn by Samuel Pearce, Bath, 1829, reproduced by kind permission of Rutter & Rutter, Wincanton

To begin with, the Rutters rented a house, probably initially from Lord Rosebery and later from Lord (Robert) Grosvenor, the 2nd Earl, who acquired almost the entire town of Shaftesbury from Lord Rosebery in 1819 for a sum thought to be between £60,000 and £70,000 (£4.9 million to £5.7 million) in 2018 prices). As well as being an investment, this acquisition enabled Grosvenor to control elections to Parliament. The Earl's purchase of the town gave him a dominant interest as he obtained 383 properties and he claimed to be a patron of the borough.[99]

John Rutter's second publication, in 1819, showed his care for the plight of the poor, consistent with his Quaker beliefs and his desire for equality and fairness. *A Brief Sketch of the State of the Poor in Shaftesbury* documented the circumstances and the plight of the poor and recommended the establishment of 'houses of industry' for 'the consideration of the inhabitants of the town of Shaftesbury, and other places'. This book is described further in the next chapter.

John Rutter was entrepreneurial. He was always looking for new business ideas and new ways of promoting his trade. A primitive version of the bicycle had been invented in France in 1790 with the name 'celerifere' or 'velocifere'. An improved version of this was developed in Germany in 1817 and was patented in England by Denis Johnson in December 1818. It was known as the 'velocipede', or colloquially as a 'hobby horse', 'pedestrian curricle', 'swiftwalker' or 'dandy horse', the last of these after its principal use by Regency dandies on the paved streets of London and the spa towns. With a curved wooden frame and iron wheels, the velocipede weighed 48 pounds (22 kilos) and was propelled by using one's feet on the ground. Johnson made over 300 velocipedes in the first half of 1819 and his son toured England in the spring publicising the new contraption. A ladies version was also introduced with a dropped frame to accommodate their long skirts. Johnson normally charged between £8 and £10 (£650 to £820 in 2018 prices) for his velocipedes.[100]

Rutter offered some examples for sale at a very much lower price - from four to seven guineas (£330 to £580 in 2018 prices), 'according to make and decorations'. In the *Salisbury and Winchester Journal* of 3 May 1819 he advertised, 'One at four guineas constantly checked for inspection; and with which any individual may be accommodated, for a short time at a reasonable charge'.[101] It is not known whether Johnson appointed Rutter as his agent or whether Rutter was granted a licence to manufacture his own velocipedes in Shaftesbury. It is more than likely that Rutter acquired one or two velocipedes and then advertised them to promote his real business of printing and bookselling. As his granddaughter, Elizabeth Rutter, later recorded, 'He was the first man to go through Shaftesbury on a hobby-horse, which caused great excitement in the town', thus adding to the proposition that this might have been for publicity purposes.[102] The velocipede was a short term fashion, lasting not much more than six months. The problem was that England's

The Dandy Horse, 1819 (Glasgow City Council, Libraries Information and Learning)

roads were so rutted that the velocipedes were mainly ridden on pavements, bumping into and causing accidents with pedestrians. After an initial flurry of success, surgeons advised against their use and some local authorities banned the machines. It was not until the 1860s that pedals were introduced and then not until the 1880s that technological, as well as road, improvements gave rise to the age of the bicycle. As with many ideas and activities, Rutter was ahead of his time.

Stemming from his egalitarian Quaker background, it was not long before young Rutter began campaigning for change in society. Early 19th century Great Britain was crying out for reform. John Rutter hated privilege, unfettered wealth and the power that went with ownership of property. He also hated the disenfranchisement that most of Shaftesbury's inhabitants suffered. One of Rutter's primary targets was the town's corporation, which comprised the mayor, who acted as the returning officer at elections, and twelve capital burgesses who were, effectively, self-appointed. Under the legal charters of the day, they also controlled the magistracy. Local government was a closed shop, a self-perpetuating oligarchy, unrepresentative of the people.

John Rutter would also have read about, and no doubt been influenced by, reports of the Peterloo Massacre in Manchester in August 1819. There, fifteen demonstrators were killed and over 400 were injured when the cavalry was brought in, at the request of the local magistrates, to dispel a crowd of over 60,000 people who were protesting against economic conditions and who were advocating political reform 'No taxation without Parliamentary representation'. In the following year, 1820, supporting this reform movement, John Rutter was prominent in seeking a candidate for the Parliamentary election to fight the nominees of Lord Grosvenor in the pocket borough of Shaftesbury. Grosvenor had acquired most of the town in 1819 and therefore controlled the election of its two members of Parliament. This foray into politics and his actions to question and reform the Shaftesbury Corporation are described further in chapter six. Aged 24, Rutter was becoming involved in political and community affairs. In 1820, it is reported that he seconded a Loyal Address from the inhabitants of the Borough of Shaftesbury to Queen Caroline on the loss of her daughter.[103]

John Rutter also printed and put his name as a subscriber to a leaflet, in November 1820, celebrating the decision to withdraw the 'Bill of Pains and Penalties' which would have brought about the divorce of Queen Caroline from George IV. This long forgotten episode created quite a stir in the country at the time, with over 800 petitions totalling nearly one million signatures in her favour. The background to this is that George had married Duchess Caroline of Brunswick-Wolfenbüttel in 1795 when he was Prince of Wales. There was an inauspicious start to the wedding which was delayed by a week due to bad weather interrupting her journey to England.[104] The marriage was an unhappy one, with each unsuited to the other. They separated the following year and she left England to live on the Continent. On the death of George's father, King George III in 1820, Caroline returned to England to become Queen. George refused to accept this and pressed the Government to introduce a bill to annul the marriage and deprive Caroline of her title. The bill was introduced to Parliament, on 5 July 1820, to give legal effect to a divorce.

The Queen had always championed liberal causes. She lived modestly and supported reform in England. Unlike King George, who was widely regarded as extravagant, selfish and dissolute, Caroline was popular. In the country she was perceived as a wronged woman, fighting for her rights. The bill was debated first in the House of Lords and was more like a trial of the Queen. Witnesses for the prosecution were mainly from Italy, where the Queen was accused of having had affairs. These allegations were largely discredited after one of her defence counsels, Henry (Lord) Brougham, quoted an Italian correspondent as saying 'There is nothing at Naples so notorious as the free and public sale of false evidence. Their ordinary tariff is three or four ducats, according to the necessities of those who sell, and the occasions of those who buy it.'[105] While the Lords passed the Bill by 123 to 95 on 6 November 1820, it was clear that the Commons would vote it down. So the Prime Minister, Lord Liverpool, withdrew the Bill.[106]

This led to much rejoicing throughout the country and, in Shaftesbury, the leaflet printed by Rutter announced that 'the 115 subscribers would be providing liberal entertainment for the labouring, and other classes in honour of the rejection of the Bill of Pains and Penalties against the Queen'. The celebration included 'a liberal quantity of Beef, Plumb-Pudding (sic), Bread and Strong-Beer'. Lord Grosvenor's contribution was five guineas (£460 in 2018 prices). Rutter contributed one guinea.[107] Despite the Bill being withdrawn, Queen Caroline was not permitted to attend George IV's Coronation on 19 July 1821 and, sadly, she died almost three weeks later, on 7 August.

Back in Shaftesbury, Rutter was growing his business. Printing work was forthcoming from various sources. As an example, John Shipley was secretary of the Shaftesbury Branch of the Bible Society whose annual reports were printed by John Rutter in 1820 and 1821.[108] Additionally, he also printed a 'selection of discourses (being speeches), delivered on various occasions by some eminent deceased Ministers of the Society of Friends'.[109]

Rutter's business interests, starting with printing, must have been profitable as, in 1822, four years after his marriage, he acquired a property. This was an indication of his modest prosperity in an age when most of the country's inhabitants rented their own homes. According to John Farley Rutter

> He bought an old cottage at Gillingham with about an acre around it, later he rebuilt the cottage and made it a very comfortable residence; he called it Farley Cottage. My mother mostly lived there and kept a little donkey and carriage in which she went to Shaftesbury. My father found this a pleasant retreat where he could throw off the cares of business. After a few years, much as he loved the cottage, increasing business and other activities coupled with the heavy expense of maintaining the property decided him, albeit reluctantly, to part with it. Lord Grosvenor bought it, naming it Grosvenor Cottage.[110]

Today, Grosvenor Cottage is a thatched cottage, still standing and still bearing this name, in Gillingham on the Shaftesbury side of the town, to the east of the River Stour.

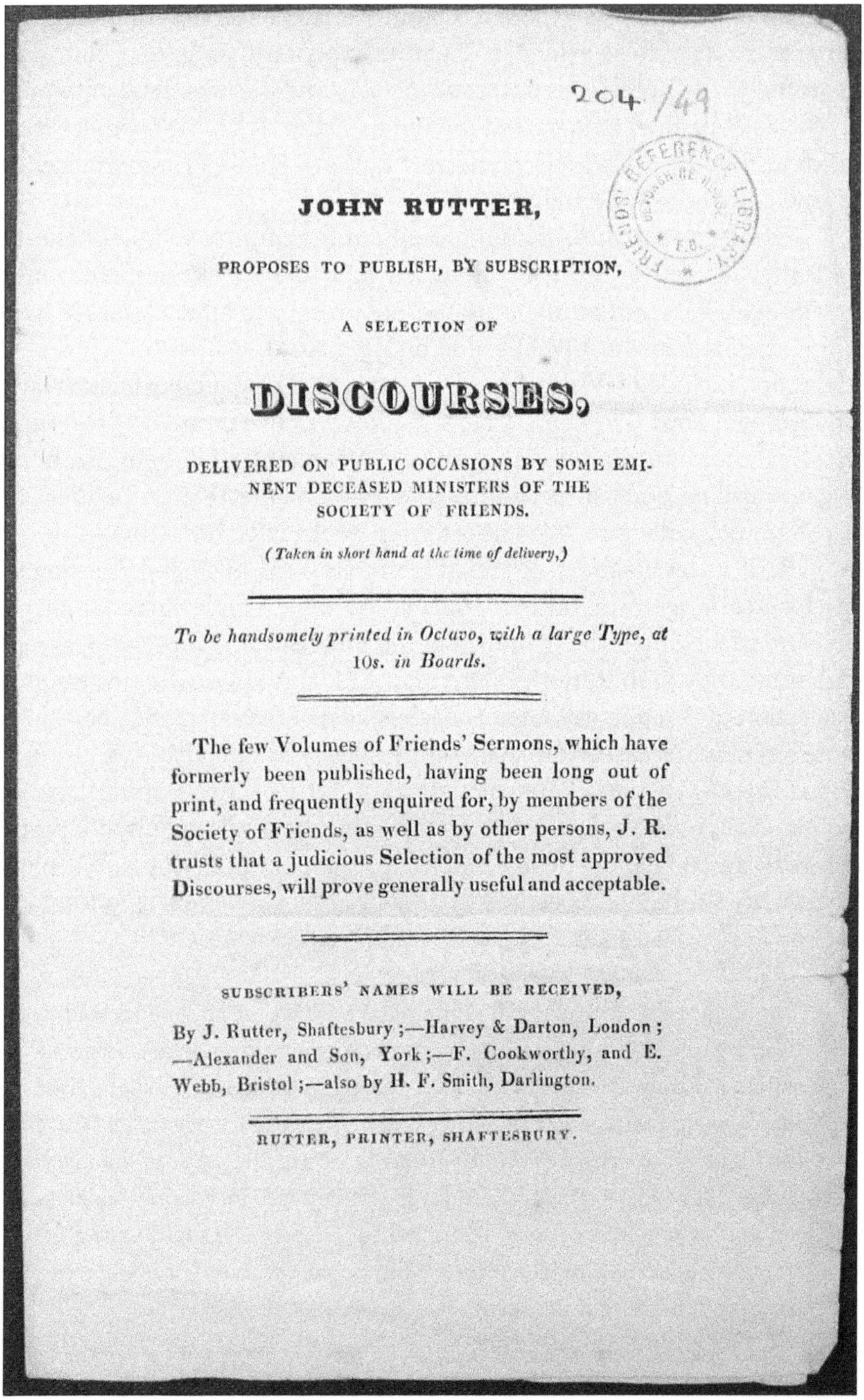

JOHN RUTTER,

PROPOSES TO PUBLISH, BY SUBSCRIPTION,

A SELECTION OF

DISCOURSES,

DELIVERED ON PUBLIC OCCASIONS BY SOME EMINENT DECEASED MINISTERS OF THE SOCIETY OF FRIENDS.

(Taken in short hand at the time of delivery,)

To be handsomely printed in Octavo, with a large Type, at 10s. in Boards.

The few Volumes of Friends' Sermons, which have formerly been published, having been long out of print, and frequently enquired for, by members of the Society of Friends, as well as by other persons, J. R. trusts that a judicious Selection of the most approved Discourses, will prove generally useful and acceptable.

SUBSCRIBERS' NAMES WILL BE RECEIVED,

By J. Rutter, Shaftesbury;—Harvey & Darton, London; —Alexander and Son, York;—F. Cookworthy, and E. Webb, Bristol;—also by H. F. Smith, Darlington.

RUTTER, PRINTER, SHAFTESBURY.

Selection of Discourses by Quaker Ministers, © Religious Society of Friends (Quakers) in Britain, (LSF tract box 204_49)

The years 1822 and 1823 were particularly busy as two of his major works came to fruition.[111] These were detailed guide books, describing Fonthill Abbey and Wardour Castle. As a result, his financial position improved further. Contributing to this, it is recorded that, in 1823, Rutter sold the copyright of the higher quality and well-illustrated *Delineations of Fonthill & its Abbey* to Charles Knight and Co., of London, for more than £500 (£60,000 in 2018 prices).[112] Rutter had other business ideas which required investment.

John Farley Rutter relates that, in the same year, 'my father continued to exert energy and push, he purchased the chemists' business of Thomas Bowder, for the stock £130 was paid. He soon made this acquisition a valuable one'.

At that time, there were two old ladies, with the surname of Mullett, who carried on business as chemists in the Market Place. They were Quakers and were fond of John Rutter 'in whose success they rejoiced' and whom they assisted.[113] Rutter had a natural gift for medicine and soon acquired quite a reputation for compounding medicines and curing people. His son records that, on one occasion, a squire by the name of Gillingham, of Cann, a separate parish to the east of Shaftesbury, sent for him. The squire thought he was going to die and told Rutter that if he cured him he would pay Rutter £500. The potions and the pills worked and the mean fellow recovered but he had neither the honesty nor the grace to fulfill his promise. It is recorded that 'he was a rank Tory' and that whenever they met, Gillingham always had a sheepish look.[114]

The contemporary engraving on page 23 shows Rutter's printing and stationery business adjacent to his chemists' shop in the Commons, an area at the end of the High Street in Shaftesbury. Rutter's rented premises faced directly onto the Grosvenor Arms, which was a demonstration of his landlord's importance and a daily reminder to him of the patronage of the wealthy peer.[115] He is also listed in Pigot & Co's 1823 Directory of Dorsetshire, as a bookbinder and printer, High Street, Shaftesbury.[116]

The following year, 1824, was occupied in distributing his book on Fonthill Abbey to the various subscribers, settling the bills to the artists and engravers, and winding up the account. John Farley Rutter, wrote that 1825 was a quiet year and that

> My father devoted his energy to developing and extending his business. He took an active part in local affairs but always maintained an independent attitude; athletic games especially cricket were entered into. Whilst an apprentice he took much interest in public affairs and widened the judgement and ability that so characterised him in after life.[117]

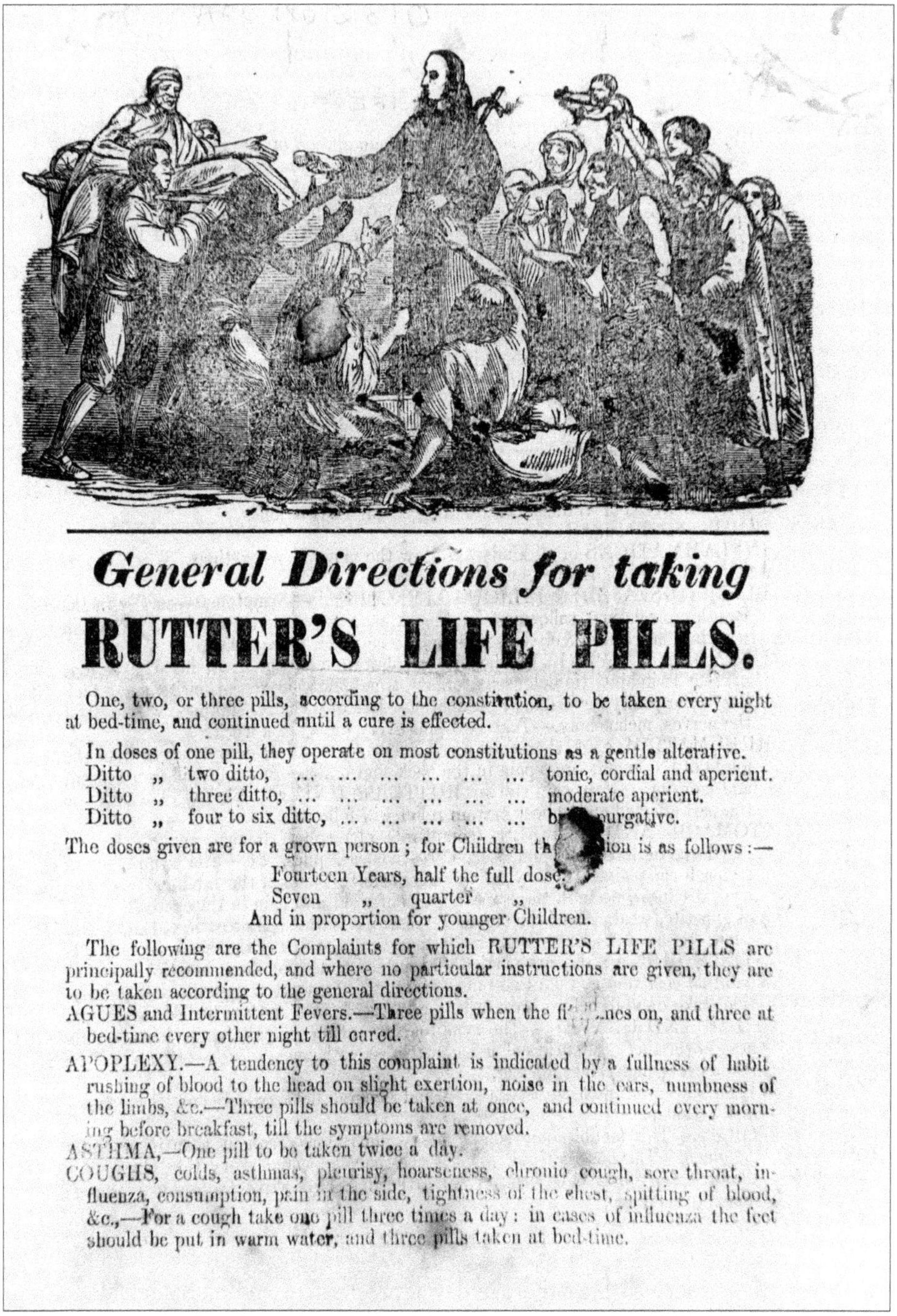

General Directions for taking

RUTTER'S LIFE PILLS.

One, two, or three pills, according to the constitution, to be taken every night at bed-time, and continued until a cure is effected.

In doses of one pill, they operate on most constitutions as a gentle alterative.

Ditto	„	two ditto, ...	tonic, cordial and aperient.
Ditto	„	three ditto, ...	moderate aperient.
Ditto	„	four to six ditto, ...	brisk purgative.

The doses given are for a grown person; for Children the proportion is as follows:—

Fourteen Years, half the full dose.
Seven „ quarter „
And in proportion for younger Children.

The following are the Complaints for which RUTTER'S LIFE PILLS are principally recommended, and where no particular instructions are given, they are to be taken according to the general directions.

AGUES and Intermittent Fevers.—Three pills when the fit comes on, and three at bed-time every other night till cured.

APOPLEXY.—A tendency to this complaint is indicated by a fullness of habit rushing of blood to the head on slight exertion, noise in the ears, numbness of the limbs, &c.—Three pills should be taken at once, and continued every morning before breakfast, till the symptoms are removed.

ASTHMA,—One pill to be taken twice a day.

COUGHS, colds, asthmas, pleurisy, hoarseness, chronic cough, sore throat, influenza, consumption, pain in the side, tightness of the chest, spitting of blood, &c.,—For a cough take one pill three times a day: in cases of influenza the feet should be put in warm water, and three pills taken at bed-time.

Rutter's Life Pills (S&DHS, D.H.C., D-SHS/Box 44.2645)

By the age of 29, Rutter had grown his businesses. A memorandum showed that the gross revenues were about £2,500 a year (almost £260,000 in

2018 prices), of which £2,000 was derived from his printing and bookbinding activities.[118] He was becoming a prominent member of the Friends as well as a political activist and reformer. His position in the community at that time is demonstrated by his name being included in the 1825 to 1829 returns of Churchwardens and Overseers of the Parish of Shaftsbury St Peter of men qualified to serve as a juror, where he was described as a 'Stationer'.[119]

John Rutter had arrived and, apart from being successful commercially, he was promoting social and political reform. Rutter had introduced a third candidate in the 1820 General Election to stand against Lord Grosvenor's two nominees in the pocket borough. Rutter was also was critical of the local government in Shaftesbury which was a 'close corporation', a self-perpetuating oligarchy. In challenging the status quo, he was making waves. He was also making enemies amongst the established elite.

In 1826, a letter was printed in his printing works and issued without his name being shown at the foot of the letter. At that time, the law provided that printers were obliged to record their name on printed material. To omit this was a criminal offence and the ruling political clique in Shaftesbury seized the opportunity to deal with this *Turbulent Quaker*.[120] He was fined £5 (£450 in 2018 prices) on each of two occasions by the local magistrates; a libel charge was brought against him; and he was sent for trial at the Quarter Sessions in Dorchester. Although he was not fined on that occasion, the legal costs and damages incurred by the plaintiff were substantial. This made a dent in his finances and was painful but not disastrous.[121] The full account of this episode is described in chapter six below.

As part of a drive to promote his bookselling and stationery business and, altruistically, to encourage reading and learning, in 1827 Rutter established The Shaftesbury Subscription Library with a Reading Room for 'newspapers, reviews and magazines'. The Library consisted of over 2,000 volumes. The Reading Room was above Rutter's shop, linked by a staircase, and was open from 'ten till five o'clock daily, Sundays excepted'. Subscription to the Library for reference and for borrowing and to the Reading Room was two guineas annually in advance. The rules of the Subscription Library provided that town subscribers could take one set of books home and country members could take two sets. In the latter case, a light box would be provided at a cost of 3s.6d 'for the safe conveyance of the books'.[122] According to John Farley Rutter, the books selected by him to form the foundation of the Library cost his father £375 (£35,000 in 2018 prices).[123]

He also sold books for other authors and historians and was in regular contact with London printers, J.B. Nichols & Son of Number 25 Parliament Street, Westminster, to obtain the printed sheets which were subsequently

THE SHAFTESBURY SUBSCRIPTION LIBRARY for Circulation and Reference, with a READING ROOM for Newspapers, Reviews, and Magazines, are now open to Subscribers, under the care of JOHN RUTTER, Bookseller.

The Library consists of nearly Two Thousand Volumes, and will be increased by the purchase of New Works of merit and general interest.

Subscription to the Library and Reading Room, Two Guineas annually (in advance), from the 1st day of January to the 31st of December; to either separately, One Guinea and Half.

N. B.—From the Society's institution on the 2d of May, to the 31st of December 1827, half a year's subscription only will be expected.

A Catalogue of the Books, with the Rules, &c. may be had on application to J. Rutter, Shaftesbury, the Librarian. [6157

Notice of Shaftesbury Subscription Library, 1827 (Gold Hill)

bound. One of these books was Sir Richard Colt Hoare's classic work *The History of Modern Wiltshire. Hundred of Dunworth and Vale of Noddre,* which Rutter advertised at £3.13s. (£380 in 2018 prices) for 'each of six parts'

> The Hundred and Town of Mere
> The Hundred of Heytesbury
> The Hundred of Branch and Dole
> The Hundreds of Everley, Amesbury, and Underditch
> The Plates of the Hundred of Dunworth are in the Engraver's Hands
> Parchment Registers for Baptisms, Marriages, and Burials, 2s per sheet.[124]

The years 1828 and 1829 were successful for Rutter's publishing activities but the strain of local politics and the legal proceedings were beginning to affect his wellbeing. He had incurred legal costs and damages amounting in total to almost £403 (£36,000 in 2018 prices) in defending the action at the Quarter Sessions in Dorchester in 1826. He decided he needed a change of scene and he spent some weeks travelling to the towns and villages of Somerset with the aim of gathering material prior to writing guides to the area.[125] These are also described in the next chapter.

Rutter was always looking for new sources of revenue to enhance his business activities. In an advertisement of January 1830 he is listed as the contact for passengers wishing to secure a passage to Philadelphia on the fast sailing ship *Cambridge* under the command of Richard Pearse at the 'first fair wind after the 25th of February'. It was further stated that 'This Ship will afford a particularly eligible opportunity for Passengers proceeding to the United States, as she has a commodious Poop and ample space between decks, which will be fitted up expressly for the purpose'.[126]

But, despite the setback in 1826, John Rutter would not let up in his campaign for social justice and political reform. He again found candidates to stand in the General Elections of 1830, 1831 and 1832 in opposition to the Grosvenor faction. The bloody accounts of these contests, particularly the 1830 campaign, after which Rutter was indicted for riot and tried at the Quarter Sessions at Dorchester, are related in chapter six. Fortunately the charges were dropped in 1831.

Meanwhile his business interests thrived in the face of attempts by the Grosvenor faction to introduce competition to drive him out of town.[127] In Pigot & Co's Trade Directory for Shaftesbury & District of 1830, John Rutter is listed under Booksellers, Stationers, Printers & Binders as operating from premises in the High Street, where he also provided the public reading room & subscription library. He is similarly listed under 'Chymists & Druggists' also in the High Street. The shops were adjacent to each other.[128]

Meanwhile, another career opportunity was presenting itself to John Rutter – that of the law.

The Corporation Act of 1661 and the Test Act of 1673 required public office holders to submit a sacrament certificate confirming, under oath, that they had taken Holy Communion according to Anglican rites. Between 1689 and 1702, the requirement to take an oath was extended, inter alia, to members of universities, teachers and lawyers. As part of their faith, Quakers refused to swear an oath. Oaths are commonly referred to throughout the Old Testament of the Bible and, in the New Testament, Jesus is recorded as issuing a command 'Swear not at all'. This was repeated by James the Apostle. The early years of Quaker history were times of plotting and intrigue. The oath of allegiance and other oaths were frequently used to trap Quakers, who were at pains to explain that refusal to swear an oath in no way meant any less allegiance to the monarch. Thus, until the abolition of the Corporation and Test Acts, in 1828, public office and the legal profession were therefore closed to those who were Friends. In that year, the obligation to swear an oath was replaced with a declaration (under the Sacramental Test Act) that the office holder would neither injure nor weaken the Church of England.[129]

After his scuffles with the law in 1826 and 1830, and following the introduction of the Great Reform Act of 1832, Rutter thought that he had achieved, or almost achieved, his objectives in terms of Parliamentary reform.

After the passing of the Sacramental Test Act of 1828, the legal profession was open to him and Rutter decided, in 1832, that he would train to become a lawyer.

This was a momentous decision which he took after much deliberation and discussion with his wife, Anne. As a trainee solicitor, John Rutter was paid little and was not permitted, under the Law Society's rules, to conduct any other business activity. Anne had always managed the shop while Rutter was busy electioneering. Being a well-educated lady, she was well liked by visitors to the bookshop and to the Subscription Library. From 1833, she took greater responsibility, notwithstanding her duties looking after her family of five surviving children. Her son, John Farley Rutter, records 'Practically my mother managed everything, and was as useful and efficient on the drug side as on the bookselling and stationary side. In the printing office, too, she was mistress of all that went on'.[130]

Born on 8 November 1820, Clarence[131] was the Rutters' eldest surviving son and, despite being just 12 years old, he was given the first offer of his father's firm. Clarence decided that, one day, he would take over the business of printing and bookselling. His younger brother, John Farley Rutter, wrote that Clarence thought that 'this would give him greater independence and would entail less labour and effort'.[132] Accordingly, in a deed of 7 January 1833, Rutter assigned his entire business interests to Rutter family members, upon trust for Clarence, until he was old enough to own them.[133] In the meantime, Clarence was sent away to a boarding school, in Kendal, Westmoreland[134], although in the school holidays he worked in the bookselling and stationery businesses in the High Street.

Mindful of the Law Society's regulations, John Rutter was anxious to demonstrate that he was no longer the owner of, nor responsible for, the printing and bookselling business. Accordingly he arranged for a notice to be issued in Clarence's name in November 1833, just before his 13th birthday, informing 'his Friends and the Public that the New Catalogue of his Subscription Library at Shaftesbury is just published, and may be had on application'.[135] The chemists' business was also carried on in Clarence's name with most interesting potions and concoctions being advertised, for example

> Rutter's Sheep-Wash: The Fly, Tick and Magot in Sheep being very prevalent this Season, C. Rutter recommends those farmers who do not use it to try this Sheep-Wash, which they will find the cheapest and most efficient Remedy yet discovered. Try also Rutter's Cow Drinks for Cleansing, Scour and Yellows and his celebrated Alternative Powders for Horses. These Powders are excellent for Horses out of condition, or

> having any of the following symptoms: viz., dulness (sic) and unfitness for work, bad appetite, a rough and staring coat; scurf, or eruption of the skin. The above valuable Medicines are prepared and sold by C. Rutter, Chemist, Shaftesbury.[136]

John Rutter undoubtedly kept an eye on things as well as studying to become a solicitor.[137] But, in practice it was, of course, Anne who oversaw the chemists' business as well as the printing and bookselling activities. Her son, John Farley Rutter, recalled one occasion which was termed a 'raid day', when inhabitants were encouraged to descend on shops to help themselves to goods at knockdown prices, as they do today at periodic sales. He wrote 'The preparations made for that day were great; twice during the day clean straw was put down to receive the mud and dirt from the tramping of so many feet'.[138]

In the 1800s, chemists and druggists dispensed published recipes and patented medicines. In many cases, they made their own, at home, and goodness knows what the ingredients were and how effective, or otherwise, the pills and potions proved to be. The lack of regulation of the industry became a scandal and there were calls for reform. This led to the foundation of the Pharmaceutical Society in 1842.

Perhaps because of this and also because of Anne's domestic commitments, John Rutter identified a partner to manage Clarence's businesses pending his coming of age. James Wallbridge, who was a chemist in Kennington Lane, Lambeth, agreed to form Rutter and Wallbridge, until Clarence could take over as the sole owner a few years later.[139]

In a letter dated 26 January 1832 John Rutter wrote to Wallbridge saying that 'I find the necessary attention to my old business too much for Mrs Rutter and I therefore want someone, willing and capable of relieving her from a large share of her present fatigue and confinement and of generally superintending the business'. He counselled Wallbridge by warning him that 'I fear your London habits etc will make your expects beyond what the business of Shaftesbury will sustain'. Rutter proposed that Wallbridge be provided with accommodation, a salary and a bonus of 5% 'upon the gross amount taken, beyond the average of the last three years – including both the Drug and Stationery Sides'.[140] Wallbridge replied in March that Rutter's offer of £75 (£7,400 in 2018 prices) a year was too little and asked for an increase to £80, with a view to closing down his business in London and starting 'at Shaston' before the end of March.[141]

A deal was done and the partnership was to last almost seven years. The chemists' business was carried on in the name of 'Rutter and Wallbridge', while the printing business carried the name of 'C. Rutter', which appeared at the foot of the first page of any printed material. His name is so described as 'Bookseller and Printer, Shaftesbury' in a notice of the British and Foreign Bible Society convening a meeting on 25 July 1837 in the nearby town of Mere for the purpose of forming a local Bible society.[142]

Then, after leaving school and returning home, aged 18, Clarence placed an advertisement dated September 1839. He announced his new found independence to 'his Friends and the Public generally' and also that

CLARENCE RUTTER

Begs to inform his Friends and the Public generally, that he has entered upon the Business of a

Chemist and Druggist,

BOOKSELLER AND STATIONER,

AT

SHAFTESBURY,

Carried on for so many years by his Father; and having been for some time past in well-conducted Establishments at Bristol and in the north of England, he trusts that the increased experience which he has thus acquired, more particularly in the careful

Dispensing of Medical Prescriptions

and Family Recipes, will ensure him a continuance of that confidence and support which the Business has hitherto received.

It is C. R.'s determination to supply his Customers with pure and genuine Medicines, at reasonable prices, and procured from the most respectable manufacturing Chemists, rather than with inferior articles at a nominally lower price.

In addition to the regular Stock of Books and Stationery, orders for both, including New Publications, are regularly sent to London every Wednesday, and parcels received in return every Saturday. Reviews, Magazines, and other periodical publications are regularly delivered to order, at the Publisher's prices, on the first day of every month.

The READING ROOM continues to be supplied with the Standard, Times, and Morning Chronicle Daily Newspapers; the John Bull, General Advertiser, Bristol Mercury, Salisbury and Sherborne Journals; and also with the Quarterly and Edinburgh Reviews, Blackwood's Magazine, and Literary Gazette. The Room is open from Ten to Five o'clock daily to Subscribers and Strangers visiting the Town and its Vicinity.

The Shaftesbury Subscription Library

Consists of nearly 2,000 Volumes, and is constantly increasing by the addition of New Works of interest in general literature and the passing Publications of the day, a printed Catalogue of which may be had without charge.

Shaftesbury, September, 1839.

Clarence Rutter, Notice of September 1839 (S&DHS, D.H.C., D-SHS/Box 44.2645) he would continue to dispense medical prescriptions as well as to operate the Reading Room and the Shaftesbury Subscription Library, consisting of nearly 2,000 volumes.[143] By this time, Clarence had become a member of the Pharmaceutical Society of Great Britain and described himself as such when advertising *Rutter's Life Pills*.[144] He also sold penny black postage stamps after they were introduced in 1840 and a sign with the words 'Stamp Office' was hung above the door to his shop.[145] In a further effort to capture business in areas of growing interest he was later recorded as having advertised musical instruments from his 'Music Warehouse', offering 'an old violin' for sale for five guineas and 'a handsome 6 stop chamber barrel organ'.[146]

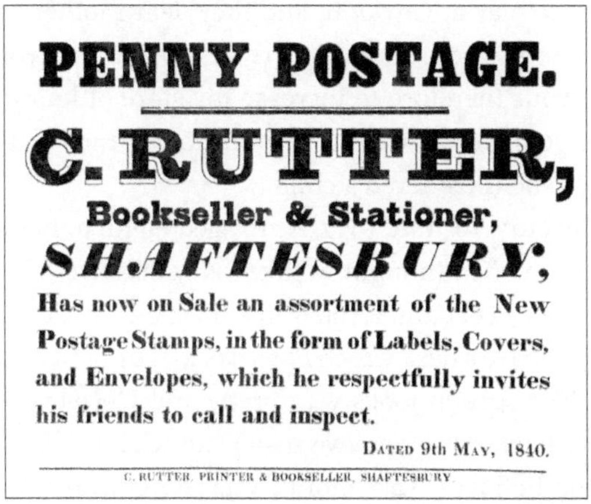
PENNY POSTAGE.

C. RUTTER,

Bookseller & Stationer,

SHAFTESBURY,

Has now on Sale an assortment of the New Postage Stamps, in the form of Labels, Covers, and Envelopes, which he respectfully invites his friends to call and inspect.

DATED 9th MAY, 1840.

C. RUTTER, PRINTER & BOOKSELLER, SHAFTESBURY

Penny Postage, Notice of 9 May 1840 (S&DHS, D.H.C., D-SHS/Box 44.2645)

As part of his change in career, John Rutter moved his family, in 1833, from the shop premises in the High Street and rented Layton Cottage, in Layton Lane, at the foot of Gold Hill, from the Marquess of Westminster. The environment at Layton Cottage was of a loving family enjoying the tranquility of a house, on the edge of the country, with a garden full of flowers and vegetables. As John Farley Rutter described 'This retired spot with its large garden suited him exactly, and he remained in it to the day of his death'.[147]

The sons were initially tutored in Shaftesbury in the Classics, History and Geography by Charles Binns[148] before being sent to Quaker boarding schools – Clarence to Kendal, John Farley to Croydon, for a short time, and Llewellyn to Croydon and then Hitchin. This last school had been founded in 1810 on the lines promulgated by the Quaker, James Lancaster, whose educational model was much admired by John Rutter, as described in chapter seven below.

Evidenced by letters exchanged between the sons (away at school) and their parents (back in Shaftesbury), the family relationships were warm and supportive. As might be imagined there was much mention of food parcels being requested from home and there were nostalgic references to the Layton Cottage garden and its produce. 'Have the figs ripened well?'[149]

Extracts from these letters give a further flavour of the focus of the family members' interests:

> Shaftesbury, 4 April 1836, John Rutter to his son, John Farley Rutter, aged 12, who was boarding at Croydon School 'Thou art now, my dear boy, getting to an age, where the importance of knowledge and of correct principles become more and more apparent; thou hast not very much longer to stay at Croydon, and they dear mother and myself are anxious that thou shouldst make the best use of thy remaining time there. Endeavour therefore to increase thy store of knowledge of every kind, and remember that when a boy gets to be nearly 14 years of age he is no longer to be considered a child...'.
>
> Shaftesbury, 16 June 1837, Ann, aged eight, to her eldest brother Clarence 'I have often thought of thee today because John (her brother John Farley) has a coat and a collar like thee, and at a distance he looks very like thee. I have a desk which Papa has lent me and I have everything complete.... The garden looks very pretty and Llewellyn (her youngest brother) have (sic) one, where we may plant what we like. It only wants a week to the holidays. Last month was the Queen's birthday on the 24 of May when we gave the Misses Westalls (her school teachers) a silver salver.... Misses Westalls invited us to tea and after tea we dance (sic) and we had cake and wine and we enjoyed ourselves very much.... your affectionate sister'.[150] The dancing and the wine must have greatly contributed to the enjoyment!
>
> Shaftesbury, 1838 (precise date not known), Llewellyn, aged six, to Clarence 'I wish thee could see my nails for I have nearly left off biting them. I have such a nice little garden for my own with three current (sic) trees and so many flowers will come up and look pretty....I cannot write any more (sic) and Mama has some rhubarb I must peel so farewell dear Clarence, I do not say Canance now...Thy affectionate little Llew'.[151]
>
> Shaftesbury, 11 February 1839, Ann, aged nine, to Clarence 'Llewellyn goes to school and asked me to buy him a little knife like the one which thee gave him before thee left'.[152] He must have lost the first one!
>
> Croydon, 23 February 1844, Llewellyn, aged eleven, to his mother 'We had a very nice walk to the Addington hills and in the evening we

had cake and coffee and after that some of us repeated some pieces of poetry and Master asked us a few riddles. We have had a good deal of snow and frost lately'.[153]

Hitchin, 10 August 1848, Llewellyn, aged sixteen, to his mother 'I hope thou are still improving in health, and that thou hast been able to take several walks down the parish with my father.....The principal reason that I wrote (sic) this letter now is that I want you to send a box of mathematical instruments, as I expect to go into mensuration (geometry) next week, having finished cube root....There is not nearly such a poor crop of apples in this part of the country as there is about us. Pears too are very plentiful and also a small kind of green gage (sic) of which we can get from eight to ten for a penny....A parcel of good things would not come at all disagreeably now, for we are hungry as church mice from between twelve to two, which is our dinner hour, and there has not been a single one arrived since I came'. Ann says that thou dost not approve of boys taking jam to school, but I should like some uncommonly, as several other boys bring some....With love to all, Thy affectionate Son'.

Then: Hitchin, 11 September 1848, aged 16, Llewellyn to his mother 'On Saturday I received thy parcel for which I am much obliged as it came just about the right time to be acceptable, but I can't say that it arrived quite safe as both the jars of preserve were broken to pieces and I only managed to save about half of each if so much, what remained was extremely good. I should advise you to send me the next in a hamper as then you will be inclined to put more things in them. Some boys have jam and mince tarts, gingerbread etc. These little things it is that constitutes in a boy's mind a good parcel'. The wording and tone of Llewellyn's letter is so reminiscent of the joys to a mother of those challenging male teenage years!

Shaftesbury, 26 October 1848, aged 27, Clarence to Llewellyn 'We shall be glad to have thee as a helper in the office and I look forward to Christmas with some pleasure'. [154]

In parallel with his legal training and continuing his desire to be of public service, John Rutter decided that he would stand for election to the new town council in the reformed Shaftesbury Corporation, following the implementation of the Municipal Corporation Act of 1835. In December 1835, he became a town councillor, a position he held for four years.[155] During this time his stature within the community was further enhanced and he led many campaigns and initiatives.

At the end of 1837, aged 41, John Rutter completed his legal training and was admitted as an attorney in early 1838. After this he began to tire of politics. He stated that he wished to devote more time to his family and to his professional work. He had, for a period of seventeen years, devoted a considerable amount of energy to elections and to political reform at both national and local level. The 1837 General Election was the last in which he was actively engaged and he stood down from the local town council in 1840. Rutter estimated that, in addition to time spent, he incurred of the order of £1,500[156] (£165,000 in 2018 prices) in election expenses. But, as John Farley Rutter, related 'my father had the happy faculty of making money with comparative ease'. He goes on to say 'He also had the faculty of getting rid of it with equal ease'.[157]

Thereafter, he devoted much of his time to the legal profession as well as to continuing his public service roles, including establishing an infants' school in St James, participating in the Peace movement, promoting the Bible Society and the Temperance movement and speaking on a variety of subjects. His desire to promote Bible reading to the poor, who were not Quakers, caused a spat with the Society of Friends in Shaftesbury. He stuck to his principles and was 'disowned'. Despite this, he and his family continued to attend regular prayer meetings at the Meeting House in St James. The circumstances of his being removed as a member are described in chapter five.

As an example of his varied interests and extensive public speaking, he was recorded in the *Salisbury and Winchester Journal* of April 1840 as having delivered a lecture at the Mechanics Institution in Fordingbridge on 'Geology, with an especial reference to Natural Theology'.[158]

Shortly after completing his five years of articles to become a solicitor, in 1837 John Rutter entered into partnership with Charles Hannen and his son, William. They practised under the name of Hannen & Rutter. At some point Charles retired, leaving William Hannen and John Rutter to continue until February 1845 when the partnership was dissolved and each continued to practise under his own name.[159] Rutter's independent firm of solicitors was the foundation, in 1837, of the present day law firms of Rutters in Shaftesbury and Gillingham and of Rutter & Rutter in Wincanton.

John Farley Rutter recorded that, in the years after John Rutter had become a solicitor, he was invited to the Marquess of Westminster's house in Grosvenor Square. The Marquess, Robert Grosvenor, told him that his agents had spent £2,000 (£220,000 in 2018 prices) in efforts to crush and ruin Rutter.[160] Interestingly, this is not a dissimilar amount to that spent by Rutter (£1,500, as referred to above) in pursuing his political and electoral agenda. John Rutter was invited to dine at Motcombe House, near Shaftesbury, by

Lord (Richard) Grosvenor (the 3rd Earl and the eldest son of the 1st Marquess) on more than one occasion but he always courteously declined. One letter read

> John Rutter feels much obliged to Lord Grosvenor's kind invitation to dinner at Motcombe House on Friday next, but the present Quiet and retired routine of life renders him unfit for such visits, and therefore hopes Lord Grosvenor will excuse his non acceptance of so tempting an invitation. John Rutter, Layton Cottage, 12 February 1840.[161]

Layton House, Shaftesbury Auction Sale, 1919 (Gold Hill)

John Rutter and his family lived at Layton Cottage for eighteen years, from 1833 until his death in 1851. These were happy times. John Farley Rutter recorded his mother serenely contented with her children around her in the garden on a summer's evening and in the summer house they built, decorated inside with sea shells and moss. 'The summer house would hold us all comfortably and occasionally we had tea it'. Rutter was an accomplished gardener – planning the layout, planting trees and then benefiting from the abundance of fruit and vegetables. His son recorded that 'A loving Christian Spirit seemed to cover the household. My father and mother lived in an atmosphere of love. I feel I am indebted to my dear parents for what I am, and for the happiness of my early life'.[162]

The Census Return of 1841 confirms Rutter living in Layton Lane. He is described as a solicitor, aged 43 (Note: he was, in fact, 44 or 45 years old, depending on the exact date of the Census enumerator's visit to Rutter's house). Living with him were his wife Anne (aged 46), son John (18) who is described as an articled clerk, daughter Ann (12), son Llewellyn (9) and two servants/maids: Maria Maidment (aged 22) and Mary Hellier (aged 21).[163] His tenancy of Layton Cottage and the surrounding gardens and buildings is also shown in Shaftesbury's Tithe Apportionment of 1846, with the relevant tithe map references[164]

605 & 606: Layton Cottage, Garden & Premises – two roods[165] (half an acre). Owner: Marquis (sic) of Westminster
607: Stable Yard etc (adjacent to Layton Cottage) – 12 perches. Owner: Marquis (sic) of Westminster
161: Part of Garden (adjacent to Layton Cottage – 12 perches. Owner: Marquis (sic) of Westminster
601 & 601a: Garden (on the north side of Layton Lane, opposite Layton Cottage) – one rood and one perch. Owner: Trustees of the Corporation

Separately, the 1846 Tithe Map shows him as the tenant of the following business premises, from which he practised as a solicitor[166]

547: House (opposite 504, on Church Lane, off the High Street) – 3 perches. Owner: Trustees of the Corporation
557: House & Premises (on Church Lane, off the High Street) – 12 perches. Owner: George Franks
504: Offices – 4 perches. Owner: Marquis (sic) of Westminster

Finally, the 1846 Tithe Map also shows that he owned a plot of land (18) on the north side of St James Street on which the Infant School had been constructed in 1840. This is described further in chapter seven below.[167]

In 1847, no doubt enjoying the fruits of labour in his legal practice, Rutter drew up plans to make significant alterations to Layton Cottage, which had previously comprised two separate and adjacent semi-detached cottages. These were merged into a single, grander house and he added a Victorian front to the north side of the house, thus doubling the dwelling in size.[168] It was a major exercise and the work was not completed until 1849[169], after which it became a very desirable gentleman's residence. His office on the High Street was ten minutes away, involving a steep walk up the picturesque Gold Hill. The house was on the edge of the country with plenty of land, in a south facing position. Grapes and figs could be grown in the garden, as well as other fruit: apples, plums, pears, damsons and mulberries. At some stage, between 1895 and 1901, the name of the house was changed from Layton Cottage to Layton House.[170]

By the time he was 50, in 1846, John Rutter had achieved much in his life. He had developed thriving stationery and chemists' businesses which he had passed on to his son Clarence. He was an author and publisher of some exceptional books. He had been an active political and social reformer. He was well known as a champion of many causes: peace, abstinence, Bible reading and education as well as public gas lighting and, even, railway construction. He was an authoritative speaker. He was now a successful attorney and a pillar of the community. To prove it he was living in a desirable house with a large garden at the foot of Gold Hill, in the parish of St Peter, adjacent to the parish of St James where the poor of Shaftesbury lived. He was close to the people for whom he cared and for whom he fought. His Quaker values did not totally prevent touches of vanity and recognition of his status. On a visit to Paris for the International Peace Congress in 1849 he acquired a fine, cream-coloured top hat. Then in 1850 he commissioned Monsieur Jacqueline, a French portrait painter, to execute an oil painting, a photograph of which adorns the front cover of this book.

Towards the end of the decade, Rutter's health started to take a turn for the worse. In a letter dated 21 August 1850, he wrote 'For nearly the whole of the present year I have been compelled by ill health to give up not only every thing (sic) of a public character but also much of my own professional bearings and I am still unable both in body and mind to do much.'[171]

From a diary kept by his youngest son Llewellyn, it is evident that his father was a very sick man throughout 1850. Despite consultations with local doctors and London specialists, and several holidays taken with his unmarried daughter Ann, his health appears to have steadily worsened. In a diary entry of 10 January 1851, Llewellyn records 'Papa still continues better but exceedingly weak from not being able to take any solid food whatever' and ' M of W (the Marquess of Westminster) called to inquire after his health and a number of the respectable persons of Shaston'.[172]

John Rutter lingered on into the spring but he died on 2 April 1851 of *hydrothorax*[173], following injuries sustained on being thrown from his carriage.[174] It was a most unfortunate end to the life of a talented and caring man.

John Rutter passed away just eight days before his 55th birthday. Clarence wrote to family and friends on 3 April with the words 'my beloved father breathed his last on Wednesday the 2nd April. His end was peace and

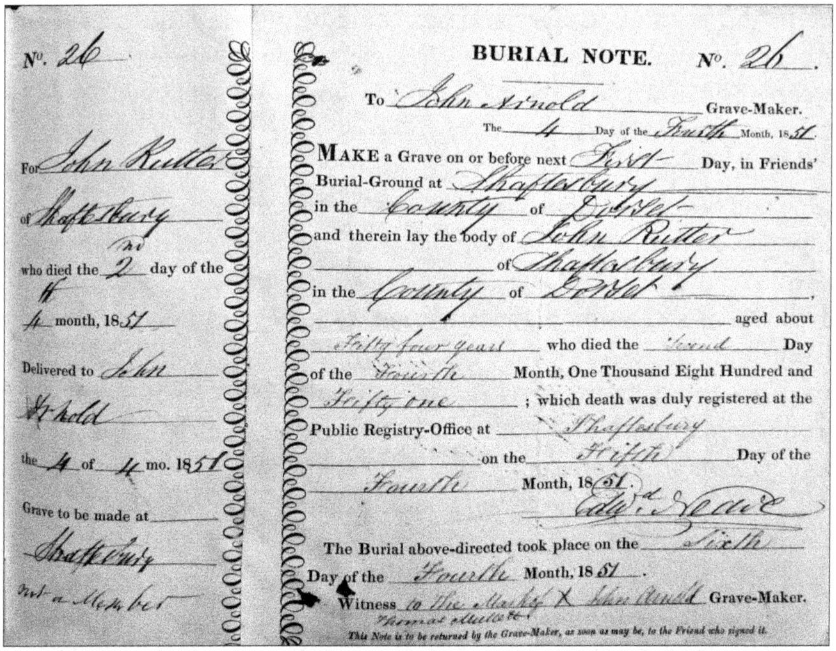

No. 26

For John Rutter
of Shaftsbury
who died the 2 day of the 4 month, 1851
Delivered to John Arnold
the 4 of 4 mo. 1851
Grave to be made at Shaftsbury
not a Member

BURIAL NOTE. No. 26.

To John Arnold Grave-Maker.
The 4 Day of the Fourth Month, 1851.

MAKE a Grave on or before next First Day, in Friends' Burial-Ground at Shaftesbury in the County of Dorset and therein lay the body of John Rutter of Shaftesbury in the County of Dorset aged about Fifty four years who died the Second Day of the Fourth Month, One Thousand Eight Hundred and Fifty one; which death was duly registered at the Public Registry-Office at Shaftesbury on the Fifth Day of the Fourth Month, 1851.

Edwd. Neave

The Burial above-directed took place on the Sixth Day of the Fourth Month, 1851.
Witness to the Mark of X John Arnold Grave-Maker.
Thomas Mullett

This Note is to be returned by the Grave-Maker, as soon as may be, to the Friend who signed it.

John Rutter's Burial Note (Burial Notes of the Shaftesbury and Sherborne Monthly Meeting, Volume 50, 1838 to 1851, D.H.C.)

joy, his anticipations of an entrance into eternal bliss we all feel opened and fully realised'[175]. He was interred on 6 April in the Quaker burial ground next to the Meeting House in St James and is recorded in the Friends' Burial Notes as 'not a member', which is further explained in chapter five below.[176]

John's widow, Anne, lived on at Layton Cottage for some years, together with her unmarried daughter, Ann, dying at the age of 88 on 13 January 1879.[177]

Like his father, Rutter's second surviving son, and the only one to marry, John Farley Rutter, qualified as a solicitor and he took over his father's legal practice after he died.

Sadly, John Rutter's eldest surviving son, Clarence, died on 3 July 1855 aged 34[178] and the businesses of chemist, druggist, bookseller, stationer and printer were advertised for sale. Terms and particulars of the sale were recorded as being available from Messrs Rutter & Rutter, solicitors, either at Shaftesbury or at the nearby town of Mere.[179] By that stage, John Farley Rutter was living in Mere and managing that office, whereas Llewellyn, also a solicitor, had stayed in Shaftesbury.[180] The businesses did not attract a buyer and, in March 1856, an auctioneer (Mr Guy) was appointed to sell the stock, fixtures and effects over seven consecutive days based on the large variety of seven different business items. These were 'musical instruments and music; stationery effects, including books, prints and engravings, as well as walking sticks; drugs, pills and ointments, the contents of the Shaftesbury Circulating Library; the two printing presses and block; and, finally, the fittings of the shop'.[181] Sadly, these businesses which John Rutter had established in his twenties and thirties did not survive long after his death. But the law firms, operating as Rutters in Shaftesbury and Gillingham and as Rutter & Rutter in Wincanton, continue to the present day.

James Everard, 10th Baron Arundell of Wardour (1785-1834)

Sir Richard Colt Hoare, 2nd Baronet (1758-1838)

4
Printer, Bookseller, Author and Publisher

After establishing his printing business in 1817, John Rutter also wrote, published and sold books. He is variously described as 'printer and stationer'. The latter description is, interestingly, derived from the stalls or 'stations' that manuscript writers and illuminators set up around St Paul's Cathedral in London in the 14th century to provide copies of ecclesiastical works, such as the Bible, and charters. The City of London livery company, The Worshipful Company of Stationers, was formed in 1403 after which its members (known as liverymen) had a monopoly, or near monopoly, over England's publishing and printing industry for the next three centuries.

Rutter took on jobbing work as a printer, making full use of the expensive equipment he had purchased. He is shown, for example, as the printer (trading as The North Dorset Press) of the Sixth Report of the Shaftesbury Branch Bible Society of 1820, with the printing costs recorded as £2.17s.6d (£240 in 2018 prices). He is similarly shown as the printer of the Seventh Report of 1821 with the cost of printing the annual report being five guineas.[182] He would have printed notices, prospectuses, advertisements as well as leaflets and the pages of books, before they were individually bound for wealthy customers.

The Rutter family's history also records that, in 1818, he purchased a library of classical and other valuable books from 'an eccentric person of the name of Bennett living at Orchard; he issued a catalogue which classified and priced the books in a manner which astonished the Shastonians' and that in 'about 1819 he rented a shop at Wincanton as a printer and stationer, this venture was not a success and was given up at the end of 1822'.[183]

As mentioned in the preceding chapter, in 1818 John Rutter penned his first work as an author. It was a description of the history of the Cranborne Chase.

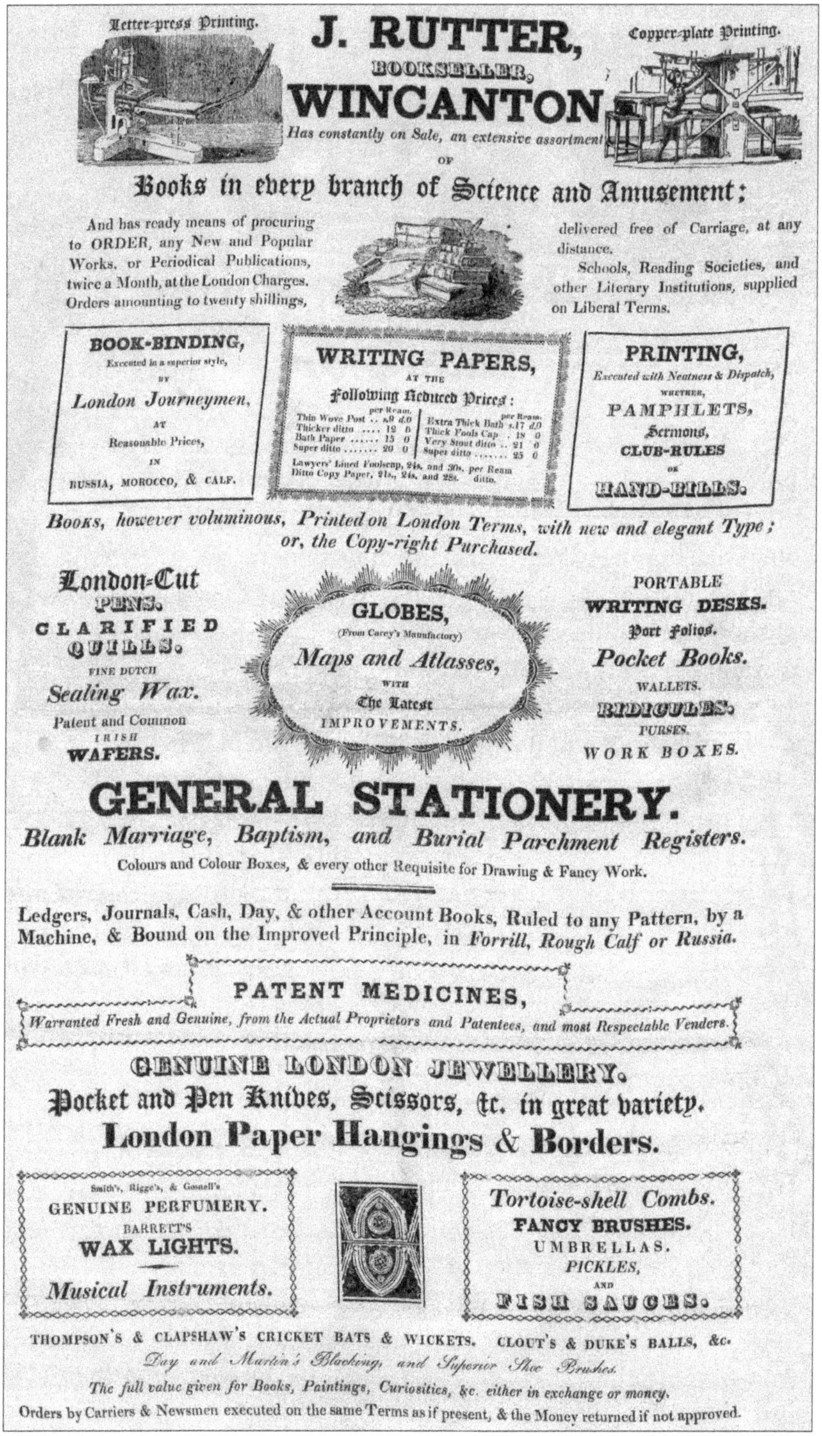

Advert for Rutter's shop in Wincanton, printed on silk (Audrey Hart-Roy)

A Brief Sketch of the State of the Poor in Shaftesbury

HIS SECOND BOOK, of 40 pages, was closer to his Quaker heart. Researched in 1818, *A Brief Sketch of the State of the Poor and of the Management of Houses of Industry; Recommended to the Consideration of the Inhabitants of the Town of Shaftesbury, and Other Places,* was published in 1819.[184]

The abolition of the monasteries (1536–40), on the instruction of King Henry VIII, removed places of refuge and curtailed the provision of food for those at the bottom end of the social spectrum. It also reduced the availability of education. The abolition was accompanied by a decline in Christian values as it took many years before the country's former Catholic faith was replaced by the new Church of England's pronouncements. At the same time, the traditional feudal system was breaking down and, with that, the age old practice of landowners being responsible for the peasants living on their land. Changes in agricultural practices, including land enclosure, were forcing more people from the countryside into towns and villages; and these changes were creating significant social problems. The duty of care, in its widest sense, in England was being transferred from the monasteries and the landowners to local communities. As a consequence of these changes, the number of poor people and their plight increased such that in Elizabethan times several acts of Parliament were passed in an attempt to deal with the rising problems.

Legislation had been introduced in the period 1530 to 1550 dealing with the punishment of vagabonds and beggars. However, it was the laws of 1552 and 1572 that dealt with the issue of the poor who thereby became the responsibility of the parish in which they lived. These laws required the poor to be registered and to be identified by one of six labels: the deserving poor, the deserving unemployed, the sick, apprentices, undeserving poor and beggars. The law also required all parish residents, with the ability to pay, to contribute funds, with justices of the peace determining the amount of contributions and overseeing the distribution of relief. In 1576, the concept of the workhouse was introduced.

The harvests of 1596 and 1597 failed and instances of illegitimacy, poverty and crime increased towards the end of the century. Action was needed to deal with this dire situation and The Poor Law Acts of 1597 and 1601 were passed. These Acts provided that England's 15,000 parishes should appoint church wardens and overseers to collect poor rates, distribute funds for relief, provide materials to generate work, establish poor houses and almshouses, and facilitate apprenticeships. Begging was curtailed. The poor rate was formally introduced as a means of raising poor relief, based as a tax on the occupiers of property.

During the 17th and 18th centuries successive pieces of legislation were passed dealing with vagrants, unmarried pregnant mothers and illegitimate children of the poor. Poor rates became the main mechanism for collecting funds which were then distributed, mainly in the form of the cash dole, for the relief of the poor. Sir Edward Knatchbull's Act of 1722–23 gave stimulus to the introduction of workhouses, managed by the parish, to provide food and shelter in return for a harsh regime of work. Organisations such as the Society for the Promotion of Christian Knowledge (SPCK) encouraged the establishment of these workhouses and, by 1732, there were probably some 700 workhouses in England.[185] The reformer, Jeremy Bentham (1748–1832), proposed the creation of a national charity to manage 250 large purpose-built workhouses. Still further, in the 18th century, legislation was introduced to supplement low wages out of the poor rate, which continued to rise and became increasingly unpopular as the 19th century dawned. The annual expenditure on poor relief in England and Wales rose from £400,000 in 1696 to £1.5 million in 1776.[186] By 1803 it was more than £4 million (£370 million in 2018 prices).[187] This increased burden on property owners and tenants was exacerbated by the growing practice of paying 'outdoor relief' as a subsidy to those in work, living outside workhouses, but with low wages.

As the Industrial Revolution progressed, farm workers migrated to the ever expanding towns, thus moving from one parish to another. Relief for the poor was becoming more complicated to administer. The population of England was also growing faster than the supply of wheat, which was reduced by poor harvests in 1789, 1790, 1792 and 1795, resulting in price increases.[188] The import of wheat was adversely affected by the French Revolutionary Wars, from 1792 to 1802, and by the Napoleonic Wars which ended in 1815. Then, in 1816, the harvest failed in a disastrous way following the volcanic eruption in April 1815 of Mount Tambora on the island of Sumbawa in today's Indonesia. The ash dispersed around the world, shutting out the sun for months and leading to lower temperatures. 1816 was dubbed 'The Year without Summer'.[189]

There were then concerns over political stability and possible social disorder. A long overdue reform of the Poor Law had been held back for political reasons during the Napoleonic Wars. Meanwhile, the total spent in England on poor relief continued to increase, from £4.3 million[190] in 1803 to £9.3 million[191] in 1818 (£760 million in 2018 prices), the year in which John Rutter undertook his review.

In Shaftesbury an almshouse for sixteen poor women had been founded in 1611 by Matthew Chubb in Salisbury Street.[192] In 1626 a workhouse was

A

BRIEF SKETCH

OF THE

State of the Poor,

AND OF THE

MANAGEMENT

OF

HOUSES OF INDUSTRY;

RECOMMENDED TO THE CONSIDERATION

OF THE

INHABITANTS

OF THE

TOWN OF SHAFTESBURY,

AND OTHER PLACES.

BY JOHN RUTTER.

SECOND EDITION.

Shaftesbury:

PRINTED AND SOLD BY J. RUTTER; SOLD ALSO BY THE NEIGHBOURING BOOKSELLERS.

1819.

A Brief Sketch of the State of the Poor, 1819 (Shaftesbury Library) established in Parson's Pool 'to provide work for the able-bodied poor and the correction of the idle and disorderly' but it does not seem to have functioned post 1660. Then, in 1663, Sir Henry Spiller founded an almshouse for men in Salisbury Street on the opposite side of the road to Chubb's.[193] The names of both Chubb and Spiller live on today in Shaftesbury as sheltered housing charities.

A poorhouse also existed in Trinity parish. The Shaftesbury Workhouse Act of 1697 established a corporation with powers to build a workhouse but there is no evidence that this was built. However, historical records indicate that at least one workhouse existed in Shaftesbury and was functioning by the early 19th century.[194] Still further, in his book of 1819, John Rutter describes an account of his visit to two workhouses in Shaftesbury in 1818.

At that time, industry in the town was on the decline with a consequential detrimental effect on the poor, many of whom were unemployed.[195] By the turn of the 19th century every parish in Dorset was supporting landless labourers who could not find, or keep, regular employment.[196] During the early 1800s, unemployment in Dorset was high, especially amongst the agricultural workforce. The average farm labourer was one of the poorest paid in the country. The number of demobbed soldiers returning to England at the end of the Napoleonic Wars, combined with the collapse in cereal and other agricultural prices, led to a deep rural depression which lasted from 1815 until the mid-1830s. The increased supply of labour, coupled with farmers' declining demand and inability to pay, led to an immediate and dramatic rise in unemployment in late 1815.[197] The combination of lack of work, poor pay and the demise of the button industry resulted in many Dorset families emigrating to America and Australia.[198] In the county the average annual amount raised from the poor rate between 1748 and 1750 was £13,790; in 1803, this had risen to £78,358 and by 1813 it was £130,048.[199] With this level of increase, there was growing pressure from householders in Dorset, as well as nationally, for reform.

In 1818, aged just 22, John Rutter was appointed to a Committee to assist the overseers in Shaftesbury to discharge their duties under the Poor Law. In the introduction to his book he wrote, 'the provision in this Town for the Poor, does not preserve them from want, or even from nakedness, but too generally induces habits of indolence and negligence, and frequently affords encouragement to vice of the grossest nature'.[200] He recommended the establishment of a well-regulated House of Industry for the destitute and claimed that thereby the poor rate would be reduced.

Rutter wrote 'industry, the groundwork of national prosperity, and of individual happiness, has decreased amongst the lower classes, in almost equal degree, with the increase of parochial allowance'.[201] For a man of liberal convictions, he sounded like a modern-day right wing politician complaining about benefit cheats when he wrote 'the support thus miserably imparted, is demanded as a right, is received with sullen and often ferocious discontent, and is the source of a thousand subterfuges and falsehoods, for purposes of deception and extortion'.[202]

Rutter estimated that, based on information on the poor rate provided to Parliament in 1804, 'about one fourth part of our resident population, in England and Wales'[203] was dependent on poor relief and might be considered to be paupers. He attributed the huge increase in the last 30 or 40 years to the 'lengthened and destructive War', the 'increase in taxation on articles of consumption', the 'effects of the late corn bill', the 'depreciation of the value of money', the 'lowness of wages for agricultural labour' and 'the present law of settlement'.[204] The 1662 Act of Settlement had sought to regularise the power of justices of the peace to remove newcomers from a parish, under certain circumstances, so reducing the parish's responsibilities.[205] Rutter blamed 'the want of religious and moral principle and general instruction among the lower classes' and 'allowing the Poor almost every thing (sic) they asked for'.[206]

Reflecting his Quaker principles, he hailed the return of peace and called for an increase in the comforts of industrious families. He claimed that a remedy in lifting the minds of the poor from pauperdom would be the result of a tendency to 'elevate the common people in their own estimation, to give each of them a feeling of personal value and worth'. In his book he sought to highlight to the townspeople of Shaftesbury the misery and deprivation of the poor living in their midst. He gave several harrowing accounts of his visits to Shaftesbury's two workhouses

> In one of these Houses, No 1, is an upstairs room, inhabited by a Woman 84 years of age, bed-ridden and almost blind, and who receives four shillings and six pence from the Parish. The general appearance of this room is wretched, and the floor and staircase are falling in.[207]
>
> No 8, A miserable hole, with part of the floor falling into a common sewer, inhabited by two Women and a Girl, who are nearly naked and emaciated; they have no bedding, and only one blanket to cover them; their general state was excessively wretched and revolting.[208]
>
> No 3, Upstairs, veiling open to the rafters, one miserable bedstead, scarcely any bed or covering, inhabited by a Widow and five young Children, and by a Man and Wife, all in one room ! The Children are almost naked, never taste any animal food, and were much distressed in the winter.[209]

John Rutter's suggested remedy was the establishment of a 'house of industry', which would be comfortable and clean, 'where the idle are employed, the profligate amended, and every age and class are taught the precepts of religion and morality'. He cited an institution in Fordingbridge established in 1808 by one Jesse Upjohn, from the well-known Shaftesbury Upjohn family. This had resulted in the amount spent on the poor being reduced from £3,284 in 1807 to £2,113 (£180,000 in 2018 prices) after it had time to operate. The poor rate was commensurately reduced from nine shillings in the pound (45%) to £7.12s.10d (38.2%). He suggested that constructing a new building would be too expensive and he recommended repairing and adapting the Angel Inn, then owned by 'a Nobleman, who has professed his willingness to do anything in his power, to promote the good of the town'.[210] The 20th century main Post Office is now on the site of the former Angel Inn which was the home of Shaftesbury's first postmaster. The nobleman was, possibly, Lord (Robert) Grosvenor who had acquired the majority of houses in Shaftesbury from Lord Rosebery in July 1819.

Rutter went on to recommend a system of management including a Master and Mistress and 'a few respectable female inhabitants'.[211] He added 'the superior judgement, tenderness, and delicacy of the female sex are indisputable, and in every respect peculiarly adapted to the want of the helpless states of infancy, and declining age'.[212] In making recommendations of the management of a house of industry and on apprenticeships, he drew on those made by Jeremy Bentham in his book *Management of the Poor* (1796) and *Pauper Management Improved* (1797). John Rutter emphasised that too much care could not be taken in choosing a Master and Mistress. He also emphasised that a key factor in the success of the house of industry would be 'the employment of the inmates'[213], for example for the men and the boys: cultivation of land, quarrying stones, carrying out water, preparing and spinning hemp and weaving it into sacks; and for the women and the girls: spinning, knitting, needlework, buttoning and plaiting straw for the manufacture of hats and bonnets.[214]

In making his recommendations, Rutter showed an understanding of the qualities required of those tasked with the management of a house of industry and of the essential features of care. He also demonstrated his ability to understand and communicate to his audience – in this case the Committee appointed to assist the overseers in Shaftesbury to discharge their duties under the Poor Law.

John Rutter's *Brief Sketch of the State of the Poor* was one of many books and papers written on this subject at that time. Various amending pieces of national legislation were introduced in an attempt to deal with the problem of the size of the poor rate and the ineffectiveness of the Poor Law.

Then, in 1832, the Bishop of London was asked to chair a Royal Commission into the state of administration of the Poor Law. The findings, which were published in 1834, concluded that poor relief benefited larger families, that immorality was encouraged by mothers having illegitimate children, that there was a disincentive to work, and that the subsidy paid to lower paid workers led to employers paying lower wages. Much of this resonates today, in the 21st century. The Commission recommended the establishment of separate workhouses for different categories of paupers, the grouping of parish workhouses into town unions to improve the quality of management, the restriction of relief to those who lived in (and submitted to the regime of) a properly managed workhouse and a central authority to oversee the implementation of the recommendations. A workhouse test was introduced such that anyone capable of living outside a workhouse would not naturally choose to live in one, as anyone residing in a workhouse would find conditions worse than those living outside.

Lord Melbourne's Whig controlled Government approved the findings and the Poor Law Amendment Act was passed in 1834, resulting in a reduction in the amount paid in poor rate nationally (from 58% in 1834 to 41% in 1850).[215] This reduction in taxes was seen as a vote winner at a time when the electoral franchise was being increased following the Great Reform Act of 1832.

Following the 1834 Poor Law Amendment Act, the Shaftesbury Poor Law Union was formed in 1835, comprising 19 parishes, with John Rutter being elected as a Guardian. As a result of the Act, the Shaftesbury Union Workhouse (Alcester House) was built between 1838 and 1840 on the western edge of the town. Just over a decade later, in 1850, it housed 250 inmates and it was a great success.[216] By highlighting the plight of the disadvantaged, John Rutter's *'Sketch of the Poor etc'* of 1819 had contributed, in some small measure, to the movement which led to the reform of the Poor Law in 1834 and to a significant improvement in the living conditions of the 'deserving poor' in Shaftesbury.

Most of the workhouse building was demolished in 1947 and replaced by housing. A small part of the east wing appears to survive as a house, No 1 Umbers Hill, on the west side of Shaftesbury.[217]

Guides to Wardour Castle and Fonthill Abbey

THE YEAR 1822 was a very busy one for Rutter's printing and publishing business in Shaftesbury as he spent much time collecting material for, and then publishing, his guides to Wardour Castle and Fonthill Abbey.

The Arundells of Wardour were a Catholic family. William Beckford of Fonthill could hardly have been described as a caring Christian, despite his obsession with St Anthony of Padua to whom he dedicated a small sanctuary. Yet both Lord Arundell and William Beckford seemed content that Rutter, a devout nonconformist Quaker, should write, publish and print an account of their properties and possessions. John Rutter was developing a track record and a reputation as an honest, reliable writer, printer and publisher. He could write well, in a clear, descriptive, knowledgeable and eloquent style. When it came to local competence and local competition in these fields, Rutter was hard to beat. Indeed his publications were of a high national standard. And, as with his *Brief Sketch of the State of the Poor,* he had worked out his audience and the manner and style in which he could successfully communicate with his readership. In the case of *Delineations of Fonthill Abbey,* he understood what readers were looking for and how much they were prepared to pay. So separate editions, which varied in length and the quality of illustrations, were printed, to meet different demands.

An Historical and Descriptive Sketch of Wardour Castle and Demesne, Wilts

In a contemporary review of new publications in 1822, *The Gentleman's Magazine* reported on the first of these two guides

> An Historical and Descriptive Sketch of Wardour Castle, the seat of Lord Arundell of Wardour, of the old Castle, and of the Arundell family; a description of the Grounds, Terrace Walk and Ruins; and a particular Account of the new Mansion and a Catalogue of the Paintings. This useful and pleasing Guide has been sanctioned by the countenance of Lord and Lady Arundell.[218]

The guide to Wardour Castle is 51 pages long and was written, published and printed in 1822 by Rutter in Shaftesbury, with four attractive engravings by Thomas Higham. It was sold in Shaftesbury by Rutter and in London by Longman, Hurst and Co; in Bath by Barret and Sons; and in Sarum (Salisbury) by Brodie and Dowding; 'as well as other booksellers'. The guide contains brief biographies of the Arundell family, descriptions of the old and new Wardour Castles and the main rooms in the new castle, as well as the very many valuable paintings and other possessions.

The origins of Old Wardour Castle can be traced to about 1300. In a patent dated 1393, King Richard II granted permission to John Lovel to build a castle at his manor. The Arundells, whose ancestors came to Britain with William the Conqueror, acquired the Wardour estate during the reign of

King Henry III (1216–72). A descendant, Sir Thomas Arundell, of Catholic stock, volunteered to fight for the Imperial Army of the Holy Roman Empire. According to Rutter, 'he served several campaigns against the Infidels, and was uniformly distinguished for his courage and skill. At the attack on Gran or Strigonium[219] he seized the sacred standard of the Turks, for which valorous act, the Emperor Rodolphus II created him a count of the Holy Roman Empire in 1595'. At a time when England was under threat from foreign powers, not least from Spain, this prompted Queen Elizabeth I's memorable remark, 'so should faithful subjects keep their eyes at home, and not gaze upon foreign crowns.....she, for her part, did not care her sheep should wear a stranger's marks, nor dance after the whistle of every foreigner'.[220] In a debate in the House of Lords on 26 April 1993, on the status of a Russian commemorative medal awarded to British servicemen, Lord Grimond recalled his understanding of the Monarch's remark as 'my dogs shall wear no other collars but mine own'.[221] Interestingly this is the version mentioned by the travel writer, Patrick Leigh Fermor, in his book *Between the Woods and the Water*, when writing about Thomas Arundell's exploits fighting the Turks in Hungary.[222] Both are frequently quoted versions of what Her Majesty actually said.

Either way, Rutter goes on to write 'Sir Thomas's value to his own country is however shewn (sic) in a strong point of view by his giving £100 (a very considerable sum in those days) towards the subscription for repelling the Spanish Armada, in which noble effort of defence, the Catholics were equally conspicuous with their Protestant brethren'. In the reign of King James I, Sir Thomas was elevated to the peerage as Baron Arundell of Wardour.[223]

Old Wardour Castle was badly damaged and made uninhabitable during the Civil War when it was besieged twice. Initially the Parliamentarians took it, after staunch defence by the retinue of Lady Blanche Arundell while her husband was away 'attending' King Charles I in Oxford. Then the castle was attacked for a second time when her son, the third Lord Arundell, returned with a large Royalist force. The Parliamentary defence was the responsibility of the appointed Governor, Edmund Ludlow, a native of Maiden Bradley in Wiltshire and an Oxonian, who had reached fame, perhaps notoriety, as one of the judges at the trial of King Charles I and as a signatory to his death warrant. Rutter amusingly described how Ludlow sought to deceive the Royalist attackers, who were besieging the castle, by arranging for one of his kinsmen to

> enter the Castle in order that he might see the strength of the garrison and the provision made for its support, but by a stratagem of the Governor, 'an dolus aut virtus', things were so ordered by removing the

> guards from place to place, filling up the hogsheads with empty barrels and covering the latter with beef and pork, and in like manner ordering the corn, that everything appeared in proportion to the real amount.[224]

However, the Royalists managed to cut the chain from the portcullis and an engineer was engaged, with some 'Mendip' miners, to dig tunnels under the walls and then blow up the castle. 'A mine was accordingly sprung and a considerable breach effected, which was immediately stormed with great impetuosity'. The garrison continued to hold out for two days but a truce was agreed 'both parties being wearied with fatigue'. A surrender was then negotiated, on the basis that none of the Parliamentarians was detained and that there was a speedy exchange of prisoners. As Rutter wrote

> Thus did Henry, the third Lord Arundell, recover possession of Wardour Castle, which had been so shaken and dismantled by these repeated sieges, as to preclude its repair, and was no longer used either for residence or defence; but its beautiful ruins, covered with ivy and situated in the bosom of venerable oaks, some of them coeval with the building, and other trees of luxuriant growth, still continue a most interesting memorial of its ancient grandeur, and form a pleasing subject of enquiry to the tourist and the topographer.[225]

As a matter of side interest, Edmund Ludlow was sent to Ireland as Lieutenant of the Horse by Oliver Cromwell who much admired Ludlow but who was also jealous of him. Still further, after the restoration of the Monarchy in 1660, when Ludlow realised that the Act of Indemnity did not apply to the judges at Charles I's trial, he left England and sought voluntary exile in Switzerland.[226]

After the family seat had been destroyed in the Civil War, somewhat ironically largely at the hands of an ancestor, Henry the 8th Lord Arundell began building the new Wardour Castle, about a mile from the ruins of the old castle, in 1768. Designed by James Paine, it is of Palladian style and was finished in 1776.[227]

Rutter devoted a full section of his guide to a description of the grounds, terrace walk and ruins. Over ten pages he described the approach and the gardens in loving detail. Showing an understanding and appreciation of topography, arboriculture and horticulture, he wrote

> The soil of Wardour Park is of a mixed kind, consisting chiefly of siliceous particles, with some calcareous and argillaceous, sufficiently

enriched by animal and vegetable matter. The luxuriance of the trees on the heights and sides of the hills shews that the latter partake of the general fertility of the soil and situation. The herbage is of fine quality, in which the dog's-tail or 'Cynosurus Cristatus' is most abundant, together with the vernal-grass 'Anthoxanthum Odoratum'; and other blade grasses, &c. are in smaller proportions.[228]

Old Wardour Castle, drawn by P. Crocker, engraved by G. Hollis, Plate XII, taken from Sir Richard Colt Hoare's The History of Modern Wiltshire. Hundred of Dunworth and Vale of Noddre, 1829 (Wiltshire and Swindon Archives, Chippenham)

Of the old castle, he described the remains and concluded that they are 'sad tokens of the prosperity which the Castle enjoyed in former days, and of the unfortunate contests which occasioned its destruction.'[229]

New Wardour Castle was, and still is, a grand house. With its neo-classical features, including a southern front of six Corinthian columns, it makes a fine statement in the Wiltshire countryside. The principal floor consists of 28 rooms 'elegantly furnished, containing a very extensive and valuable collection of paintings, mostly of the foreign schools'. Rutter described the main rooms and then listed each of the 249 stunning paintings, illustrations, items of furniture and objets d'art. These included paintings by well-known artists: Poussin's *Jacob's Meeting with his Son Joseph*; Rubens' *Portrait of St Jerome*; Caravaggio's *A Shepherd playing on the Bagpipes with an Ass and Dog standing by him*; Rubens' *Hugo Grotius*; Raphael's *Holy Family*; Pieter Bruegel the Elder's *Dutch Village*; and Rembrandt's *Feeding a Horse*. The words used by Rutter to describe each painting and object, together with the additional information given, show his appreciation of the subject matter. He also listed the Arundell family portraits and miniatures by painters including van Dyck, Labruzzi and Hussey.[230]

New Wardour Castle, drawn by J. Rutter, engraved by T. Higham, 1822 (DZSWS 1983.1503)

Of particular interest is a Grace Cup or wassail bowl, formerly belonging to Glastonbury Abbey. Rutter surmised that it probably came into the hands of the Arundell family at the time of the dissolution of the monasteries. He recorded that it was secreted by Lady Arundell when the old castle was besieged in the Civil War. But John Rutter's description of this precious object, supposedly of Saxon origin, merits repeating as it is eloquent and informative

> This curious specimen of ancient workmanship is composed of oak. It is in the form of a modern tankard, containing two quarts, of ale measure. The liquor was divided into equal quantities by eight pegs

> within the vessel, placed one above the other; four of which remain, and the holes where the others are fixed are still discernible. A number of figures in basso relievo ornament the cover and body of the cup, and the crucifixion, with the Virgin Mary, St. John, and the two cherubs, are represented in carved work above the lid. A representation of a bunch of grapes forms the knob on the handle. The twelve apostles are round the body, of whom St. Peter bears a key, St. John a chalice, Judas a purse, and each of the others holds an open book. The name of each of the twelve is inscribed beneath his figure upon a label, under which is some representation of animals and flowers. The three feet of the cup are in the form of couchant lions.[231]

In this sketch of Wardour Castle, John Rutter, then aged 26, was demonstrating a keen interest in the countryside, grand buildings and beautiful objects, which he described so well. His biblical upbringing made him familiar with some of the religious subject matter of the paintings. His written appreciation of what he saw demonstrates an education in fine art, architecture and literature. These attributes are remarkable in someone who was orphaned at the age of ten.

According to John Farley Rutter, 'In 1823, John Rutter published his *Guide to Wardour Castle* in 98 pages'.[232] This longer version, the year after the first edition, included a more comprehensive catalogue and more illustrations.

As a sequel to this story, in 1934 the 16th Baron Arundell started repairs to the castle estate and initiated a new planting scheme. Then in 1936, Old Wardour Castle, which had been largely destroyed in the Civil War, was placed in the guardianship of the Ministry of Works (later English Heritage). After the 16th Baron's death, in 1944, new Wardour Castle and its immediate surroundings were sold to the Society of Jesus. In 1961 the new castle became Cranborne Chase School, which closed down in 1990. In 1992 it was sold into private ownership and has now been divided into self-contained apartments.[233]

Description of Fonthill Abbey and Desmesne, Wiltshire – An illustrated history and description of Fonthill Abbey and Delineations of Fonthill & Its Abbey

In the case of Fonthill Abbey, John Rutter had to move fast. The vast and spectacular neo-Gothic abbey, designed by James Wyatt, had been built between 1796 and 1818 and contained William Beckford's priceless collection of paintings, sculptures, furniture, library and objets d'art. There, Beckford, a wealthy man whose reputation had been tarnished by a homosexual scandal with a young boy, lived alone with few visitors. The declining sugar revenues from his Jamaican estates and his lavish lifestyle had caused him to borrow to finance the completion of the enormous and extravagant Abbey and to acquire the priceless treasures stored there. In debt to the tune of £145,000[234] (£15 million in 2018 prices), Beckford was falling out of love with Fonthill and turning his mind to his next project. He decided to sell everything, via an auction, to generate the funds. Even after 26 years, at the time of the sale in 1822, the Abbey was still not totally complete, with some apartments unfinished.

Beckford had been socially ostracized following reports, in 1784, of an alleged homosexual affair with the eleven year old William 'Kitty' Courtenay, later the 9th Earl of Devon. Letters of an intimate nature between the two were leaked to the Press. Until 1861 such a relationship would have been a capital offence, although aristocrats who were caught avoided this extreme punishment by leaving the country. A criminal prosecution was never brought against Beckford. Instead he spent many years in voluntary exile on the Continent, in Switzerland, Portugal and France. There he gained a taste for Gothic architecture and he collected truly magnificent works of art.

Fonthill Abbey began as a Gothic folly in the woods of the estate where his father had built a most attractive Palladian mansion, Fonthill Splendens, beside a lake. The mansion was however damp and, according to John Rutter, 'very low, and after the lake had been made, subject to frequent fogs'.[235] Beckford's plans for the folly grew in size until it came to be his main house, a huge museum to house his possessions. Work on its construction began in 1796 and continued for over twenty years, during which time Beckford gradually took up residence, finally knocking down Fonthill Splendens and selling its contents in 1807.[236]

In his new cathedral-like abode, through paintings of monarchs and coats of arms, he sought to display his perceived noble lineage in a grandiose attempt to show that he was a person of standing. Beckford even employed a dwarf, dressed in 'gold and embroidery', one of whose jobs was to open the doors of the Great Western Hall to guests. An impression of the immense oak door valves (35 feet high, weighing more than a ton) 'was accentuated by his tiny and grotesque figure'.[237] Fonthill Abbey was an extreme example of folie de grandeur.

It was known that, because of his social isolation, Beckford was reclusive. He took the extreme measure of building a high wall, known as 'The Barrier', six miles long and allegedly ten feet high, encompassing 500 acres, to prevent anyone from entering his property.[238] He had always been interested in the idea of a retreat in which he could spend time reading and contemplating, away from the world. He was also very fond of animals, particularly dogs, and hated the idea of hunting and of his estate being a killing field.

Beckford entertained few visitors. However, Admiral Nelson, together with Sir William and Lady Hamilton, spent Christmas 1800 as guests at Fonthill Splendens. A spectacularly theatrical evening was planned, with a torch lit procession accompanied by minstrels through the woods to the partly finished Abbey. Nelson's mistress, Emma Hamilton, then eight months pregnant, gave a rendition of her 'attitudes', a sort of mime, based on Emma, semi-naked, posing as classical figures in alluring costumes.[239]

On another occasion, in 1806, Sir Richard Colt Hoare, Bt. (1758–1838) of nearby Stourhead asked to see the Abbey and was shown around, allegedly by William Beckford. When his fellow Wiltshire landowners heard of this, they reprimanded Sir Richard, who explained that it was no more than a desire to see Fonthill Abbey and its contents; he protested that his meeting with the owner was 'accidental and to him unexpected'.[240] But Beckford and Hoare had so much in common that an interesting and productive conversation would undoubtedly have taken place. They were similar in age, Sir Richard being 22 months older. Both had large estates. Both had enjoyed two grand tours and many years travelling on the Continent, as well as writing about their journeys and sharing other interests. Both were avid collectors and readers of books. Both had commissioned Turner to produce watercolours: Sir Richard of Stourhead, Stonehenge and Salisbury Cathedral (in 1798 to 1800), Beckford of Fonthill (in 1799).[241] So perhaps Sir Richard's response, when questioned, was merely to avoid opprobrium.

It was also reported that Beckford lived alone in his Abbey and used only one of its bedrooms. His kitchens prepared food for twelve guests every day, although he always dined alone, with servants in full livery waiting on him.[242] It was clear that Beckford was living way beyond his means. He had spent a fortune building Fonthill Abbey and collecting a huge and impressive array of paintings and fine art. He had also started to grow out of love with the Abbey and his attention was focussed on his next project, in Bath.

John Rutter obtained an introduction to William Beckford, probably through Sir Richard Colt Hoare who was later a subscriber to, and promoted, Rutter's higher quality edition *Delineations of Fonthill & Its Abbey*. Beckford invited Rutter to Fonthill Abbey to make a description of the exterior, interior and possessions prior to its intended ten-day auction sale in September 1822 under the auspices of James Christie of Pall Mall. Rutter was clearly astonished at the size of Fonthill Abbey, the magnificence of the interiors, the opulence of the furnishings and the sheer volume of precious objects. It was possibly the most ambitious and eccentric building of the 19th century and undoubtedly influenced the neo-Gothic architectural styles of the subsequent Houses of Parliament and of St Pancras Station and its hotel, now the St Pancras Renaissance Hotel, designed by George Gilbert Scott.

Rutter wrote of Fonthill Abbey 'from the earliest hour that the interesting mansion, which is the subject of the following paper, became accessible to the world, the author felt a drawing ambition to prepare a description of it for the public eye'. Detailed sketches were made by Rutter and the artist George Cattermole for later engraving by Thomas Higham, John Cleghorn and others; a few of these were aquatinted. The result, a 72-page guide book, (frontispiece & vi + 66 pages) entitled *A Description of Fonthill Abbey, and Demesne, Wilts; The Seat of William Beckford, Esq. Including a List of its Numerous and Valuable Paintings, Cabinets, and Other Curiosities,* was published in 1822.

Fonthill Abbey – South West View, 1823, drawn by J. Rutter, engraved by T. Higham, 1823 (DZSWS 1983.2653)

In a contemporary review of new publications in *The Gentleman's Magazine, A Description of Fonthill Abbey and Demesne* was referred to as

> Well calculated as a Guide to the Visitor of that princely mansion. It gives a historical sketch of Fonthill Gifford and its possessors; a description of the Abbey Grounds (selected in a great measure from Mr. Storer's Work,

> but without mentioning its source); and an account of the Paintings, Cabinets, and other curiosities; concluding with a brief notice of the outer Grounds, and of the former Mansion. It is embellished with a very good S.W. view of the Abbey.[243]

Previously closed to visitors but, in the summer of 1822, open for viewing prior to the sale, the Abbey attracted the public's interest and fascination. Beckford's lifestyle, the alleged scandals over his sex life, his enormous collection of paintings and fine art, the sheer size and grandeur of the building made Fonthill an alluring place to visit. In his classic work, *The History of Modern Wiltshire. Hundred of Dunworth and Vale of Noddre*, Sir Richard Colt Hoare described the scene

> No place perhaps ever excited the public curiosity so much....at length, in the year 1822, the general curiosity was gratified; the gates were opened, and crowds assembled from all quarters to view this long-forbidden ground....But I shall not enter into any description, either of the Abbey or its precincts, as they have been so amply and correctly described by Messrs. Briton and Rutter, in their respective publications....no one, after viewing this work of genius and of taste, returned ungratified'.[244]

With its soaring neo-Gothic halls crammed full of Renaissance paintings, exquisite furniture, a library, sculptures and fine objects d'art, there was frenzied interest from the public. 7,200 copies of Christie's illustrated catalogue were sold for a guinea each (£110 in 2018 prices) as up to 700 people visited Fonthill Abbey each day during August and September 1822.[245] Rutter's publication *A Description of Fonthill Abbey and Demesne, in the County of Wilts* similarly sold well and it ran to a sixth edition in the same year.[246] The first edition differs from the other five in having 72 pages. It also differs in the description of the order in which one might tour the interior of the Abbey. There were also minor changes after the second edition.[247] Each of the six editions was of 8vo size, having just one illustration, and sold for 3s.6d.[248] One can imagine the large number of visitors clutching the sale particulars and also Rutter's guide book as they walked through the rooms and wondered at the spectacle of Fonthill Abbey and its contents.[249]

Immediately prior to the planned date of the auction (starting 17 September 1822) Christie postponed the event twice (eventually to 8 October), at Beckford's insistence. However on 6 October, hand bills were circulated cancelling the auction.[250] William Beckford had always hoped for a private sale. Indeed he had been in discussion with the agent of his daughter, Susan's,

Fonthill Abbey – Interior of the Great Western Hall, 1823, drawn by Geo. Cattermole, engraved by J.C. Varrall, published by J. Rutter, Shaftesbury (S&DHS, D.H.C., D-SHS/ Box 43.3363)

husband, the 10th Duke of Hamilton. But the wily factor was wary of the condition of the Abbey and Beckford's efforts were rebuffed. In the autumn of 1822, the pre-auction hype had, no doubt, been intended to encourage another potential purchaser to come forward, at a higher price than might be realised from the auction proceeds of just the contents. Behind Christie's back, Beckford had been negotiating with a rival auctioneer. Henry (known as Harry) Phillips, who used to work for Christie, had found a private buyer. Beckford sold the Abbey, all its precious contents and 5,000 acres of land for £300,000 (£31 million in 2018 prices) to a wealthy Scottish trader, John Farquhar, who had made his fortune selling gunpowder to the East India Company, 'having attained the particular favour and confidence of the late Warren Hasting, Esq'.[251] Christie must have been furious at being led along, with the loss of a large commission. The public felt cheated. But these sentiments did not seem to worry Beckford. It is believed that he realised a handsome profit on his total outlay for the building of the Abbey and on the acquisition of contents over the previous 25 years.[252] Indeed, shortly after Beckford's death in 1844, his first biographer, Cyrus Redding wrote in the *New Monthly Magazine* that Beckford had told him that 'My whole outlay on Fonthill was £273,000, some hundreds over that sum it may be, no more. This was scattered over sixteen or eighteen years in the expenditure'.[253] Beckford was pleased to be rid of it and to be able to pay his debts. His attention had also moved to his next project – life in Bath and the construction of yet another tower (now known as Beckford's Tower) on Lansdown Hill.

The following year, in September and October 1823, Harry Phillips organised at Fonthill Abbey a 37-day sale by auction of over 4,000 books, many objets d'art from the Abbey and also much brought in from elsewhere. The demand from the public to see the Abbey and its contents was again very great and, according to the *Literary Gazette* of 30 August 1823, Phillips sold 2,000 tickets for 10s.6d. each (£55 each in 2018 prices). It is thought that nearer the date of the auction this number was well exceeded and *The Times* reported

> He is fortunate who finds a vacant chair within twenty miles of Fonthill; the solitude of a private apartment is a luxury which few can hope for... The beds through the county are (literally) doing double duty – people who come in from a distance during the night must wait to go to bed until others get up in the morning. ..Not a farmhouse – however humble – not a cottage near Fonthill, but gives shelter to fashion, to beauty, and rank.[254]

In the run up to Phillips' auction in September, Rutter published *A New Descriptive Guide to Fonthill Abbey and Demesne*. This was an extensively revised version of the 1822 guide, *A Description of Fonthill Abbey and Demesne*. The new edition comprised a frontispiece, engraved title page & viii + 98 pages. It was priced at four shillings and announced in the *New Monthly Magazine* of September 1823, suggesting that this subject continued to be of great public interest. Higher quality versions of this edition were available at between one and three guineas, depending on size and the number of illustrations.[255]

The auction sale was a great success, realising £330,000. Even Beckford bought back some of the items which he had sold to Farquhar the year before.

But, Farquhar's euphoria was not to last long. Just two years later, on 21 December 1825, the central high tower of the Abbey collapsed in a storm, destroying a large part of the rest of the building with it. An evening newspaper of 24 December reported

> The tower fell...destroying the Hall, the whole of the Octagon, and great part of the Galleries, North and South, together with the first crimson room, having quietly descended into the fountain court, leading the grand entrance standing, with the organ in 'statu quo', and the statue of the late Alderman Beckford in its niche.[256]

Sir Richard Colt Hoare arranged for a drawing to be made by John Buckler of the Abbey in ruins, complementing the two large drawings which Buckler had made earlier of the Abbey in its perfect state. Sir Richard commented 'the tower, from its excessive height, was out of all proportion'.[257]

Over the years, there has been much speculation as to the cause of the collapse. There were complaints about dishonest builders. It was alleged that the architect, James Wyatt, was negligent and had been too busy attending to the affairs of the King (George III). It was suggested that Wyatt was a womaniser and that, when on site, he was often drunk. Then, Wyatt died in 1813 as a result of an accident when a carriage in which he was travelling overturned; the Abbey had lost its main architect, although Wyatt's sons provided advice after this. It was also alleged that Beckford had interfered too much with the building works and was forever changing his ideas and the plans of construction. There is some truth in this as Fonthill Abbey was originally intended to be a small Gothic folly but then it grew into an enormous monument. It was variously suggested that the architectural plans were at fault – that originally the tower was to have been made out of wood, whereas the foundations were inadequate for the later stone construction; or that a dubious system known as 'compo-cement' or 'Roman cement' had been chosen, comprising a timber frame stuccoed with render. It was alleged that the foundations may not have been deep enough but then, on the top of the hill, the builders would probably have struck rock after digging down just a few feet. The central tower had collapsed twice during construction. After the second collapse, the exterior of the Abbey was faced, at Beckford's instructions in 1806/7, in stone to replace the crumbling cement. Repair-work and rebuilding was constantly necessary.[258]

In an early commentary of the tower's collapse, in the *Gardener's Magazine* of 1835, the editor, John Claudius Loudon, wrote that the following seemed likely

> The first tower, the height of which from the ground was 400ft., was built of wood, in order to see its effect: this was then taken down, and the same form put up in wood covered with cement. This fell down, and the tower was built a third time, on the same foundation, with brick and stone. The foundation of the tower was originally that of a small summer-house, to which Mr. Beckford was making additions when the idea of the abbey occurred to him; and this idea he was so impatient to realise, that he could not wait to remove the summer-house, to make a proper foundation for the tower, but carried it up on the walls already standing. The kinds of masonry, brickwork, and carpentry which were used may be easily ascertained from the parts remaining. Nothing can be worse: the walls are carried up in some parts of brick, in others of

Fonthill Abbey in Ruins, 1825, drawn on stone by William Westall, after a drawing by John Buckler, engraved by William Westall, printed by C.J. Hullmandel (Fonthill Estate Archives)

> stone, and in others of studwork, sometimes enclosed in stone or brick casing, but always of the very worst description of workmanship......To those who are acquainted with the details of building, and especially with the practices of the worst London builders, the exhibition here is most amusing in a scientific point of view; and one may easily conceive that the work has been chiefly carried on by men in a state of intoxication.[259]

Beckford himself related to Cyrus Redding that the foreman had told him that the tower was very insecure and that the only solution was to take it down and rebuild it from the foundation. He continued 'It was a source of continual apprehension to me. I was like Damocles with the sword over his head'.[260]

More recently, two theories have been advanced as to the real causes of the collapse of the central tower.

First, Simon Thurley, the academic and architectural historian and a former Chief Executive of English Heritage, has propounded an explanation. When he was preparing for the Channel Four television series *Lost Buildings of Britain*, he decided to include Fonthill Abbey as one of the six case studies. In doing so he wished to clear up the mystery of why the great tower fell and he employed Keith Weston, a historic buildings engineer from English Heritage, to investigate. Using ground penetrating radar, the scan showed that the foundations were two metres deep, very wide and solidly packed. They dispelled the notion that the foundations were not deep enough. Weston then analysed the drawing of the cross section of the Abbey from John Rutter's *Delineations*. They concluded that the lower walls were too thin for the weight of the higher walls. After the tower collapsed for the second time and was rebuilt in wood covered with 'compo-cement' or 'Roman cement', the stucco began cracking and peeling off again. To prevent a third collapse, Beckford instructed the builders to construct the upper half in masonry, which was too heavy for the lower half to bear. It was not the foundations that were at fault but Beckford's decision to change the construction materials, without adequate support from the lower portion of the Abbey's walls. Thurley exonerated James Wyatt and concluded that Beckford only had himself to blame.[261]

But a more interesting, and new, explanation has been put forward by Philip Proctor of Shaftesbury architects, Proctor Watts Cole Rutter. He has suggested that the timber structure of the tower developed dry rot from the ingress of water through the stucco coating which had cracked as the huge tower swayed in the wind. Proctor examined the evidence and concluded that the timbers suffered in this way and could no longer bear the weight of the masonry. He points to comments in Beckford's letters, reproduced in Boyd

Alexander's book, *Life at Fonthill 1807–1822: From the correspondence of William Beckford*, translated and edited by Boyd Alexander:

> *Tuesday 7 February 1815: The dampness of this sublime abode is so great that everything will rot. Today, visiting the tabernacles or cribs in the Lancaster Gallery with wretched Rottier, I found them all covered with lichen and stalactites like Fingal's cave; the lacquer was covered with a white beard*[262]... Proctor comments that this is a good description of dry rot.
>
> *Friday 10 February 1815: My tower swayed*[263]...Proctor comments that the swaying of the tower would have resulted in the compo-cement cracking.
>
> *Saturday 24 June 1815: There is a very mild warmth, accompanied by a damp mist everywhere*[264]...Proctor comments that these were perfect conditions under which dry rot flourishes.
>
> *Sunday 25 June 1815: Oh God, what a summer, what a June – if this really is June and summer! Last night the voice of November was heard increasingly in all the chimneys*[265]... Proctor adds that, if the timbers were wet, the lack of heat in June 1815 would have prevented them from drying out properly.
>
> *Monday 13 November 1815: I'm almost stunned, not only by the deplorable impotence of Rottier but by the horrible din of the winds last night. I didn't sleep a half-hour in succession – I thought I heard sobs and lamentations, cannon shots, bomb explosions, and all the delights of the battles of Borodino or Waterloo*[266]...Proctor comments that this was the timber shrinking as it aged (the tower would have been built out of new 'green' timber) and the stucco cracking.
>
> *Sunday 31 August 1817: Every instant the weather seems to get worse – one moment cold, the next hot, always damp and nearly always windy; never any sun, never anything that reminds one of Summer*[267]...Proctor is confirmed in his view that the wet timbers would never have had time to dry out and dry rot would have resulted.

The weather in England and Wales during this period was exceptionally cold and wet. From 1809 to 1819 there were, generally, harsh winters and unsettled cold and wet summers. The spring of 1818, in particular, experienced high rainfall leading to flooding in many parts of the country.[268] The poet Keats wrote from Devon

> We are here still enveloped in clouds — I lay awake last night listening to the Rain with a sense of being drowned and rotted like a grain of

> wheat. There is a continual courtesy between the Heavens and the Earth. The heavens rain down their unwelcomeness, and the Earth sends it up again to be returned to-morrow.[269]

Proctor observes that further information about the instability of the main tower is based on the decision to build such a powerful east wing to buttress the tower. He draws attention to the 'The Year without Summer' in 1816, referred to above, which was also the year in which Mary Shelley wrote Frankenstein, adding

> Clearly the weather that gave rise to Frankenstein created perpetual dampness. With the cracks caused by timber movement and from the winds, and not much sun to dry anything, that is the perfect recipe for dry rot. Once it starts and with this form of construction it will continue to eat away at the timber, reducing its strength.[270]

Proctor also refers to Beckford's letter of Monday 26 April 1819, where Beckford despaired over the state of collapse of the small tower which housed his bedroom. Proctor concludes by pointing out that the main tower fell towards the south-west which is evidence that the timber frame had greatest weakening from dry rot on the side of the prevailing wind and rain, but with some sun to warm the moist wood, thus encouraging dry rot fungus.

Both theories seem highly plausible. Indeed it is most likely that the cause of the demise of Fonthill Abbey was a combination of the two. Beckford was fully aware of the instability of the central tower, which had already fallen down twice during construction. He was concerned about a third collapse. He had, in any event, fallen out of love with the Abbey and was anxious to get shot of it. Being cynical, it is probable that the proposed auction by Christie, with all its promotion and hype, was intended to attract a sole purchaser. After all, what would Beckford have done with the Abbey if he had sold all its magnificent contents.

It is highly unlikely that a comprehensive structural survey was undertaken by Farquhar to whom Beckford sold the Abbey. Indeed Farquhar had rushed into purchasing the Abbey, signing the contract within two weeks of viewing it.[271] Was he aware of the construction problems? Probably he was but, being commercial, imagined that he could realise more from a sale of the contents, building and estate separately.

As mentioned earlier, after acquiring the Abbey in October 1822, Farquhar auctioned the contents in September 1823. Then, after the collapse of the central tower in 1825, he tried to dispose of the remains of the damaged building but was unsuccessful, before dying intestate in 1826. After his death, the estate was divided up and sold in October 1829 in three parts, one of which included the ruined Abbey. According to Sir Richard Colt Hoare, the proceeds of sale of the Fonthill Estate, including the Abbey and its valuable effects amounted to £290,000.[272]

After the Abbey and the western part of the estate were acquired by the Marquess of Westminster in 1844, most of the remains of the buildings were demolished.[273] Only the Lancaster Tower (of the North Wing) remains to this day. Between 1846 and 1852 the 2nd Marquess commissioned William Burn to build a new large mansion, approximately 300 yards south east of Beckford's folly. Confusingly also named Fonthill Abbey, this building was requisitioned by the Army in 1941 and demolished (blown up) in 1955.[274]

Meanwhile, back in October 1823,[275] John Rutter had published, by subscription, *Delineations of Fonthill & Its Abbey*. This longer book of 153 pages (frontispiece, illustrations & xxvi + 127 pages), with proofs and etchings, was dedicated to 'The most Noble Susannah Euphemia, Duchess of Hamilton and Brandon, Marchioness of Douglas and Clydesdale'. Susan was William Beckford's younger daughter who had married Alexander Hamilton in 1810 and, on the death of his father in 1819, Hamilton became the 10th Duke. This more extravagant edition has a morocco leather spine and tips with 13 plates, three of which are hand coloured illustrations of an extremely high quality, with 15 beautiful wood-engraved illustrations in the text. There is a folding lithographed estate map which is hand-coloured in outline. As with the earlier guide, many of the architectural drawings and sketches were made by Rutter for engraving by Thomas Higham, among others. The quality of the drawings demonstrates Rutter's not insignificant artistic ability. The book was printed at Rutter's works in Shaftesbury. In addition to the 78 copies of a higher quality India paper edition, there were over 500 subscribers who bought almost 650 copies of the large paper and small paper editions. All the subscribers were listed at the end of *Delineations*. Amongst the more prominent names who acquired the India paper edition were Lord Arundell, the Duke of Bedford, the Marquess of Bath, Earl Grosvenor, the Earl of Macclesfield, Lord Suffield and four members of the Hoare family, including Sir Richard Colt Hoare.[276] Sir Richard personally promoted Rutter's work. In a letter to the Reverend Daniel Lysons, when sending him four rails (water birds), he wrote 'We are likely to have a good & minute account of Fonthill - by Rutter, who wrote the guide and it has been patronized by the second abbot'(Farquhar). He then asked if some of Lysons' friends would honour him with their names by buying other sizes: 'Large paper proofs. 2gns' and 'Small paper 1gn'.[277]

In an attempt to judge the market and to interest subscribers, Rutter had earlier, in September 1822, advertised this higher quality version in the *Salisbury and Winchester Journal* as *A History and Description of Fonthill Abbey*. It was described as being available in two sizes: demy quarto at 15s. and royal quarto at one and a half guineas (£166 in 2018 prices), available from Longman and Co in Paternoster-row, Taylor in High Holborn and Ackermann in the Strand, as well as being sold by 'all Booksellers'.[278]

During the latter part of 1822 and in the early months of 1823 there had been a race for the publication of the first fully illustrated guide book to Fonthill Abbey. The two contenders were John Rutter and John Britton, a historian and author, who wrote about architectural antiquities and the countryside.

Britton had been introduced to Beckford much earlier than Rutter. They had met in 1798 when Britton was working on his book *The Beauties of Wiltshire* (1801) in which he acknowledged that Beckford had provided the second of the two plates illustrating Fonthill Splendens and its grounds. Beckford collected many of Britton's publications including his series in *Architectural Antiquities* (1807–1814) and *Cathedral Antiquities* (1814–1835).[279] Beckford wrote critically about Britton, as was his custom when writing about most people he met or who worked for him. But he also admired his work, writing 'Britton has shewn (sic) me some really delightful drawings by a certain Mackenzie, of a delicacy, a richness of colour, a harmony, a -----: in short they are celestial...'[280] Britton began working at Fonthill in August 1822, with his artist, George Cattermole. The task was far greater and took far longer than he calculated. On top of this, Beckford had very definite ideas as to the guide's content and emphasis. In a letter to Britton of 3 October 1822, Beckford suggested that in the illustrated guide he should omit mention of the past manor and the present churches 'neither of which as you will fully observe perhaps may want merit or mention'. Instead he offered his 'quarterings' (coat of arms) for the title page because they are picturesque enough and 'will make as fine a sprawl as that displayed in front of the south court'.[281] Beckford was showing his vain and egotistical nature as he endeavoured to ensure that the contents of the book were focused on his creations alone.

Britton was furious when he heard that Rutter was planning a rival illustrated work. He wrote to him on 1 October 1822, accusing him of deceit and 'expecting you to be a fair, honourable, & candid tradesman'.[282] On 3 October 1822, Beckford's friend, Gregorio Franchi, wrote to Britton, whom Franchi supported, saying, 'his (Rutter's) work will never be sanctioned or encouraged by M. Beckford'.[283] But Britton was not at all comforted when his own artist, Cattermole, defended Rutter's integrity and right to compete.

It transpired that Sir Richard Colt Hoare had been encouraging Rutter after introducing him to the Abbey's new owner, John Farquhar, who was similarly encouraging and supportive of Rutter.[284]

Rutter visited London to stimulate interest in his illustrated work among the capital's booksellers and publishers, including J.B. Nichols & Son of Number 25 Parliament Street, Westminster. Nichols had inherited his father's printing business and for very many years was the editor of the *Gentleman's Magazine*. Until Richard Clarence died in 1826[285], when Rutter was in London he stayed at his parents-in-laws' house, Number 94 Minories, just east of the City. In a letter from this address to Nichols to arrange for a notice to be placed in the next issue of the *Gentleman's Magazine*, Rutter added 'J Britton makes such a puff about his favours at Fonthill Abbey', indicating the competition and level of irritation which had developed between the two author-publishers.[286] In a manuscript note made by Nichols, Rutter's twelve drawings of the Abbey are referred to as having been 'finished on the spot, in a very superior style, and are now in the engraver's hands'.[287]

In October 1822, *The Literary Gazette* advertised Rutter's impending work of the *History and Description of Fonthill Abbey* which 'speedily will be published', together with a brief account of the work.[288]

When both books were published in 1823, contemporary reviewers made comparisons and generally preferred Rutter's *Delineations* for its descriptions and beautiful engravings.[289] *Delineations* was reviewed in the *Gentleman's Magazine*, which proclaimed, 'Upon the whole we pronounce this publication a very correct and able account of the Abbey and its demesnes; and when we consider its many excellent illustrations, it cannot be esteemed a dear work... no visitor has returned from the Abbey without pleasure and admiration'.[290] In terms of detail, the *Gentleman's Magazine* added 'Each (that is Britton's and Rutter's) has also given ground-plans of the Abbey, of which that of Mr Rutter is the best'.[291] Still further, the magazine commented that 'we find that the engraved plates of Mr. Rutter may be considered superior, both in choice of subject, and able execution'.[292]

Thomas Moore, who wrote about the life and poetry of Sheridan, visited Shaftesbury on 21 July 1826. He described John Rutter as 'the Quaker bookseller' who thrust a copy of 'this splendid work' (*Delineations of Fonthill & Its Abbey*) into his carriage as he was driving off, saying it was a mark of his respect for the independent spirit Moore had shown in his description of the life of Sheridan.[293]

In his article, *The Troubled Gestation of Britton's 'Illustrations of Fonthill'*, Stephen Clarke observed in 2000 'Rutter's text is far more detailed, describing the Abbey room by room with general comments and separate sections on architecture, furniture and heraldry. His summary of the interior amounts to fifty-eight pages, compared to Britton's eighteen'. When comparing the illustrations, Clarke concluded that, despite both publishers sharing a number of the same artists, 'it is hard to deny Rutter's superiority'. Even Britton praised Rutter's Estate Plan and preferred Rutter's plates.[294]

In the preface to this higher quality edition, John Rutter wrote

> The satisfactory performance of his task (even to himself) he has found to be much more difficult than he had anticipated; not from any impediment thrown in his way by the late proprietor, or by the present possessor, for their kindness and liberality have been unlimited and uniform; not from a want of patronage, for he has to make his acknowledgements to a much larger body of nobility and gentry and friends than his most sanguine hopes had dared to calculate upon; but from the colossal magnitude of the principal object, the endless number of its details, and the inexhaustible stores of its precious contents.[295]

In *Delineations,* Rutter described the distant view of Fonthill Abbey as one approached Salisbury from London, 'Looking across the barren plain and over a wooded country beyond, we see an object of extraordinary height and magnitude, rising out of the side of one of the highest hills on the horizon. It is the tower of the Abbey, at a distance of twenty miles'. The entry to the estate from the main Salisbury to Exeter road was via an ornate Baroque gateway, ascribed to Inigo Jones. Then one journeyed past an ornamental lake, next by an inn named the Beckford Arms and Fonthill Gifford church, then along the Barrier (a ten foot high wall) designed to deter strangers (and even neighbours) from trespassing on the estate, to a gate which led to the long Western Avenue and thence to the grand porch of the Abbey. Each of the major rooms was detailed in Rutter's book: the enormous and lofty Great Western Hall, the Grand Saloon or Octagon, the Great Dining Room, the Crimson Drawing Room, the Grand Drawing Room, the Lancaster Turret with the Lancaster State Bedchamber and the Lancaster Gallery, St Michael's Gallery and St Edward's Gallery. In total 72 rooms were listed and their precious contents described.[296]

The interior décor of Fonthill Abbey comprised rich colours of scarlet, crimson and deep blue. There were heraldic images and much stained glass creating patterns of light in each room and on the sculptures, furniture, draperies and tapestries. There were objects of great provenance, for example two armoires designed by Le Brun (1619–1690) from the collection of the Duc d'Aumont (1709–1782) and two crystal cabinets, in the style of Camillo

Maderno, belonging to Pope Paul V (1550–1621). These were complemented by many exceptional paintings by Veronese, Rubens and Breughel.

In the galleries, portraits of medieval kings of England and knights were a testament to William Beckford's pretension to royal connections. Rutter described the bosses and heraldic emblems on the oak ceiling of King Edward's Gallery, the seven Gothic windows, the stained glass, the antique furniture and the books. He commented 'This gallery has been designed for the purpose of commemorating the names of those individuals of Mr. Beckford's ancestry, who have been honoured with the illustrious knighthood of the garter', the highest order of chivalry, created in 1348 by King Edward III. Saint Michael's Gallery had a fan-vaulted ceiling of a design copied from the cloister of Gloucester Cathedral. Rutter described its lavish decoration as 'a specimen of the richest combinations, which the genius of gothic architecture has yet invented, beautifully contrasted with the artificial gloom of the opposite gallery, by terminating in an oriel-window of painted glass, exposed to the rays of a meridian sun'.[297]

As a Quaker whose beliefs include simplicity and equality, Rutter must have found Fonthill Abbey a rather alien, but fascinating, place. The extravagance of the building and its contents must have grated. With his views on morality, he cannot have found Beckford's alleged actions and moral behaviour acceptable. Yet, he documented what he saw in a most professional manner and his descriptions were carefully accurate as well as imaginatively phrased. His use of English was excellent and persuasive.

John Rutter was, overall, generous in his description of Fonthill with its 'colossal dimensions and costly materials'. But he couldn't resist the occasional critical and caustic remark

> In this building, with what sacrifice of domestic comfort we shall afterwards inquire, the late possessor has devoted the whole, except the offices in the basement, and a few attics, to the splendid purpose of producing a succession of architectural scenes of infinite variety.[298]

Still further, he wrote

> All the Abbey, with all its Towers, furnishes but about eighteen bed-rooms, thirteen of which, from their almost inaccessible height, their smallness, their want of light and ventilation, from one or all these causes combined, are scarcely fit for their intended use; and of the other five, not one has a dressing room. The defects of the Basement in regard to the offices, must have been evident from the sketch we gave of its

> contents. There are no means of baking, washing or brewing within it, and these operations are therefore performed in a temporary out-house.[299]

In a reference to dining, John Rutter couldn't resist another dig when he wrote, 'Until very recently, the Oak Parlour was the only room for the service of dinner, with the important recommendation of being the furthest apartment from the kitchen !' (Sic: Rutter's exclamation mark).[300]

When it came to describing the grounds of Fonthill Abbey and its walks, Rutter was complimentary, showing the interest he had in the countryside, trees, flowers and things of natural beauty. Indeed he became quite poetic, quoting Chaucer, Spenser and Fletcher as well as verses from Milton's *Paradise Lost* and *Paradise Regained.* He was enraptured by the ambiance of the Abbey in its setting as 'around a holy calm diffusing'.

According to John Farley Rutter, *Delineations* was

> A very fine illustrated work, and its compilation and literary part must have taken up a considerable amount of his time; it was printed at his press in Shaftesbury. The total cost was about £1,000 [£120,000 in 2018 prices], whether he made money or lost on this book I do not know, probably the latter. Most of the architectural drawings were by his own pen and show that he might have succeeded in that line had he so desired.[301]

John Farley Rutter's assessment of the financial outcome of *Delineations* may have been a little pessimistic as 78 copies of the India paper edition were printed, realising just short of £200 in total (£24,000 in 2018 prices) and a further 650 copies, at least, of the large and small paper editions were sold to subscribers. In addition, it is further recorded that his father then sold the copyright of *Delineations of Fonthill & its Abbey* to Charles Knight and Co., of London, for more than £500 (£60,000 in 2018 prices).[302] Rutter must also have earned a reasonable amount from the sale of the six editions of the earlier guide, *A Description of Fonthill Abbey and Demesne,* in 1822.

As previously mentioned, John Rutter acquired the freehold of a cottage in Gillingham in 1822, so he must have felt sufficiently financially confident at this stage in his career to make this purchase. In addition, he acquired the chemists' business of Thomas Bowder, paying £130 (£16,000 in 2018 prices) for the stock.[303]

In October 1823, the auction sale by Phillips comprised 4,000 lots of books and of other contents of the Abbey, as well as many items brought from elsewhere.[304] The Abbey's fascination was to prove an excellent venue for a grand sale.

Some of Beckford's paintings, books and objets de vertu, had been retained by him for his new home in Bath or were reacquired by him at this second auction. On his death in 1844, these precious possessions passed to his younger daughter, Susan Euphemia, who was married to the 10th Duke of Hamilton. They were divided between Hamilton Palace and Brodick Castle (on the Isle of Arran), then owned by the Duchy. With the famous sale of the contents of Hamilton Palace in 1882, to pay off the 12th Duke's debts, much of the Beckford inheritance was dispersed. The contents of Brodick Castle survived and it remains the largest collection of Beckfordiana in the world.[305]

The statue, by John Francis Moore, of William Beckford's father, *The Alderman,* was given by Beckford in 1833 to the Worshipful Company of Ironmongers in whose Hall it can be seen on the landing at the top of the stairs. *The Alderman* was Master of the Ironmongers livery company in 1753.

It is clear that John Rutter was truly taken by Fonthill Abbey as shown by the following remarks 'the Abbey cannot be contemplated without emotions that have never been excited by any building erected by any private individual in our times' and 'we know no modern erection which deserves such unqualified praise'. Indeed Rutter was amazed by what he saw. It is also clear that he knew how to record this. He had a good knowledge of English, architecture and fine art. He could relate to what he had seen. He knew how to write and to embellish. He knew how to excite his readership in an immensely readable, high quality publication.

With its attention to detail, clarity of writing and quality of illustrations, *Delineations of Fonthill & Its Abbey* is regarded as one of the great architectural publications of the early 19th century. There are copies of *Delineations* in the Royal Collection and it is now a valuable item in any library. It is one of John Rutter's many achievements and a lasting souvenir of his career as an author and stationer. If Rutter had done no more in life than write and publish *Delineations of Fonthill & Its Abbey* he would still be remembered today for this single accomplishment.

The Defence of John Rutter

IN 1826 JOHN Rutter was charged with printing a letter without showing his name at the foot of the printed paper. He was fined £5 (£450 in 2018 prices) at his first attendance in Shaftesbury's Magistrates' Court on 14 August 1826. Because his plea for defence was cut short and because he thought he had not been fairly heard, on 9 September 1826 he printed and published *The Defence of John Rutter*. On 5 October 1826 he was fined a further £5 for the same offence. Rutter's fight for political reform in Shaftesbury and the contents of *The Defence* are described in chapter six.

The Shastonian

On 2 October 1826, after his brush with Shaftesbury's political clique and his Court fines, Rutter printed the first of four issues of a critical and satirical periodical, *The Shastonian*. It was edited by another reformer, author and political agitator, James Acland (1799–1876). Acland later became well known in Bristol as the editor of *The Bristolian* and then in Hull for criticising the established elite in local government and among the merchant class. Like Rutter, he wrote about corruption and the abuses of the unreformed corporations which governed many English cities and the alleged misdemeanours of local magistrates and public servants.[306]

In *The Shastonian,* although much of the content was written by John Rutter, Acland was careful to point out that he was the editor, so shielding Rutter, as much as he could, from the ruling elite who controlled Shaftesbury and who sought to punish Rutter for his actions. The content of the first three issues of *The Shastonian* is not dissimilar in style to the modern day *Private Eye*.

Swyer versus Rutter. A plain narration of Shastonian occurrences without comment

In 1826 and 1827, John Rutter wrote a record of the political and electoral environment which existed in Shaftesbury from the scandalous General Election of 1774 until the General Election of 1826, following which Rutter was tried for libel at Dorchester. He described the events leading up to the 1826 election, the proceedings (and fines) of the Shaftesbury Magistrates Court and the events before and during the Dorchester trial in front of the King's Bench.

He also listed the total expenses which he incurred in defending this action, amounting to almost £403[307] (£36,000 in 2018 prices), most of which were to compensate the plaintiff for his costs as well as damages. This unfortunate episode in John Rutter's life is described further in chapter six.

Unpublished Works: An Historical and Descriptive Account of the Town of Shaftesbury

IN 1827, RUTTER wrote large parts of a book, which was never published, about Shaftesbury. Manuscript notes and written material for each of the six parts are held at the Dorset History Centre and the Gold Hill Museum.[308] The six parts were typed and bound in 1972 and facsimile copies are available at Dorset's libraries. They covered the following subjects:

Part I – Names, Derivations & Antiquity, General Description – including History

Part II – Manufactures, Wells and Waterworks, Streets and Lanes, Buildings – Ancient & Modern, Markets & Fairs

Part III – The Borough, The Corporation – History

Part IV – Charities, Manors &c – Lush's Blue Coat School, Free School, Almshouses

Part V – The Abbey – Foundation, History

Part VI – Parochial History – Shaftesbury's 12 churches (today merged into two parishes: St Peter and St James), names of rectors over the years and church accounts

In Part II, Rutter described Shaftesbury's once prosperous trades which have all but disappeared. In former times, the town was well known for its woven products, knit (knitted) stockings, buttons and the special 'Lindsey Weaving', which was coloured dark blue with alternating white stripes. This was particularly sought after for winter clothing. At one time there were eight tanyards in the parish of St James and, at the time of his writing, there was just one left. The shoemaking trade was still thriving partly as a consequence of apprenticed boys from the Blue Coat School or the Charity School, although shoe production was no longer as lucrative after the introduction of a leather tax. Also the practice of Poole merchants hiring Dorset lads for fishing in Newfoundland waters had declined, with cheaper labour being available in Ireland. In summary, Shaftesbury's industries and its businesses were suffering and the number of those classified as poor had increased. The only successful elements of the economy were the shopkeepers whose shops in the High Street and the triangular Commons had all been recently renovated. They benefited from the numerous markets and fairs which attracted farmers from many miles around. While some inns had closed in recent years, the Grosvenor Arms, renamed from the Red Lion after its acquisition by the Grosvenor family, had been enlarged and improved and 'is said to be equal in accommodation to any Inn on the Western Road'.

Being on a hill, with no natural springs at its summit, Shaftesbury had always had a problem in ensuring sufficient water for its inhabitants. As Thomas Hardy wrote in *Jude the Obscure*

> Its situation rendered water the great want of the town; and within living memory, horses, donkeys and men may have been seen toiling up the winding ways to the top of the steep, laden with tubs and barrels filled from the wells beneath the mountain, and hawkers retailing their contents at the price of a halfpenny a bucketful.[309]

Lower down the hill, on the southern slopes, the parish of St James fared better as it had both springs and wells. Over the years, several attempts had been made to create a piped water supply from the Wincombe Ponds, one mile to the north east of town to the centre of Shaftesbury. At the time of his writing, discussions were taking place about the practicality of supplying the town with good spring water situated below the hill by means of a small steam engine and a hydraulic ram. Earl Grosvenor had offered £1,000 as a contribution if other subscribers could be found.[310] But this initiative foundered because of the complexity of the task, which was not finally achieved until 1852.[311] Traditionally, though, water had been carried to the town from the wells in the valley to the north, from Enmore Green in the parish of Motcombe, by agreement with Lords of the Manor of Gillingham. In addition to paying for the water, a tradition grew up of the Mayor and townsfolk of Shaftesbury processing to Enmore Green once each year in a ceremony where a 'Byzant' or 'Besom' was presented. Rutter described this eloquently as follows

> The Mayor is required, on the Monday before Holy Thursday, to dress up a prize Besom or Bezant as it is called, being something like a May garland in form, with gold and peacock feathers; and to carry it to Enmore Green, a place below the hill in the parish of Motcombe, accompanied with a band of music, and present it, together with a raw calves' head, and a pair of gloves, to the Lord of the Manor, who generally receives the presents by his Steward. A couple called the lord and lady of the Bezant

> dance within an enclosed space, and twelve penny loaves and three dozen of beer are distributed among the people. The ceremony being over, the Byzant is restored to the Mayor and brought back to the town by the Sergeants at Mace. It was formerly the custom for the ceremony to conclude in the evening by a ball for the inhabitants of the town and neighbourhood, given by the Mayor and Corporation; but this practice has been laid aside for some years, and the whole, with little exception, has become a trifling and ridiculous remnant of the ancient festivity.[312]

Now rather out of date, but interesting, the text of Rutter's book on Shaftesbury would provide much information for anyone researching the history of the town and wishing to learn more about Shaftesbury in the 1820s.

At the front of the manuscript notes is a printed introduction in which Rutter wrote that, for the last seven years, he had been accumulating materials for a *History of the County of Dorset*. He intended selling the complete work, in three volumes, for 'twenty shillings each' (£95 in 2018 prices).[313] This work was never completed.

The Prevalence of Vagrancy in some of the Western Counties of England and the formation of Mendicity Societies

In the early 19th century Mendicity Societies were established to help reduce begging and vagrancy by providing basic refuge and sustenance for anyone deemed worthy of support, for example someone travelling from one village or town to another in search of work. Those travelling about the country could be given pass-tickets to help them obtain a bed when they arrived in another place. Anthony Ashley-Cooper, the 7th Earl of Shaftesbury, was a great supporter of this movement.

Rutter had been engaged with the Mendicity Society of Shaftesbury since its formation in 1821 and was the Honorary Secretary.[314] In December 1827, he printed and sold a booklet, just 16 pages long, dealing with vagrancy and begging. The booklet documented examples, across the country, of rising levels of begging. He introduced the booklet by revealing that the practice of 'Vagrancy and Importunate Mendicity' had greatly increased throughout the country, except in those towns where Mendicity Societies had been established. There were recommendations from many people, including magistrates, of 'Mendicity Societies', as there was circumstantial evidence that they helped to reduce the incidence of 'vagrancy and importunate mendicity'. Rutter referred to the declining interest in the Shaftesbury Society but that a revival was taking place and a general collection had been launched to raise funds.[315]

Then, in January 1828, he printed the sixth annual report of the Mendicity Society for the Shaftesbury District, referring to the need to defer the annual meeting with a view to 'procuring a more general attendance' but also to afford an opportunity for replenishing the funds of the society, 'which had for some time been exhausted, and a considerable debt incurred'. He reported that during the year to October 1827, 628 men, women and children had been relieved with food and/or lodging and 80 refused. This represented a small increase on the previous year. He concluded that there was an evident necessity of 'relieving wearied and distressed travellers' and that the credit of the town and district is 'at stake'.[316]

Delineations of the North West Division of the County of Somerset

DURING THE 1820S, Rutter had access to the extensive topographical library at Stourhead, the stately home with its world famous gardens and lake near Mere in Wiltshire, then owned by Sir Richard Colt Hoare. Apart from possessing a large library Colt Hoare, as he was known in the family, was an author and historian. He spent much time in the last three decades of his life writing about the history of Wiltshire. His classic work *The History of Modern Wiltshire,* also bound and titled as *The Modern History of South Wiltshire,* was printed by J.B. Nichols & Son between 1822 and 1844. Thus Hoare, Rutter and Nichols were known to each other in the field of publishing and printing.

In a letter to Nichols of December 1827, Rutter referred to a visit to Stourhead where he recorded that Sir Richard was 'in excellent health and spirits'.[317] In a further letter to Nichols of 3 October 1828 he referred to another visit with the comment 'I saw our good friend Sir Richard Hoare a few days since, he is gone today to Bath for a month'.[318] Also in 1827 Rutter printed 25 copies of Richard Colt Hoare's 78-page 'Letter, stating the true site of the ancient colony of Camulodunum'. This letter was addressed to The Philosophical and Literary Society at Bristol and contradicted the claim made by the Reverend Mr. Skinner that Camulodunum, the capital of the British King Cunobeline, was Camerton in Somerset. Based on Hoare's analysis of the Roman battles, archaeological remains and historical commentaries, Sir Richard argued that the site was Colchester in Essex.

John Rutter enjoyed writing about the towns, villages and countryside of Wessex. In 1828 he made two excursions to Somerset and had planned to publish the book in the autumn of 1828.[319] However, this was delayed. In a letter of 2 June 1829 to J.B. Nichols & Son, he requested an advertisement to be placed in the *Gentleman's Magazine,* to be paid for by Longman & Co, who handled Rutter's publications in London. He referred to the delay due to his 'regular business' and added that Sir Richard Hoare 'was kind enough to promise me a set of the Fonthill prints to increase the Illustrations to my own copy of my work on the Abbey, for which I shall be most obliged to him'.[320]

In 1829, *Delineations of the North West Division of the County of Somerset* was published. A facsimile edition was republished in 2009 by Amberley Publishing, with an introduction by Robert Dunning. In researching material for *Delineations of Somerset,* Rutter had carefully documented what he saw on his travels and he embellished his descriptions with stories related to him about past inhabitants and interesting historical facts. The finished guide extended to over 350 pages and contained 30 vignettes and 13 engravings obtained from the owners of the properties mentioned in his book, including drawings lent to him by the High Sheriff of Somerset, J.H. Smyth Pigott, of Brockley Hall, a fine early 19th century mansion south west of Bristol.[321]

He also arranged for the Dorset poet, William Barnes (1801–1886), then running a school in nearby Mere, to prepare some vignettes on blocks for printing. Barnes has also previously produced a wood-cut for *The Shastonian.* In return, in 1829, Rutter published Barnes' book on Latin grammar entitled *The Etymological Glossary, or Easy Expositor for the Use of Schools and non-Latinists, wherein the greater part of the English words of foreign derivation are so arranged that the learner is enabled to acquire the meaning of many at once.* Barnes was an educationalist and later a clergyman but he is best known for his poetry, in particular poems in the Dorset dialect, as well as his descriptions of the lives and customs of Dorset people. Barnes also wrote the *Dorset Dialectal Dictionary*. He was conscious of the power of the language of his native county, which he believed to be a purer form of English, based on the Wessex dialect of Anglo-Saxon England. Thomas Hardy, whom William Barnes tutored, regarded him as an equal, and Lord Tennyson, Gerard Manley Hopkins and other poets wrote of his abilities. His best known works are *Poems of Rural Life in the Dorset Dialect* (1844), *Homely Rhymes* (1859) and *Poems of Rural Life in Common English* (1868). A statue of William Barnes was erected outside St. Peter's Church, Dorchester in 1889. Barnes' Christian faith, together with his support for the labouring rural poor of Dorset, would have created a bond between him and Rutter.[322]

Rutter was writing in an era before the advent of railways. Tourism from the major cities had yet to develop to any great degree. However, in Somerset, towns such as Minehead, Burnham-on-Sea, Weston-super-Mare and Clevedon were in easy reach of both Bristol and Bath and were attracting visitors who wanted some fresh sea air or wished to indulge in the new found activity of sea bathing.[323] *Delineations of Somerset* describes country houses which were open for public viewing, caverns (such as Banwell Caves), seaside tourist resorts, priories and churches. The guide was intended to appeal to a wide range of potential buyers but could also be customised for individual subscribers who wanted more, or larger, illustrations of their houses, described as 'gentleman's seats'. Being a printer, Rutter could easily arrange short print runs to accommodate these particular wishes. To promote this facility, a prospectus was issued to attract subscribers who were offered higher quality versions of the guide for between 10 and 25 shillings (£50 and £130 in 2018 prices). In total over 500 subscribers helped defray the initial printing and publishing costs, which his son, John Farley Rutter, estimated to be about £500 (£52,000 in 2018 prices) before a single copy was sold.[324]

Brockley Hall, 1829, drawn by J.C. Buckler, published in Lithography by J. Rutter, Shaftesbury (S&DHS, D.H.C., D-SHS/Box 42.3016)

A separate edition was published in 1829 for Longman, Rees of London, entitled *Delineations of the North Western Division of the County of Somerset and of its Antediluvian Bone-caverns.*[325]

In *Delineations of Somerset* Rutter gave a short history of each town and village, with references to its Saxon or Norman origins and any royal connections. Of Long Ashton Manor he related that the grandson of Richard Choke, afterwards the eminent Lord Chief Justice of England

> Sold the manor in 1506, to Sir Giles Daubney, knt. having previously given the church house, now the Angel Inn, with land to feoffees [trustees], for the use of the parish, so long as a prayer should be offered up on every Sunday, in Long Ashton church, for his own soul and those of his deceased ancestors.

When describing Brockley Hall, he listed the 83 paintings by old masters, including Caravaggio, Da Vinci, Holbein, Murillo, Rubens and Titian. Demonstrating his love of the countryside, he wrote poetically about the approach to the fine mansion

> Brockley Hall is surrounded by shrubberies and pleasure grounds, extending a considerable distance, including the romantic scenery of Brockley Coomb. A carriage drive extending more than three miles, has been formed through the grounds. It commences at the bottom of the glen, through which it pursues its way, turning to the right, to the high ground above, which has been extensively planted. It continues its winding course along the very edge of the cliffs, on a level with the tops of the trees, which grow on precipitous sides, through which are caught some fine views of the opposite rocks, rearing their naked heads above the surrounding foliage.[326]

For the tourist interested in the increasingly popular seaside towns, John Rutter described the growing attractions of Weston Super Mare (*sic*)

> The fishermen's huts have almost disappeared, and the town now contains about two hundred and fifty houses; a large portion of which are respectable residences; but notwithstanding this, the general appearance is little inviting to the stranger, especially in gloomy weather, or when the ebb of the spring tide leaves open, large tracts of beach. But on a fine summer evening, when the tide is in, nothing can be more beautiful than the scene which it presents; numerous groups walking on its smooth and extensive sands, intermingled with a variety of carriages, horses, fishermen wading with nets, and the villages enjoying the exhilarating breeze after the fatigues of the day; all these combine to render the scene interesting to the feelings, and cheering to the spirit.[327]

Rutter captured, some 200 years ago, the very essence of a British seaside resort today – sombre and foreboding in winter; exciting and inviting in summer. He did not hold back from describing the negative as well as the positive experiences that one might encounter. The factual integrity of his authorship shines through. He is not just trying to market a dream. The professionalism of his journalism demonstrates his values and his ability to communicate.

At the end of the book, Rutter included more than 60 pages of appendices describing, in great detail and with great authority, the geology of Somerset, a translation into English of the Latin names of botanical species and a list of some of the sea birds with English and Latin names. He further described the ancient and pre-Roman fortification The Wansdike; the Roman road from Uphill, on the Bristol Channel near Weston-super-Mare, to Old Sarum, near Salisbury; and then finally the 'Roman and British Stations and Antiquities, within the District'.[328] This is a learned work, demonstrating the breadth and range of his reading and knowledge.[329] It is a product of which Nikolaus Pevsner, writing some 125 years later, might have been proud.

After publishing *Delineations of Somerset,* Rutter then offered for sale the illustrations, both in a collection and separately. Using the text and his printing facilities, he also published the following guides.

The Westonian Guide

The Westonian Guide was printed and published in 1829. It included the following

> At the request of the Bookseller at Weston Super Mare, who considers it calculated to impart useful information to the visitors at that rapidly increasing watering place, and to make more generally known, the attractive objects of interest in its vicinity. The arrangement has been made with the view of rendering the Guide useful to the tourist; the first chapter is supposed to conduct him from the city of Bristol, to the favourite resort of its inhabitants, Weston Super Mare; the next is confined to a description of that place; the five following are arranged in the form of as many day's excursions, from Weston, as a centre; the latter part of the seventh re-conveys the tourist to Bristol.[330]

The Westonian Guide, of 88 pages is a shortened version of *Delineations of the North West Division of the County of Somerset* with a greater focus on Weston-super-Mare. It was intended to appeal directly to Bristolians who might be attracted to visit Weston to enjoy the pleasures of this seaside town: walking, sailing and fishing, shooting, sea bathing, hot and cold bathing and enjoying the '*salubrious air*'. Rutter described arrangements for sea bathing

> The bathing machines are well built, and are kept clean and neat; they are constantly in attendance, except at very low tides, and may be driven to any requisite depth into the water; females being accompanied, if required, by careful and experienced bathing women.[331]
>
> Bathing has been practised from the earliest periods of society, either as a religious ceremony, for cleanliness, or for comfort and pleasurable gratification; and more lately for its salutary effects in contributing to the general health. Its primary action causes the sensation which is called a 'shock'; the direct consequences of which vary extremely, according to the constitution, or general state of health, at the time.[332]

Weston Super Mare, with bathing machines, 1829, drawn by J.W. Brett, Bristol, engraved by Thomas Higham, published by John Rutter (S&DHS, D.H.C., D-SHS/Box 42.3016)

The guide was available from Longman, Rees & Co in London, Richard Hill of the Library, Weston-Super-Mare and Booksellers of Bath and Bristol. It was clearly popular as a second edition was published in 1840 entitled *A New Guide to Weston-super-Mare.*

Banwell and Cheddar Guide
The Clevedon Guide

In the same year, 1829, John Rutter also published two further short guides, *Banwell and Cheddar Guide* (78 pages) and *The Clevedon Guide* (52 pages), the text of each was similar to that in *The Westonian Guide* and intended for more tailored audiences. For example, he repeated a description of Leigh Court which had featured in *Delineations of Somerset*. This grand Grecian mansion was designed by Thomas Hopper for Philip John Miles and built between 1814 and 1817. As Rutter recorded, it had a distinguished picture collection, which included a pair of paintings by Claude Lorraine, *The Landing of Aeneas* and *The Sacrifice of Apollo*, which had been commissioned by the Altieri family and which had once belonged to William Beckford at Fonthill.[333]

Banwell Church, 1829, drawn by J.C. Buckler, engraved by Thomas Higham, published by John Rutter (S&DHS, D.H.C., D-SHS/Box 42.3016)

History of the Shaftesbury election of 1830

John Rutter wrote and published an account of the election campaign in Shaftesbury of the 1830 General Election. This described the pernicious activities of Lord Grosvenor's agents in managing the campaign for his two chosen candidates who were elected as Shaftesbury's two members of Parliament. The account explained how the Shaftesbury electorate was coerced. Rutter was also critical of Grosvenor as a self-professed Whig, allegedly in favour of Parliamentary reform. This is described below in chapter six.

5
John Rutter the Quaker

Quaker history and beliefs

In his childhood, with a Quaker upbringing, Rutter would have learnt about George Fox (1624–91), the founder of the Religious Society of Friends. Born in Leicestershire into a hard-working and relatively prosperous family, George studied the Bible but was not enamoured of the structure and rigid form of Christian teaching through the Church of England. In 1647, he came to believe that people could have a personal experience of God, which he called the 'Inner Light'.[334]

George and his Quaker Friends were products of the English Civil Wars (1642–1651) and the Commonwealth of England (1649–1660). The Church of England was associated with the losing Royalist side and during the period of the Commonwealth its bishops were abolished and its prayer book, the Book of Common Prayer, was banned. There was no legal requirement for the public to attend church services.

George Fox preached with zeal to many hundreds of people in England, particularly in the new nonconformist stronghold in the north of the country and abroad, in America and on the Continent. His followers became 'Friends of the Light' and the Society of Friends was born.

George Fox encouraged his followers to tremble at the Word of God, perhaps quoting Isaiah chapter 66 verse 2 'For all those things hath mine hand made, and all those things have been, saith the Lord: but to this man will I look, even to him that is poor and of a contrite spirit, and trembleth at my word'. He also quoted Psalm 119 verse 120 'My flesh trembleth for fear of thee; and I am afraid of thy judgements'. From this, the name 'Quaker' was derived.

Fox sought simplicity, humility, abstinence and a life without sin. He abhorred luxury. Principles of equity and fairness and his rejection of the established church were translated into a criticism of tithes and church taxes, a campaign for social equality and a rejection of war, oppression, injustice and the swearing of oaths. This led him to be imprisoned many times for preaching principles and beliefs contrary to accepted ecclesiastical practice.

George Fox, (1624-1691) by Thomas Fairland, printed by Darton 1822, © Religious Society of Friends (Quakers) in Britain, (LSF 94_AXL 33)

In 1652 George Fox climbed Pendle Hill in Lancashire, the place from which the Pendle Witches derived and whose trial 40 years earlier had resulted in most of them being convicted of murder by witchcraft and hanged. Perhaps the recent memory of these tragic and inhuman trials inspired what followed. In his diary, Fox wrote

> As we travelled we came near a very great hill, called Pendle Hill, and I was moved of the Lord to go up to the top of it; which I did with difficulty, it was so very steep and high. When I was come to the top, I saw the sea bordering upon Lancashire. From the top of this hill the Lord let me see in what places he had a great people to be gathered. As I went down, I found a spring of water in the side of the hill, with which I refreshed myself, having eaten or drunk but little for several days before.[335]

In 1656, in an exhortation to the Friends, he wrote

> Be patterns, be examples, in all countries, places, islands, nations, wherever you come, that your carriage and life may preach among all sorts of people and to them; then you will come to walk cheerfully over the world, answering that of God in every one.[336]

Like George Fox, Quakers were persecuted in the 17th century. Many were arrested and imprisoned or emigrated to North America. During the years after the Restoration and the re-established Church of England, the situation became worse for Quakers and it has been estimated that the total number of sufferers by imprisonment and distraint in England and Wales was more than 15,000.[337] A higher estimate of over 20,000 names has also been given, of whom at least 450 died in prison or from the direct effects of imprisonment.[338] The more usual distraints made against Quakers were either for tithes or church taxes not paid or for Court fines. It was a criminal offence, under the Conventicle Act of 1664, to hold religious assemblies of more than five people, other than from an immediate family, not conducted in accordance with the Book of Common Prayer and thus outside the auspices of the Church of England. The law was aimed at discouraging nonconformism and strengthening the position of the established church. Anyone holding or being present at a meeting was liable to prosecution which would result in a heavy fine.[339]

In 1689 the passing of the Toleration Act in England granted freedom of worship to nonconformists and meant that being a Friend was no longer treated as a criminal offence. However, some of the old legislation remained on the statute book and, technically, nonconformity remained an illegal activity. Religious liberty had been conceded, but civil equality had not – prison might still await those who refused to pay tithes or to take the oath of allegiance. Quakers were urged by their fellow Friends to refuse both.[340]

The movement continued to grow and, in the 1680s, a Quaker, William Penn, founded Pennsylvania as a safe haven for Quakers in North America. The death of George Fox in 1691 was a blow as the emerging global Society had lost a leading member. But others emerged and the movement grew in England, the American colonies and on the Continent of Europe.

Passages from the Bible that influence Quaker beliefs and behaviour include verses 22 and 23 of chapter five of the Epistle of St Paul to the Galatians

> But the fruit of the Spirit is love, joy, peace, longsuffering, gentleness, goodness, faith,

> Meekness, temperance: against such there is no law

and verses 52 and 53 of chapter one of the Gospel according to St Luke:

> He hath put down the mighty from their seats, and exalted them of low degree.
> He hath filled the hungry with good things; and the rich he hath sent empty away

Today, the basic Quaker testimonies are expressed as truth, equality, peace, simplicity and community. Education was valued by Quakers as a true preparation for life in all its respects. One 'Advice', for the benefit of Friends, of 1737 read

> In the Education of their children take care, as suitable opportunities and occasions may offer to let them be Instructed in some Modern Tongues as French, High and Low Dutch, Danish, &c. that so when they are grown up they themselves if traders to foreign countries, may reap the benefit thereof, and as it shall please the Lord to dispose and incline them, may be of service to the Church.[341]

From its early days, the Society of Friends became involved in social reform. The equality and brotherhood of all men were fundamental beliefs. In the late 18th century, in the newly created United States of America, this desire for equality evidenced itself in Quaker communities abandoning the practice of owning slaves and promoting the abolition of slavery. Then, as the industrial revolution took hold in the 19th century, the Friends became engaged in seeking equality and social justice through reforms in working conditions, education, prisons, public elections and the conditions of the poor.

For many years, Quakers could not become members of Parliament as any successful Quaker candidate would not sign an oath of allegiance to the Crown. For similar reasons, Quakers did not enter the legal profession which, in any event, they regarded with mistrust as it was English law which was being used by their oppressors to abuse them. The Corporation Act of 1661 and the Test Act of 1673, which required public office holders to submit a sacrament certificate confirming they had taken Holy Communion according to Anglican rites, were abolished in 1828. The Representation of the People Act, known as the Great Reform Act, was passed in 1832. Thus elected MPs were permitted to make a declaration to affirm that they were telling the truth rather than to swear an oath in order to be admitted to Parliament. These reforms led to Joseph Pease becoming the first Quaker MP in 1832.[342] Similarly, Quakers began to train as lawyers to exploit the English legal system to argue against and to prevent discrimination.

Because politics and the law were closed to Quakers until the 1830s, in the 100 years before this, Quaker entrepreneurs began managing shops, establishing small businesses and forming banks, where their reputation for honesty and integrity made them trusted and brought commercial success. The concept of business being pursued solely in the interest of the owners to the exclusion of other stakeholders is a foreign one to Quakers. They have always wanted to ensure that everyone – workers, suppliers, customers – all benefit from success. The trades which Quakers pursued also had to be 'innocent', not contributing to war.

The major UK chocolate manufacturers (Fry's, Cadbury's and Rowntree's) stemmed from modest Quaker origins around the time of the Industrial Revolution: Joseph Fry (1761 in Bristol), John Cadbury (1831 in Birmingham) and Joseph Rowntree (1869 in York).[343] Similarly, the major banks Barclays and Lloyds had Quaker origins.

Barclays took its name from James Barclay who joined the firm in 1733, having married the daughter of one of the bank's two founders, John Freame and Thomas Gould, who established themselves as goldsmith bankers in Lombard Street in the City of London in 1690. Barclay, Freame and Gould were all practising Quakers. John Freame served as clerk to the Yearly Meeting (the Quakers' annual gathering attended by representatives from all over the country) and published a book *Scripture Instruction* which was used in Quaker schools. He also campaigned for greater toleration for Quakers, achieving the right to make an affirmation rather than swear an oath, and the right to be prosecuted before magistrates rather than in the church courts. James Barclay's grandfather, Robert, was known as 'The Apologist' because he wrote a book explaining Quaker beliefs, entitled, *Apology For The True Christian Divinity*. Barclays' regional network was formed from amalgamations of small Quaker banks which had been established in the 18th century: for example, Alexander's (1744 in Needham Market), Backhouse's (1744 in Darlington), Taylors & Lloyds (1765 in Birmingham) and Gurney's (1770 in Norwich).[344]

Lloyds Bank (originally founded in Birmingham as Taylors & Lloyds in 1765) undoubtedly owed much to the Lloyd family's Quaker connections as well as their strong work ethic. As leading members of the Society of Friends, the Lloyd family was close to many of the most influential and pioneering members of that community. One of those was Elizabeth Fry, the prison reformer. Elizabeth was the daughter of John Gurney and Catherine Barclay, both from prominent Quaker banking families. She went on to marry yet another Quaker, the banker Joseph Fry.[345]

There have been other famous Quakers who have made significant contributions to British industry. These include Abraham Darby, who was the first person to produce pig iron in a blast furnace from coke rather than charcoal, in 1709; The pharmaceutical company, Allen, Hanburys & Barry, was formed in 1824 and, in 1841, William Allen became the first President of the Pharmaceutical Society; the shoe company, C&J Clark, was founded in Street, Somerset, in 1825; and then Huntley and Palmer, both from the west of England, came together in Reading in 1841 to make biscuits.[346]

Rutter as a Quaker

RECORDS OF QUAKERS in Shaftesbury date from the end of the 17th century, when William Fry of Ashmore gave land in the Wiltshire-Dorset border hills for a Quaker burial ground. At that time, Quakers were not permitted to be interred in churchyards. The first Shaftesbury Quakers met in people's homes, in barns or in the open air. Then, in 1746, a Meeting House was built in St James, on the south side of Shaftesbury, set back against the hill with the land in front used for burials.[347]

After the young fifteen year old John Rutter moved from Bristol to Shaftesbury in 1811, he would have spent much time, as a practising Quaker, at the Friends Meeting House in St James. His marriage on 7 July 1818 to Anne Burchett Clarance (1791–1879) strengthened his Quaker ties. She had been educated at the Friends School at York and they met when she was employed as a governess to the children of the Shaftesbury Quaker, John Shipley, to whom Rutter had been apprenticed.

Some 100 years after John and Anne married, their granddaughter, Elizabeth Beaven Rutter (1857–1942), the fourth child of their second son, John Farley Rutter (1824–1899) wrote about her paternal grandparents

> John Rutter and his wife both wore the Quaker dress of the day, he with silk stockings and garters and she with her grey Quaker bonnet, silk gown, white tippet and shawl. Together they must have been a very handsome couple. I never saw my grandfather but remember my grandmother well. My grandfather was a thorough Friend and spoke as a Friend to everyone. He had a good presence and as a speaker was fluent and attractive with a fine, persuasive voice which created confidence. His energy was not spasmodic and fitful, but quiet, constant and persistent,

> carrying everything before him. He had great concentration of thought and could throw off business worries and occupy himself with some other absorbing work. From a phrenological sketch we gather he had balanced qualities and ought to succeed in everything he undertook. He had great faculty for making and keeping friends.[348]

John Rutter was a committed Friend and, on one occasion, he represented the Dorset & Hants Quarterly Meeting at the national Yearly Meeting in London. He was strongly evangelical in his interventions at the Yearly Meetings of the late 1830s.[349]

The Yearly Meeting of the Religious Society of Friends approves, from time to time, an updated guide for the use of Friends. The guide, *Advices & Queries,* is intended as a reminder to each individual Friend of the insights of the Society. Some of the *Advices* are particularly evident in the life and behaviour of John Rutter

> Live adventurously. When choices arise, do you take the way that offers the fullest opportunity for the use of your gifts in the service of God and the community? Let your life speak
>
> Every stage of our lives offers fresh opportunities. Responding to divine guidance, try to discern the right time to undertake or relinquish responsibilities without undue pride or guilt
>
> Remember your responsibilities as a citizen for the conduct of local, national, and international affairs
>
> If pressure is brought upon you to lower your standard of integrity, are you prepared to resist it?
>
> Consider which of the ways to happiness offered by society are truly fulfilling and which are potentially corrupting and destructive
>
> In view of the harm done by the use of alcohol, tobacco and other habit-forming drugs, consider whether you should limit your use of them or refrain from using them altogether.[350]

Capital punishment

SINCE THE FOUNDATION of the Society of Friends, Quakers have objected to capital punishment. In 1682, William Penn reduced the number of capital offences in Pennsylvania. But, in the 18th century, Great Britain experienced a dramatic increase in capital punishment. More and more crimes, such as the petty one of pick-pocketing, were made punishable by death. By 1765 these had risen to about 160 and by 1810 to 222. Towards the end of the 18th century, campaigns began and speeches were made, aimed at reversing this trend. The Quakers were very much at the heart of this movement.

Rutter was one of many Quakers contacted in April 1830 to approach bankers in the south west with a view to putting their names to a petition seeking the removal of capital punishment for forgery.[351] The subsequent Forgery, Abolition of Punishment of Death Act of 1832 abolished the death penalty for all offences of forgery, except for forging wills and certain powers of attorney. It also reduced the number of capital crimes to around 60.

Between 1832 and 1837, successive Governments introduced bills to reduce further the number of capital crimes. Shoplifting and sheep, cattle and horse stealing were removed from the list in 1832, followed by sacrilege, letter stealing, returning from transportation (1834/5), forgery and coining (1836), arson, burglary and theft from a dwelling house (1837), rape (1841) and, finally, attempted murder, in 1861.

By 1861, the number of capital offences had been reduced to just four by the Criminal Law Consolidation Acts of that year. These crimes were murder, high treason, piracy with violence and arson in the Royal Dockyards. After this, it was reduced to just two capital offences, namely murder and treason, for which criminals would be put to death.

Rutter and his Quaker Friends had taken a key role in the struggle to eliminate capital punishment, which was finally abolished in the United Kingdom in 1965.

Bible reading

But Rutter was also something of a rebel. It is clear that he did not like structure and procedure which interfered with a simple understanding of the truth and compliance with it in daily life. He became an admirer of Isaac Crewdson who had caused controversy among Manchester Quakers by advocating that too much emphasis was placed by Quakers on the 'Inner Light' at the expense of Biblical guidance and authority. In a book *A Beacon to the Society of Friends,* published in 1835, Crewdson criticised the American Quaker, Elias Hicks (1748-1830), who had caused a schism in the American Society of Friends in 1827 by claiming that the most important principle of worship was 'obedience to the light within'. Crewdson had been born into a Quaker family in Kendal in the Lake District and, after becoming a successful cotton mill owner in Manchester, he drew more to the faith and was appointed as a Quaker Minister. He attracted a large following and, after leaving the Hardshaw East Monthly Meeting of Friends in Lancashire, in 1836, he created a breakaway movement known as the 'Evangelical Friends' who were also termed 'Beaconites'. The Beaconites introduced certain traditional rituals, such as baptism by water as opposed to 'inner baptism' as practised by Quakers, and promoted Bible studying meetings. This alternative version of Quakerism did not survive after Crewdson's death in 1844 but it created divisions within families and in some business partnerships.[352]

Perhaps influenced by his mother's Methodist faith, John Rutter was attracted to these ideas. For many years he had printed leaflets and reports for the Shaftesbury and Gillingham Auxiliary Bible Society and was recorded as the Secretary of the Society in notices printed by his son Clarence in 1834 and 1838. At the first of these, a collection was made in aid of the Negro Testament Fund. The Notice explained that 'in consequence of the extinction of slavery throughout the colonies of Great Britain in August 1833, a copy of the New Testament and Psalms would be given to every liberated negro capable of reading. These are estimated at 130,000 copies, the expence (sic) of which will be not less than £20,000'. (A staggering £2.2 million in 2018 prices).[353]

Rutter's '*Letters in Defence of the Bible Society to L. Neville*' appeared at London in 1836 in reply to Neville's accusations against the British and Foreign Bible Society and against Dissenters, published by James Dinnis of Paternoster Row, 1836.[354]

Elizabeth Rutter wrote

> The Bible Society held a warm place in his interests, he was appointed the Secretary of the local auxiliary 2 May 1833, a position he retained until 1845. His religious life was one of deep conviction; he carried it into his business and everyday life, even as a boy, and as a Friend was punctual in attending all Meetings of the Society, to which he was deeply attached.[355]

During the summer months of 1838 and 1839, John Rutter organised Bible readings for the poor who lived in the vicinity of the Friends Meeting House in St James Street, Shaftesbury. As many as 100 people gathered together to hear the Holy Scriptures being read, with plain, practical explanations. Rutter initially held these readings at the Meeting House. In a letter dated 19 April 1839, Ann Elizabeth wrote to her brother, Clarence, that 'Papa has begun to have meetings at our Chapel, and the people seem to like to come very much'[356]. However, it sounds as though he did not consult his fellow Friends or the Elders at his local Monthly Meeting in Shaftesbury or else he rubbed someone up the wrong way. There were complaints from the Shaftesbury Friends about this and the General Meeting of Quakers for Dorset and Hampshire passed the following resolution in November 1839

> This meeting, having been informed that the Meeting House in Shaftesbury has been used by a member of our Society for the purpose of conducting Public Worship in a manner inconsistent with our principles, thinks it right to express its disapprobation thereof, and to call on the Shaftesbury and Sherborne Monthly Meeting to prevent a continuance of the practice.

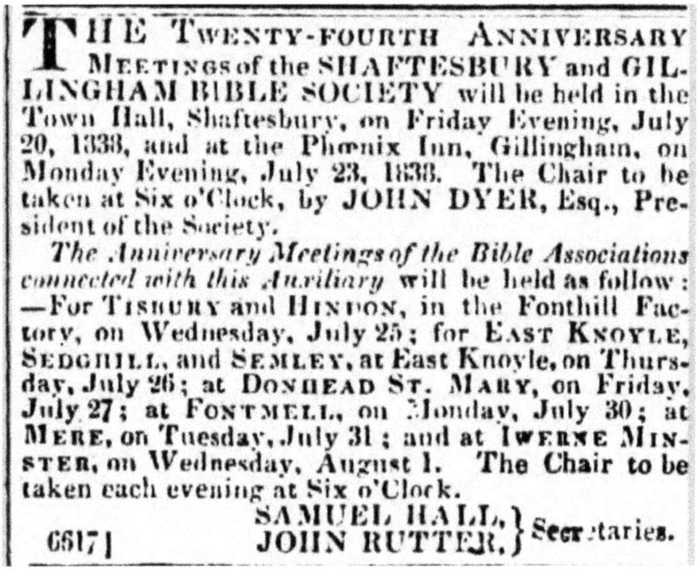

THE TWENTY-FOURTH ANNIVERSARY MEETINGS of the SHAFTESBURY and GILLINGHAM BIBLE SOCIETY will be held in the Town Hall, Shaftesbury, on Friday Evening, July 20, 1838, and at the Phœnix Inn, Gillingham, on Monday Evening, July 23, 1838. The Chair to be taken at Six o'Clock, by JOHN DYER, Esq., President of the Society.

The Anniversary Meetings of the Bible Associations connected with this Auxiliary will be held as follow: —For TISBURY and HINDON, in the Fonthill Factory, on Wednesday, July 25; for EAST KNOYLE, SEDGHILL, and SEMLEY, at East Knoyle, on Thursday, July 26; at DONHEAD ST. MARY, on Friday, July 27; at FONTMELL, on Monday, July 30; at MERE, on Tuesday, July 31; and at IWERNE MINSTER, on Wednesday, August 1. The Chair to be taken each evening at Six o'Clock.

6617] SAMUEL HALL, JOHN RUTTER, } Secretaries.

Bible Society Notice – Salisbury & Winchester Journal, 16 July 1838. With thanks to The British Newspaper Archive (www.britishnewspaperarchive.co.uk)

During the first half of 1840, correspondence passed between Rutter and William Binns, a representative of the Monthly Meeting, requesting Rutter to cease holding Bible readings at the Meeting House as this was contrary to Friends' practice. Rutter responded that he 'felt it his duty publicly to invite attention to the Gospel of Jesus Christ'. However, he eventually acceded to the wishes of the Monthly Meeting and wrote, on 11 June 1840, to advise them that the poor people were now assembling at another place, namely the Infant School Room in St James, which Rutter had recently founded (see chapter seven).[357]

This prompted the next Monthly Meeting, in December 1840, to bring a second accusation against Rutter, not for using the Friends Meeting House but for attending and taking an active part in other Bible reading meetings. Binns wrote to Rutter on 16 February 1841 asking him to refrain. Rutter responded that there was nowhere else in Shaftesbury where poor people could meet and hear the scriptures, except the parish church. He advised that he 'could not feel satisfied to refrain from speaking of the love of God'. The Monthly Meeting of 30 March 1841 concluded that 'our testimonies on the subject of Divine Worship and Gospel Ministry are infringed upon by John Rutter' and 'tenderly & affectionately recommends (sic) him to refrain from attending the said meetings'.[358] He was informed of these Minutes. However, Rutter replied that he could not desist. On 10 August 1841 the Monthly Meeting, attended by John Rutter's son Clarence, declared 'its discontinuity with John Rutter's proceedings' and accordingly 'discontinues him a member of our Religious Society'.[359] This was a blow but, as when a boy at school, he maintained his principles at great cost to himself. Despite being disowned, for the rest of his life he and his family continued to worship at the Friends Meeting House in St James. His family remained members of the Society. Rutter claimed that his disownment could not alter their belief in the principles of Friends. Separately, there is unconfirmed, circumstantial evidence that Rutter was later 'baptised by Lush's father-in-law in a chapel in Little Wyld Street in London'.[360]

It is clear that Rutter held firmly to his beliefs, namely that the word of God should be available to the poorest in society. He did not wish to be bound by the strictures and rules of any organisation, not even the Quakers, who themselves had rebelled against the prescribed form and procedures of the established church. He was prepared to fight for any cause which he thought to be just and he continued to earn the reputation, in some quarters, of being troublesome. He became *The Turbulent Quaker*. Yet, Rutter was far from being turbulent, which the dictionary describes as 'characterized by conflict, disorder, or confusion; not stable or calm'. He was very measured in what he did, having given careful consideration to each issue. To repeat what his granddaughter, Elizabeth Rutter, wrote 'his energy was not spasmodic and fitful, but quiet, constant and persistent, carrying everything before him'.

It has been suggested that Bible reading as proposed in *A Beacon to the Society of Friends* was twenty years ahead of its time and that by the 20th century some Quaker evangelicals had reached a position close to that of Crewdson in the 1830s. For many, Rutter's actions would also today be regarded as ahead of their time.

Religious freedom

THE FIRST HALF of the 19th century witnessed changes in attitude and in the law towards religious groups who were not part of the Church of England. After the traumas of the Reformation and the subsequent English Civil War, and following the Restoration, the Corporation Act of 1671 and the

Test Act of 1673 had introduced legislation which enhanced the position of the established church. They provided that the holding of public office in England was conditional on the swearing of an oath to the King and to the Protestant English Church. They provided for the signing of a declaration denying the Catholic doctrine of transubstantiation. Catholics, nonconformists and non-Christians were excluded from public office. In the 1820s there was a growing campaign for these two Acts to be repealed and the Sacramental Test Act was passed in 1828. The Catholic Emancipation Act of 1829 followed, providing that Catholics could sit as MPs in Parliament and hold public office. A further 30 years passed before Jewish emancipation was achieved when the law restricting the oath of Parliamentary office to Christians was changed. During these years there was much debate about religious freedom. Nonconformists and dissenters objected to church rates and the tithe – and to the Anglican monopoly on marriages and funerals. In 1836, when the Whigs were returned to office, the rights of other religions were enhanced through The Tithe Commutation Act, The University of London Royal Charter and the Dissenters' Marriage Act. Despite these legislative changes, dissenters were still barred from the ancient universities of Oxford and Cambridge. Discrimination had not yet been totally removed.

This was the environment, in 1838, when the 'General Union for the Promotion of Religious Equality' was established in London. The publication describing its formation stated that it was the duty and right of every man to worship his Creator and Redeemer; that it was unjust to compel anyone to adhere to a particular faith; and that political office or patronage based on conformity with any particular church or sect was an impediment to 'the propagation of the Gospel'. Its objects were, inter alia, to secure cooperation between friends of religious liberty; to watch over legislation to promote religious liberty; and to promote and support religious liberty in the country, in Parliament and throughout the world.[361] Its formation did not go without criticism. *The Inquirer* of January 1839 claimed that the General Union 'is intended to effect the downfall of the Established Church and to take away its pre-eminence by making all sects equal'.[362] Other magazines claimed that the 'religious equality' being sought was merely a pretence for 'political liberty' and 'political ascendancy'. It was claimed that the General Union threatened the very existence of the Christian faith in England. Those Anglican clergymen who put their name to the formation of the Union were also heavily criticised.[363]

As a believer in social equality and religious freedom, John Rutter was attracted by the General Union. It is reported that he chaired a meeting in Wareham in December 1838 for the purpose of forming a branch association to cooperate with the society in London. The meeting was addressed by

Church of England rectors from Weymouth, Corfe and Wareham, showing that the concept of religious equality was not restricted to the nonconformist movement.[364]

The General Union fizzled out but the drive for social and religious equality continued. Today, religious freedom is enshrined in the United Nations' International Covenant on Civil and Political Rights 1966, Article 9 of the European Convention on Human Rights and the UK's Human Rights Act 1998. As ever, Rutter was ahead of his time.

The Temperance movement

JOHN RUTTER WAS also a keen supporter of the temperance movement and an early pioneer. In September 1834 he acted as Provisional Secretary of a Temperance Society after it had been agreed at a public meeting that a branch should be established for Shaftesbury and the surrounding district.[365]

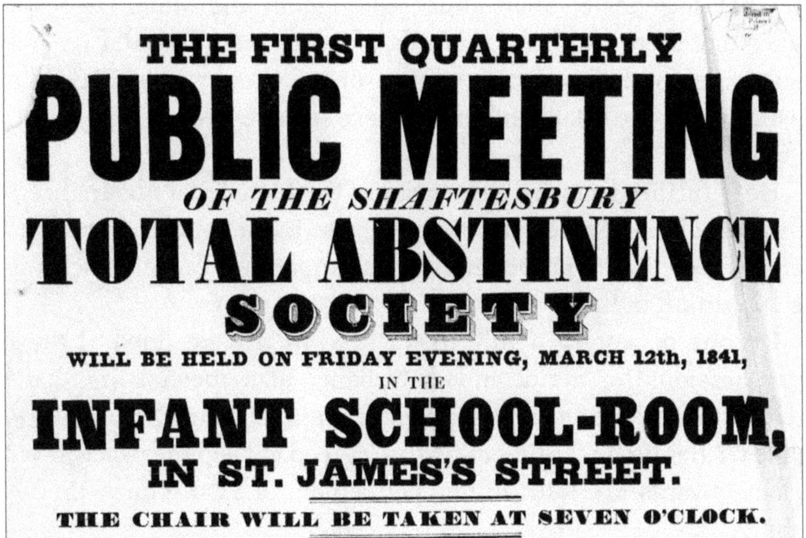

THE FIRST QUARTERLY

PUBLIC MEETING

OF THE SHAFTESBURY

TOTAL ABSTINENCE

SOCIETY

WILL BE HELD ON FRIDAY EVENING, MARCH 12th, 1841,

IN THE

INFANT SCHOOL-ROOM,

IN ST. JAMES'S STREET.

THE CHAIR WILL BE TAKEN AT SEVEN O'CLOCK.

Several Members of the Society will address the Meeting.

NOTE.—*The Entrance will be exclusively by the end door of the School-Room.*

☞ No Collection will be made.

C. RUTTER, BOOKSELLER AND PRINTER, SHAFTESBURY.

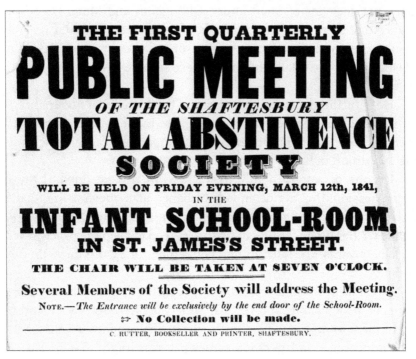

Notice about a Total Abstinence Society Meeting, 12 March 1841, printed by C. Rutter, Shaftesbury (S&DHS, D.H.C., D-SHS/Box 44.2645)

In 1835, 'The Total Abstinence Friendly Society', commonly called 'The Rechabite Tent' after the biblical descendants of Rechab, who were forbidden to drink wine or live in cities, was founded in Salford, near Manchester.

This Society provided benefits to its subscribing members in the event of sickness or death in 'distressed circumstances', providing members 'signed the pledge neither take himself, nor offer to others, intoxicating liquors' and 'providing no intoxicating drinks are introduced at the funeral'. The Shaftesbury Total Abstinence Friendly Society was founded in 1840, with Rutter's encouragement, and its rules were printed in 1842 by John Rutter's son, Clarence. The society later took the name of 'King Alfred's Tent'.[366] Rutter also wrote an introduction to a leaflet entitled *An Abstract of the Acts of Parliament relating to Friendly Societies* in which he is described as a member of the Shaftesbury Tent of the IOR (Independent Order of Rechabites).[367]

In June 1842 John Rutter addressed a gathering of 1,400 supporters of the temperance movement in the nearby town of Mere. Although a hall had been booked for the occasion, its capacity was 600 people and, in order not to disappoint anyone, a large yard was lent by one of the friends and the 'tea meeting' was held in the open air. Rutter gave a report on the three temperance societies of Shaftesbury, Gillingham and Mere. He advised his audience that there had been upwards of 1,600 members and 90 reformed drunkards, many of whom there was reason to believe were converted to God, 'and who but for the establishment of these societies would have died in their sins!'[368]

He is further recorded in a notice of the Mere Total Abstinence Society as being one of the speakers at a meeting, also in Mere, on 11 October 1842.[369] Rutter was a dedicated proponent of the temperance cause, which met with some opposition in the town.

On one occasion, in July 1843, three men were fined at the Dorset Quarter Sessions for a riot and disturbance at a meeting in Shaftesbury where the principles of total abstinence from intoxicating liquors were being advocated. After being found guilty they 'agreed to keep the peace towards all, especially towards Mr. John Rutter, gentleman, of Shaftesbury, in £5, for 12 months'.[370]

A year later, the *Sherborne Mercury* reported that Rutter had addressed a meeting of the Rechabite and Teetotal Society of Sherborne, after a procession through the town accompanied by the Rechabite band from Gillingham.[371]

Interestingly and perhaps somewhat amusingly, *The Ipswich Journal* reported in January 1837 'Removal of Temptation – Last week some thieves broke into the premises of Mr. Rutter, a Member of the Temperance Society, of Shaftesbury, and stole three dozen of very choice wines'.[372] This prompted Rutter to prepare a notice offering '5 Guineas Reward' (£550 in 2018 prices) to anyone who would give information leading to the conviction of the offender. It was prefaced by an account of the theft 'from two to three dozen bottles of port and white wine were stolen from Mr. Rutter's Cellar at Layton Cottage, and carried through the door-way leading into Layton Field'.[373] Being charitable, one assumes that the port and the wine were being stored prior to transfer to the chemists' shop operated by Clarence Rutter and that the wines were for medicinal purposes only. But then, Clarence was still in his late teens and was he a teenage tearaway? Or, is it possible that the wine in question was owned by Clarence's partner, James Wallbridge?

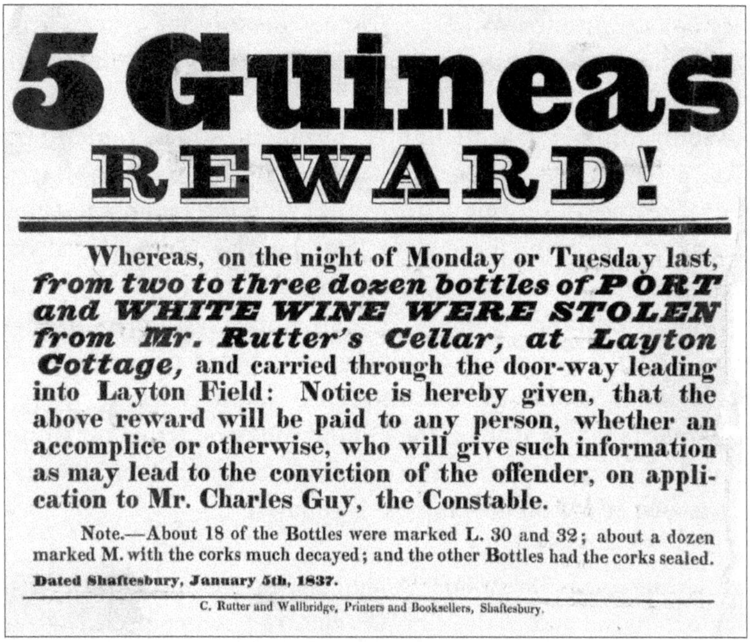

5 Guineas
REWARD!

Whereas, on the night of Monday or Tuesday last, *from two to three dozen bottles of PORT and WHITE WINE WERE STOLEN from Mr. Rutter's Cellar, at Layton Cottage,* and carried through the door-way leading into Layton Field: Notice is hereby given, that the above reward will be paid to any person, whether an accomplice or otherwise, who will give such information as may lead to the conviction of the offender, on application to Mr. Charles Guy, the Constable.

Note.—About 18 of the Bottles were marked L. 30 and 32; about a dozen marked M. with the corks much decayed; and the other Bottles had the corks sealed.

Dated Shaftesbury, January 5th, 1837.

C. Rutter and Wallbridge, Printers and Booksellers, Shaftesbury.

Notice of reward for wine stolen, 5 January 1837, printed by C. Rutter and Wallbridge, Shaftesbury (S&DHS, D.H.C., D-SHS/Box 44.2645)

While the provision of insurance dates from earlier times, it was not until the 19th century that friendly and life assurance societies developed in a major way. The growing middle classes demanded greater financial protection for their families in the event of injury or death. In November 1839, Robert Warner was incensed when he applied for life assurance and was informed that the premium would be higher because 'you are a teetotaller; and the directors consider teetotal lives are worse than ordinary lives'. As a result, he set up his own insurance company, The United Kingdom Total Abstinence Life Association or Temperance Provident Institution.[374] According to the company's first advertisement in 1840, its founding objects were to 'afford to persons who entirely abstain from intoxicating beverages, the benefits of the temperance and industry, more fully than is practicable in societies composed of persons of all classes indiscriminately'[375]. Warner took out the company's first policy in January 1841. The company drew attention to the increased longevity of temperance lives by proudly stating that it had received only three claims by the end of 1844 with just under 1,000 policies on the books.[376] As a solicitor, John Rutter was familiar with insurance and assurance products, sometimes acting as agent, and he is shown as one of the patrons of The United Kingdom Temperance Provident Institution in 1842. The Institution's literature pointed out that the average consumption of intoxicating liquors in the UK was estimated to be £2 10s per person per year (£270 in 2018 prices) and recommended that this would be better spent on a premium for life assurance.[377]

As John Rutter's granddaughter, Elizabeth Rutter, remembered 'John Rutter was a very active Temperance worker. On August 4th, 1846, he, with five others, formed a Committee for conducting the business of the World's Temperance Convention; three days later he was a speaker at a meeting in Covent Garden Theatre'.[378] This event was reported in the *Journal of the American Temperance Union* and John Rutter is quoted as saying 'The movement which they were now making was based upon the principles of charity and philanthropy'. He became more eloquent asking 'Were they not the true Samaritans, who, when they found the poor drunkard wounded and robbed by strong drink, poured the oil of consolation into his wounds'.[379] In another account of the proceedings, it is reported that

> Mr J. Rutter, of Shaftesbury, congratulated the meeting upon the improved position of their principles since it was first formed by a few zealous men working in Preston. He had seen an instance in which a gentlemen of birth and attainments, married to a lady of equal worth, was reduced to the greatest misery and the wife to death in consequence of indulging in moderate drink. Surely such an example was sufficient to induce all Christians to avoid the temptations of drinking, and also to persuade their friends to do so.[380]

John Rutter spoke often at Temperance events. He was listed as one of the speakers on teetotalism at a 'Grand Temperance Festival' to be held at Bristol Zoological Gardens on Whit Tuesday, 13 June 1848. In the notice he was described as one of the 'talented advocates of the cause'. Thousands were expected to attend and would be entertained by two 'efficient bands of music'.[381]

On 19 July 1850, the members and friends of the Temperance Societies of Shaftesbury, Mere, Wincanton and Gillingham enjoyed a 'Pleasure Trip' to

Stourhead by special permission of the owner, Sir Hugh Hoare, Bt. Joined by the Gillingham Temperance Band, the 'Party of pleasure' visited King Alfred's Tower at Stourhead and were addressed by John Rutter on 'the principles and practice of true Temperance'.[382] King Alfred's Tower had been built in 1772, the inspiration of Henry Hoare II of Stourhead, who wished to commemorate the end of the Seven Years' War with France and the accession of George III in 1760. It was built near the location of Egbert's Stone, where it is believed that King Alfred the Great rallied his Saxon troops before defeating a Viking army nearby at the Battle of Edington in AD878. There is a commanding view over the countryside from the 160 feet high tower which was restored in 1986 and is owned by the National Trust.

In his book *Temperance Pioneers of the West,* published in 1888, Thomas Hudson, a proponent of the Temperance cause, wrote

> Mr John Rutter was a man of commanding presence, and an able and convincing speaker. He was, moreover, a well-informed man on a variety of subjects; was the author of an Illustrated History of Somersetshire, and from the reputation he had gained, was accounted a valuable acquisition to our ranks. This gentleman was also the first elected President of the Shaftesbury Temperance Society, a distinction which he continued to hold until his lamented death in 1851, at the comparatively early age of fifty-five. He became a solicitor of good standing and considerable practice.[383]

Abolition of slavery

THE MOVEMENT TO abolish slavery was essentially led and promoted by the Society of Friends.[384] In 1783, Quakers established the Friends Committee to promote the Abolition of the Slave Trade. Thomas Clarkson, a prominent Quaker, recruited William Wilberforce to the cause and the Society for the Abolition of the Slave Trade was formally established in May 1787 with the aim of bringing about Parliamentary reform[385]. Nine of the original twelve members of the Committee were Quakers and five went on to play a central role[386]. The political climate during the French Revolutionary Wars prevented successive British Governments advancing the cause of abolition but, finally, under increasing pressure and the leadership of Wilberforce, who was the Committee's Parliamentary spokesman, the Abolition of the Slave Trade Act was passed in 1807. A further, important piece of legislation was introduced in 1833 intended to abolish slavery in the British Empire.

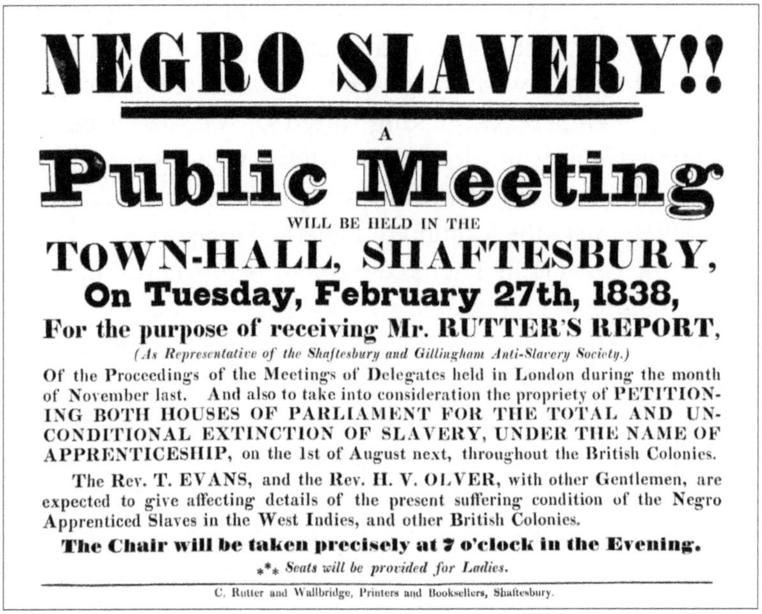

NEGRO SLAVERY!!

A

Public Meeting

WILL BE HELD IN THE

TOWN-HALL, SHAFTESBURY,

On Tuesday, February 27th, 1838,

For the purpose of receiving Mr. RUTTER'S REPORT,

(As Representative of the Shaftesbury and Gillingham Anti-Slavery Society.)

Of the Proceedings of the Meetings of Delegates held in London during the month of November last. And also to take into consideration the propriety of PETITIONING BOTH HOUSES OF PARLIAMENT FOR THE TOTAL AND UNCONDITIONAL EXTINCTION OF SLAVERY, UNDER THE NAME OF APPRENTICESHIP, on the 1st of August next, throughout the British Colonies.

The Rev. T. EVANS, and the Rev. H. V. OLVER, with other Gentlemen, are expected to give affecting details of the present suffering condition of the Negro Apprenticed Slaves in the West Indies, and other British Colonies.

The Chair will be taken precisely at 7 o'clock in the Evening.

**** Seats will be provided for Ladies.*

C. Rutter and Wallbridge, Printers and Booksellers, Shaftesbury.

Notice of Meeting on 27 February 1838 about Negro Slavery, printed by C. Rutter and Wallbridge, Shaftesbury (S&DHS, D.H.C., D-SHS/Box 2645)

However it was far from clear that this had happened. After two visits to the West Indies, another abolitionist, Joseph Sturge, published two papers *Narrative of Events Since the first of August 1834* and *The West Indies in 1837*, confirming the continuation of slavery in a new form. In 1837 he founded, together with another prominent Quaker, Samuel Bowly, the Central Negro Emancipation Committee in order to seek to combat the system of indentured apprenticeships of bonded labour which had developed in the West Indies. This led to further abolitionist legislation in 1838.[387]

In Shaftesbury, as might be expected, John Rutter was engaged in supporting the campaign to abolish slavery in all its forms. He is recorded as a speaker in Mere in March 1838 when he explained the 'oppressive and deceptive operation of the Apprenticeship System' in the West Indies, which system had been introduced after the abolition of slavery in the British colonies in 1833.[388]

He drafted a petition to Parliament entitled *Negro Apprenticeship Slavery and Address to Queen*, which was approved by the Shaftesbury Town Council at its meeting on 18 May 1838.[389] Still further, Rutter arranged for the Shaftesbury Friends to contribute funds amounting to £9.50s (£1,000 in 2018 prices) to the Central Negro Emancipation Committee.[390]

The peace movement

EXPRESSING HIS QUAKER beliefs, John Rutter was also very supportive of the peace movement and attended two of the International Peace Congresses, the very first, in July 1843 in London, and the third congress in August 1849, in Paris, when Victor Hugo was the President.[391]

Amusingly for someone who had been brought up as a Quaker to cherish simplicity, humility and frugal living, during his visit to Paris, John Rutter purchased a fine top hat - not black or sombre grey in colour, but cream. Perhaps, when confronted with what Paris had to offer, he just got carried away, as Englishmen often do when abroad. The hat is covered in silk plush and is of the 'Empire Period' (roughly 1800 to 1850) when top hats, which were straight-sided and much taller than they are today, were referred to as 'stovepipe hats'. The cream top hat is now in the possession of a descendant, Simon Rutter, and carries inside the inscription 'Paris'. The fine leather box in which it is kept has a Waterloo sticker on it.[392]

More seriously, in the final year of his life, he attended a 'Peace Congress Demonstration', in Bristol in October 1850, together with a fugitive slave (Dr Pennington), Edmund Fry and delegates of the Frankfurt Peace Congress which had been held in August 1850. At this public meeting, John Rutter made the following remarks 'It was strange that it should be necessary in the present day to stand up and prove that war was a curse and peace a blessing'. He advocated, to cheers from his audience, that 'war was opposed to christianity, and he was prepared to show that it was impossible for a man to be a soldier, or a fighting sailor, and yet profess to be a christian, without the most striking inconsistency'. He called the existing system of law in England 'a disgrace' and said that, as a lawyer, 'if the people waited to procure a reformation and an improvement in that respect, they must take care not to send lawyers to Parliament'.[393] Interestingly, after a decade as a professional solicitor he was not averse to challenging and criticising his own. He might justifiably be called a rebel to the greater cause. To some he was just plain *turbulent.*

The conversations at these Peace Congresses proved to be very fruitful and formed the backdrop to the formation in 1863 of the International Committee of the Red Cross which persuaded governments to adopt the first Geneva Convention in 1864.[394]

John Rutter – a Quaker to the end

NOTWITHSTANDING HIS DIFFERENCES with the Society of Friends in Shaftesbury, John Rutter remained true to Quaker testimonies for the rest of his life. He continued to attend Meetings of the Friends. The problem was that he was a free spirit. He did not like to be constrained by the strictures of any organisation.

John Rutter's strongly held beliefs led him to be active in support of the poor, education, social and political reform, abstinence, and the anti-slavery and peace movements. Despite being disowned, he followed the values espoused by the Society of Friends and lived his life accordingly.[395]

Because of his disownment by Shaftesbury and Sherborne Friends, his death was recorded in the Monthly Meeting Burial Notes as 'not a member'. Despite this, instructions were given by the Friends to a grave-maker, John Arnold, to prepare a grave for his body in the Quaker burial ground next to the Meeting House in St James Street, where he was interred.[396] Even in death, John Rutter's determination and perseverance as a dissenting Quaker could not be denied.

His son, John Farley Rutter recorded in his note book, which Elizabeth Beaven Rutter repeated in *The Rutter Family*, a prayer which Rutter often said:

> Heavenly Father, Thou has taught us the duty and the privilege of drawing near unto Thee, and of asking for thy guidance and instruction. May it please Thee in Thy mercy in Christ Jesus to regard us who are now assembled professedly for the purpose of worshipping Thee in Spirit and in Truth, to give us that wisdom from above which every one of us stand so greatly in need of and to strengthen us to overcome our proud Spirits by Thy Divine Spirit.[397]

The first Friends Meeting House in Shaftesbury, built 1746, in dilapidated state in the 1970s before being renovated to become a private house. John Rutter is buried in the Burial Ground in front of the house, in an unmarked grave

6
Reformer and Political Activist

SHAFTESBURY'S RIGHT TO be represented at a national government level in England dates from the Model Parliament of 1295 when the borough was entitled to send two representatives (burgesses) to London. For reasons explained below, over the centuries, a democratic tradition did not emerge in the town. The 1665 Charter governing its constitutional electoral system encouraged nepotism and corruption. In *The History of Parliament (1820 to 1832)*, Shaftesbury was described as 'A borough of notorious venality and intractable politics'.[398]

By the time John Rutter arrived in Shaftesbury in 1811, the town's council was a self-perpetuating oligarchy and, for national elections, it was regarded as a 'pocket borough' entitled to return two MPs and controlled by two aristocratic landlords. In the mid-18th century, they were Lord Shaftesbury and Lord Ilchester who, between them, owned most of the town and the surrounding countryside. The two peers agreed not to compete against each other and were able to sell the right to stand for election to potential candidates who typically paid £2,000 (about £400,000 in 2018 prices) for each Parliamentary seat. Those elected might expect jobs and sinecures, with significant monetary gain, as well as status and sometimes titles. At that time, payment for the right to stand for and represent one of these pocket boroughs was not illegal, although bribing the electorate was already a criminal offence. However, bribery and the treating of voters, through the provision of food, drink and lavish entertainment, were widely practised. Such expenses would often increase the total cost of securing a seat by a further 50% to 100%. Thus, the actual cost might be as high as £4,000[399] (about £800,000 in 2018 prices). For these national elections the electorate comprised those who paid 'scot and lot'. 'Scot' was a tax on an inhabitant while 'lot' was based on the value of the house, whether owned or rented. It was assessed on the individual's ability to pay. The right to vote was vested in every inhabitant renting to the value of 40 shillings per annum and paying rates and taxes. Their votes were secured either by being 'bought', through the provision of a loan or treating, or by the voters being threatened with eviction from their rented houses if the landlord's

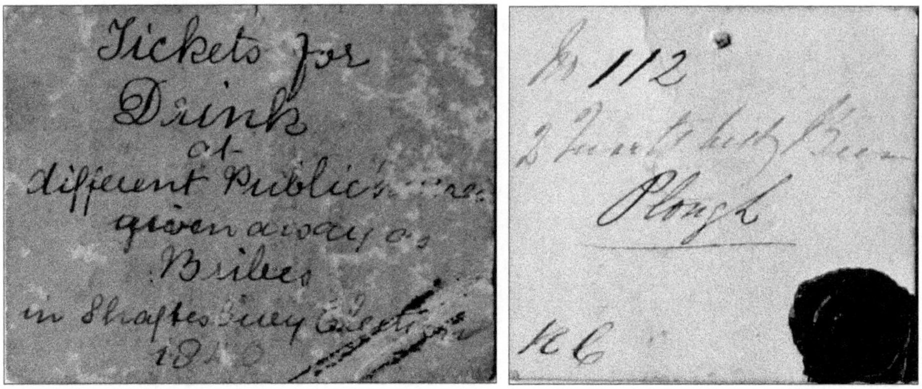

Tickets for drink at different public houses given away as bribes in Shaftesbury Election. Ticket No 112 on the right is for '2 Quarts best Beer – Plough' (Gold Hill)

chosen candidate was defeated. A small clique at local level acted as agents to ensure that the electoral process was managed to the satisfaction of the landowners. However, as the 18th century progressed, because elections were invariably so obviously fixed, increasingly a third candidate was encouraged by some of the electorate to stand against the two chosen candidates.

In 1774 and 1785, respectively, Shaftesbury was to experience two scandals which caused it to develop a growing and sustained reputation as an undemocratic and politically corrupt town.

1774 General Election

THE 1774 SCANDAL arose during a heated Parliamentary contest when an independent candidate, Hans Winthrop Mortimer, stood unsuccessfully against Francis Sykes and his fellow Indian nabob, Thomas Rumbold. Sykes had been elected in 1771, standing on Lord Shaftesbury's interest. After his Lordship's death Sykes built up his own interest in the town and secured control of the corporation. Rumbold was Ilchester's candidate. The election results were: Sykes: 284; Rumbold: 248; Mortimer: 112; the total votes cast being 634 (each voter being able to cast votes for two candidates, if they wished). Sykes and Rumbold were alleged to have paid 20 guineas (almost £3,000 in 2018 prices) to each voter to secure support.[400] It was later recorded by Thomas Oldfield, a historian, that

> A person concealed under a ludicrous and fantastical disguise, and called by the name of Punch, was placed in a small apartment, and through a hole in the door delivered to the voters parcels, containing twenty guineas each: upon which they were conducted to another apartment

> in the same house, where they found another person called Punch's secretary, who required them to sign notes for the value received: these notes were made payable to an imaginary character, to whom was given the name of Glenbucket.[401]

A satirical cartoon entitled *'The Shaftesbury Election or the Humours of Punch'* depicted the malpractices at this election. Three compartments in the upper part of the print showed the interiors of a house which were labelled Punch's Room, Secretaries' Room and Agents' Room.[402]

The Shaftesbury Election or the Humours of Punch (Gold Hill)

A subsequently convened committee of the House of Commons investigated the alleged malpractice and concluded that Sykes and Rumbold had not been properly elected and that they should be prosecuted for bribery and perjury. A criminal case was never brought against them and thus they were, unbelievably, free to stand in the next election. The committee which tried the petition drew the attention of the House to the 'most notorious bribery and corruption' which had been practised; and a bill to incapacitate certain voters was brought in, but eventually dropped.[403] Mortimer was deemed to have been duly elected to one of these two seats and then successfully brought a civil case of bribery against Sykes. He was awarded £11,000[404] (equivalent to about £1.6 million in 2018 prices), on 22 counts of £500 each in damages, which sum he used to purchase properties in Shaftesbury, so enhancing his chances of controlling the electorate and of being elected in future. Despite this, six years later, in 1780, both Sykes and Rumbold (now Sir Thomas, following a spell abroad as Governor of Madras) were elected as the two members of Parliament for Shaftesbury but Rumbold (only) was again unseated for electoral corruption. Sykes was made a baronet in 1781. Mortimer served as the other MP in 1775 & 1776 and again from 1781 to 1789. Still further he was able to secure the election of a colleague, John Drummond, in 1786, without contest.[405] Shaftesbury was, indeed, a pocket borough, with a rotten reputation to match it.

Shaftesbury a 'close' corporation

THE SECOND SCANDAL, in 1785, resulted from a concentration of power in the Court of Common Council of Shaftesbury in the hands of one capital burgess[406], Charles Pinhorn, who abused his offices to enjoy and provide lavish hospitality. He avoided paying rent on his property, as well as failing to pay quit rent to Lord Shaftesbury for fourteen years and neglecting to ensure the proper administration and financial accountability of the Corporation and related charities. The problem arose as much from a systemic failure of the structure of governance of the Corporation as it did from the lack of integrity and honesty of Mr Pinhorn. The town was governed by a Common Council of capital burgesses under a charter of 1665, which had been granted by King Charles II. It was a 'close' corporation, which at that time meant that only Church of England communicants were entitled to hold public office. These provisions emanated from the Corporation and the Test Acts of 1661 and 1673 respectively, which were designed to ensure loyalty to the Crown and curb the involvement of Catholics and nonconformists in public office. These constraints were not removed until the Sacramental Test Act of 1828.

The members of the Common Council were the Mayor and the capital burgesses who appointed the Recorder (the legal officer) for a term 'during the pleasure of the Corporation'. When a vacancy arose on the Council, due to retirement or death, a new capital burgess was appointed by the Mayor, the Recorder and a majority of the capital burgesses. There existed no power under the Charter to remove a capital burgess. The Mayor was elected annually, shortly before Michaelmas, by the Common Council and was chosen from among the capital burgesses, serving for a term of one year, mirroring the custom elsewhere. The Mayor could not be re-elected until three complete Mayoralties had elapsed. At the end of his term of office, the outgoing Mayor was automatically appointed as the Common Warden, who was an officer of the Corporation, to serve for the following year. This practice encouraged corruption as the Common Warden was, in effect, the chief executive who was responsible for receiving revenues, from Corporation and other charitable properties, and paying all the salaries and other bills. Thus, after stepping down as Mayor, the former incumbent of that office was in a position, as Common Warden, to account for his own expenditure in the year when he was Mayor. There was no independent review or audit and the Court of Common Council was a self-perpetuating oligarchy whose members monitored their own affairs. They renewed leases of properties owned by the Corporation, collected rents, and administered many of the town's charities. There was also an annual event (a celebration involving a feast, known as the 'Bezant Ceremony') to thank the neighbouring village, Enmore Green, for the provision of water to the hill-top town of Shaftesbury. The cost of this expensive affair was met out of Corporation funds. In addition, each new Mayor was entitled to a grand annual feast to celebrate his inauguration.[407] The magistracy was not independent of the executive since, according to the laws of the day, the town's three magistrates were the Mayor, the most recent Past Mayor and the Recorder. Thus the town was controlled by a small political clique, accountable to no-one.

Mr Pinhorn served as Mayor in 1770, 1775, 1779 and 1783 and, consequently, held the office of Common Warden in 1771, 1776, 1780 and 1784.[408] These were perfect conditions under which he could exploit the privileges of the two offices for his own financial benefit. The cost of the two feasts mushroomed from £40 in 1744 to £111 in 1770/71 (about £19,000 in 2018 prices).[409] Bills for wine were rendered from the Three Swans Inn in connection with small events and in celebration of the King's Birthday; these amounted to £33 (about £6,000 in 2018 prices) in 1781/82.[410] The annual rent which Pinhorn failed to pay on his house, Puckmore, in Motcombe, owned by the Corporation, amounted to £45 (about £7,000 a year in 2018 prices).[411] Apart from self-ingratiation and embezzlement of public funds, his actions resulted in nothing being spent on the public good. There was inadequate maintenance and repair of the Town Hall and the School House, no pitching of streets, as well as a reduction in the number of almsmen and almswomen being cared for. Relief to the poor all but disappeared as did a legacy of £100 (about £17,000 in 2018 prices) bequeathed by George Foyle to fund donations.[412] After many years the fraud and the inefficiency were addressed in 1785 by a group of capital burgesses, led by Thomas Tucker. Pinhorn was never elected Mayor again but, since he could not be dismissed, he continued as a capital burgess until he died in 1795.[413] He was never charged with fraud or misappropriation of public funds. During the 1770s Mr Pinhorn had been all powerful. One of the few instances when his wings were somewhat clipped was the visit by John Wesley to Shaftesbury. Wesley came to preach in the town many times. Pinhorn attempted to stop him from preaching by sending one of the town's constables to restrain him. Wesley's retort was dismissive 'While King George gives me leave to preach I shall not ask leave of the Mayor of Shaftesbury'.[414]

By confronting Pinhorn, Shaftesbury's Court of Common Council had sought to clean up its own house but without being transparent and thus without exposure to public censure. Some progress was made in dealing with creditors and with some aspects of the Corporation's finances. The back pay of quit rents, amounting to £271 (almost £40,000 in 2018 prices) to Lord Shaftesbury, was settled and the finances of the Corporation were rebuilt by charging exorbitant fines (premiums) for the renewal of Corporation leases.[415]

Over the centuries, the Shaftesbury Corporation had come to own a number of properties which were leased or let out. The length of each lease was typically the life of the lessor or 99 years, whichever was the shorter. For a lease for life, the tenant would pay an initial capital sum, known as a fine, or an annual rent, or more often both. Two other people would normally be named in the lease. These were often relatives of the tenant. As long as one of these two remained alive, the tenant, provided he (or rarely she) observed the terms of the lease, would remain in possession of the property. If any one of those named died, then a new lease was required and could be granted with a new life added but this would usually require the payment of another large fine. It was a nasty scam for extracting more money from the population of Shaftesbury, while enhancing the coffers of the Corporation.[416]

Despite all of the above, the presentation of accounts and the financial administration of the Corporation remained deficient and the priorities for expenditure did not, sadly, extend to the poor. In comparison, £47 (well over £5,000 in 2018 prices) was spent in 1798 on new colours and other expenses for the two Volunteer Corps and another 20 guineas (almost £2,500 in 2018 prices) was provided, in 1803, towards equipping the Shaftesbury Volunteer Infantry. Little was expended on repairs to the almshouses or on pitching the streets or on any other services for the public good.[417]

Sadly the containment of Pinhorn's excesses did not put an end to the practice of the capital burgesses lining their own pockets and perpetuating the Corporation's existence. It did not prevent further nepotism and corruption in Shaftesbury's Court of Common Council. The position actually got worse before it improved. Another capital burgess, Edward Buckland, became as dominant as Charles Pinhorn. In 1804, he took on the role of Receiver of Rents as well as Town Clerk and arranged for his sons and friends to take on various offices and roles in the Corporation and on the Court of Common Council. During the Buckland era the fines from the renewal of leases continued to increase dramatically, from £670 (about £120,000 in 2018 prices) in the period 1750 to 1787 to £2,369 (around £200,000 in 2018 prices) in the period 1798 to 1835.[418] This enabled greater sums of money to be expended on largesse than during the time of Pinhorn. Some small efforts were made to contain excess. For example, the Mayor's expenses were limited to £60 per year from 1827 (£5,500 in 2018 prices)[419] but this compared to a more modest £10 in the mid-17th century. The Recorder, a lawyer, Charles Bowles, who has been described as a kindly Pickwickian figure and an honourable and respected citizen, served in that office from 1804 to 1827, before he was forced out by the Buckland faction. He did his best to introduce propriety. But the Court continued to be controlled by a small clique of Edward Buckland, Philip Chitty (Buckland's son-in-law) and William Swyer, who also acted as agents to the wealthy landowner Lord Grosvenor.[420]

As noted earlier, in 1819 Grosvenor had acquired Lord Rosebery's 383 properties in Shaftesbury for a sum thought variously to be £60,000 or £70,000 (about £5 million in 2018 prices). Together with the properties owned by the Corporation, this represented two-thirds of the houses in Shaftesbury. Thus the political clique of Buckland, Chitty and Swyer, as agents, controlled the two seats in Parliament as well as the borough of Shaftesbury. To add to this, they appointed Lord Grosvenor as the Recorder in 1828, after ousting Charles Bowles.[421] The three Shaftesbury magistrates comprised the Mayor, the immediate Past Mayor (who became the Common Warden) and the Recorder. Therefore Lord Grosvenor and the key burgesses controlled the judiciary as well as the Corporation and Parliamentary representation. The dominance of Buckland, Chitty and Swyer continued for the first three decades of the 19th century. It finished with William Swyer's death in 1831 and after Philip Chitty lost the Grosvenor agency in the same year. The reforms introduced by the Great Reform Act of 1832 and the Municipal Corporations Act of 1835 further sealed the end of the Buckland era. In these dying years, the members of the Court of Common Council sought to amend and address the Corporation's priorities. They provided £400 (£50,000 in 2018 prices) for the rebuilding of Chubb's Almshouse (for women)[422] and a similar amount, through the waiver of a loan, to the trustees of the Spiller's Almshouse for the same purpose.[423] By doing this the capital burgesses saw themselves as great reformers, although sceptics might claim that the expenditure was part of a public relations exercise to deflect attention from their own personal financial excesses. In 1834 an enquiry was launched into the municipal government in England and Wales, of which more below. At that time, there were four Bucklands among the thirteen members of the Corporation and a fifth Buckland was Town Clerk.[424] The resulting Municipal Corporations Act of

1835 put an end to the self-perpetuating oligarchy and helped to contain the excessive expenditure and personal abuse of public funds.

1820 General Election

UNTIL 1820 JOHN Rutter had been content to focus his efforts on his printing and publishing business. But in the society in which he lived, he saw many injustices. The Peterloo Massacre in Manchester in August 1819 would have influenced his thinking about the need for political reform. As a Quaker, Rutter was concerned with equality, fairness and justice. He had already written a booklet in 1819 on the state of the poor in Shaftesbury.

By the time of the general election in 1820, triggered by the death of the monarch, George III, Rutter had begun to focus his attention on the lack of democracy and inadequate representation both at a national level in Parliament and at a local level in the Shaftesbury Corporation. It seems that, notwithstanding his parents dying when he was young, John Rutter had been well-educated and well versed in liberal values and political ideology via his schooling, the influence of his older sisters and his fellow Quakers at the Meeting House. His awareness of political issues would have been furthered by reading the works of the 18th century liberal writers John Locke and Thomas Paine. He would have been seized by the idea that the legitimacy of a government is obtained via the will of the people, freely expressed.

According to John Farley Rutter

> In 1820 *(Note: it was actually 1819)* Earl Grosvenor purchased the Borough of Shaftesbury; this gave him a dominant interest as he obtained over 383 properties and claimed to be a patron of the Borough. He appointed a tyrannical and unscrupulous agent[425] who proclaimed that all the tenants were expected to yield their wishes and political views to the Patron. My father was a great lover of freedom of speech and action and his soul rebelled against political slavery. Many of the voters were of a very low type and were easily managed by drink and bribery judiciously given. Others felt indignant at the way the agent acted, he treated the tenants as if they had been slaves. As a result when the first election occurred my father was chosen to go to London to find a candidate who would fight the nominee. He chose Mr Merest of Lydford Hall, Norfolk, who made a gallant fight but the nominee of the Grosvenor interest was returned. After this effort for freedom of election the unfriendly feeling against my father began. It was always apparent, but in after years it merged into violent opposition and a determination to ruin him in business.[426]

Robert Grosvenor, 2nd Earl Grosvenor and 1st Marquess of Westminster (1767-1845)

After Lord Grosvenor acquired Lord Rosebery's interests in Shaftesbury, his local agents, under instruction from the Chief Agent John Jones of London, initially adopted a much tougher approach. Rather than providing lavish entertainment to the electorate, tenants were threatened with eviction if they could not demonstrate that they had voted for the preferred candidates.[427] John Rutter is reported as saying in an election speech 'These are the genuine sentiments of my heart, for when Lord Grosvenor purchased this Borough, he neither purchased my person, my principles, nor my vote'.[428]

In an election handbill written and printed by Rutter, there was a mock dialogue between Grosvenor and Jones where the Earl comments on how compliant the Shaftesbury voters are, with no expenses and no treating. The agent boasts that he has arranged this 'by dominating the Body Corpulent with friends' and claiming that he could get 'the dutiful and obedient tenants in that Borough....to return your black footman or even your Grey Charger'.[429] It was not until 1872 that votes were cast in secret[430] and, thus, the threat of expulsion from one's home was very real for those tenants who did not comply with their landlord's electoral wishes.

At the 1820 General Election, Lord Grosvenor's candidates, The Hon. Edward Harbord and Abraham Moore, were returned as the two members of Parliament. In 1821 Harbord inherited a peerage and another of Grosvenor's candidates, Ralph Leycester, was elected in his place. Also in 1821 Moore, who had left for America owing a considerable amount to Earl Grosvenor, resigned his seat. Lord (Robert) Grosvenor arranged for his third and youngest son (confusingly also named Robert) to stand in the by-election which he won in April 1822, at a cost of £495 (£52,000 in 2018 prices).[431] Young Robert Grosvenor, aged just 21, was a Whig and, like his father, supported liberal petitions to Parliament and reforming legislation. These included criminal law reform (June 1822), an anti-slavery petition (March 1826), revision of the Corn Laws (April 1826) and Parliamentary Reform (April 1826). At the General Election in June 1826, Robert Grosvenor did not stand again in Shaftesbury but, instead, was elected to represent the city of Chester.[432] Although young Robert had espoused similar sentiments to his electorate and to those of Rutter, even in a pocket borough such as Shaftesbury, the inhabitants objected to a candidate being foisted upon them. After Rutter's efforts in the 1820 election, Lord Grosvenor's agents were forced to agree that in future more deference and consultation was to be paid to the town's voters.[433] However this did not alter their approach of ballot rigging and intimidation.

John Rutter did not let up in his criticism of the controlling clique who, he considered, did not handle Lord Grosvenor's affairs well. In his view, they were continually seeking to strengthen their influence through patronage, arranging for their own cronies to be appointed to key positions within the Corporation and the town – and feathering their own nests. In one celebrated instance, in 1824, the clique succeeded in removing James Shrimpton, the innkeeper of the Red Lion (subsequently renamed the Grosvenor Arms), which was leased from the Earl, and replacing him by a friend of theirs named Harriss. Rutter led the campaign against this, writing to Grosvenor in support of Shrimpton[434], who had moved to the Bell Hotel which he owned.[435] The dissatisfied voters supported Shrimpton and took their custom to the Bell, causing a loss of trade to Harriss who subsequently went bankrupt and left the town.[436]

As part of this struggle, the Recorder, Charles Bowles, resigned as Grosvenor's agent and ceased all participation in the management of his lordship's properties. Rutter was one of those who put his name to the motion thanking Bowles for having endeavoured to prevent the expulsion of Shrimpton.[437] Bowles later referred to John Rutter as 'the champion of the oppressed'.[438] The capital burgesses who formed the clique were not amused by Rutter's continual opposition and this was the atmosphere pertaining when the dramatic events of 1826 occurred.

The 1826 incident

At first sight, the circumstances that led the bitter clashes in that year seem quite tame and innocuous but the daggers were out for Rutter who was an outsider in every respect. He was not of Shaston parentage. He was a dissenter. Worse still, he was out to change the status quo and to put an end to the comfortable, nepotistic and fraudulent lifestyle which the ruling clique of the Corporation enjoyed.

Lord Grosvenor sought to establish his position as patron of the town by donating funds for a new Town Hall and a new Market Hall, removing its medieval predecessors which were inconveniently situated in the middle of the High Street, by then much busier than in former times. On 2 August 1826, at the ceremony of laying the first stone of the new Town Hall, Grosvenor provided entertainment for the town's residents. His agents, the ruling Buckland clique, divided the invitees into two groups: the favoured, who were considered to be gentlemen, were invited to dine at the Grosvenor Arms and the less favoured, the tradesmen, were invited to drink wine at 'inferior inns'[439], all at the Earl's expense. Invitations were issued by the Mayor, William Swyer. John Rutter was the subject of a cruel hoax, as he was invited to the latter treat. Rutter was affronted and, perhaps wishing to get the agent into trouble, personally hand delivered a letter to Grosvenor's Motcombe House writing

> J. Rutter feels obliged by Lord Grosvenor's invitation to drink wine at his expense at the Bell Hotel this evening, but begs to excuse himself, not only on the ground of his general habits of abstemiousness, but still more so from his not having been accustomed to associate with the greater portion of that class of individuals enumerated in the list which was shewn (sic) him. Shaftesbury, 8th Month 2nd, 1826.[440]

The Bell Inn stood on part of the site of the present main car park in Shaftesbury and gave its name to the adjoining Bell Street, where the archway that formed the entrance to the old fire station can be seen and is now the front of an estate agent's premises. The inn was acquired by Lord Grosvenor in 1828 and ceased to operate as a public house soon afterwards.[441] The building was demolished to make a new cattle market in the late 19th century, another of the many benefactions to Shaftesbury by its principal landowner, Lord Grosvenor.

On receipt of Rutter's letter Grosvenor was sympathetic and forwarded it to his agents at the Grosvenor Arms to put the matter right[442]. But worse was to follow.

Thomas James Bardouleau, a lawyer's clerk, in the firm of Bowles, Chitty & Chitty, had also received an invitation to the tradesmen's event and was deeply offended. He wrote a letter to the Mayor demanding that his name be struck off this lesser, demeaning list. In his letter, Bardouleau was much more strident than Rutter had been. He wrote

> Mr. Wm. Swyer, Sir, I have known you merely from being in possession of a Catalogue of your Acts; and I feel that a most gross insult was intended me, when you were pleased to billet me at the Bush. I am neither a Horse, nor a Tenant of Lord Grosvenor's. I have as yet never eat nor drank at my Lord Grosvenor's expense, neither shall I do so now, unless at his Lordship's own table. I desire that my Name immediately be, by yourself, struck from such List, or I shall most certainly avail myself of a Public opportunity to express my just indignation. One word of advice, which you ill deserve from me, 'Noli irritare Crabrones'. I shall wait your reply till two o'clock. Your humble Servant, Thomas James Bardouleau.[443]

In providing advice to the Mayor in Latin, translated as 'Do not stir up the hornets', Bardouleau perhaps sought to demonstrate his education and, therefore, his status and his justification for inclusion in the list of those invited for dinner at the Grosvenor Arms. Then, having received no reply from Swyer by the stated time, he went to John Rutter's printing shop to arrange for his letter to be printed prior to circulation in the town.[444] This was carried out by one of Rutter's staff who omitted to record the printer's name on the printed page, as required by an Act of Parliament. Apparently John Rutter took a cursory glance at the letter before handing it to his workman. He was, perhaps, preoccupied with his own thoughts about refusing the Earl's invitation to drink wine at the Bell Inn.[445] Unknowingly, John Rutter was set up for a fall and he was snared. Buckland, Chitty and Swyer knew that they had him in a trap and were determined to exact full damage and retribution. They were out to punish *The Turbulent Quaker*. Rutter was prosecuted for omitting his name on the printed version and received the following summons

> John Rutter, of the Borough of Shaftesbury, Printer, personally to appear, &c. &c. to answer the complaint and Information of William Swyer, for that the said John Rutter did on the 2nd day of August instant, print a

certain paper intended to be published and dispersed, purporting to be a Letter from one Thomas James Bardouleau to the said William Swyer, without having printed the name and place of abode of him the said John Rutter in legible characters upon the front of such paper, the said paper not being within any exception enumerated and set forth in and by any Act or Acts of Parliament contrary to the statute in that case made and provided, &c. &c.[446]

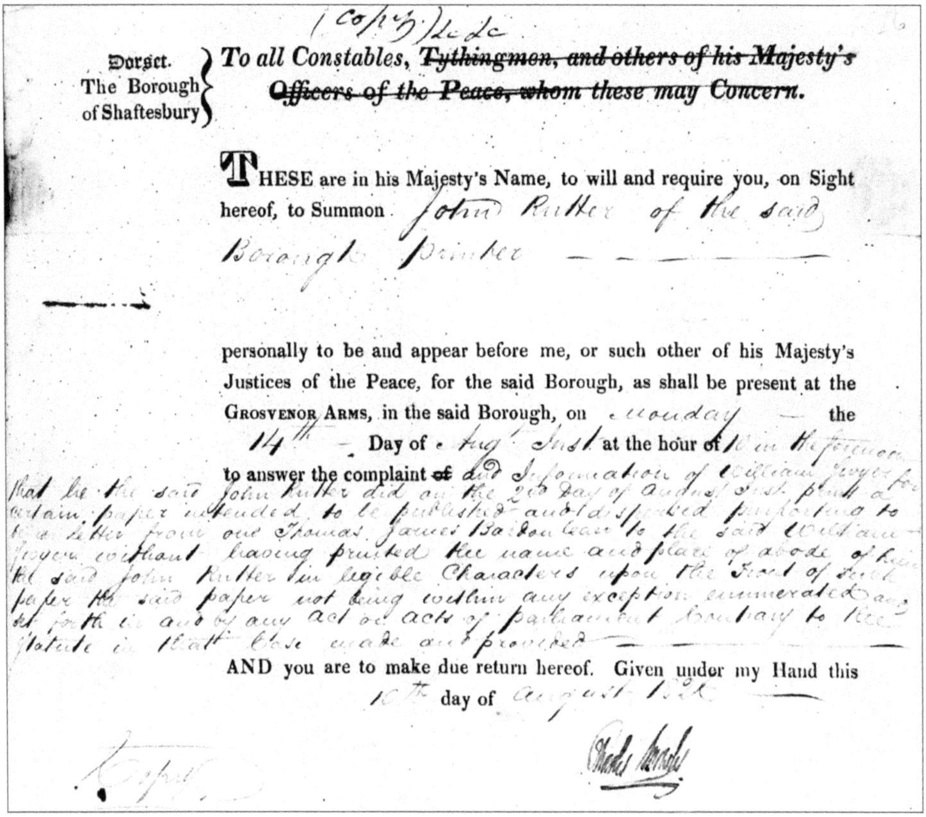
(Copy) ...

Dorset. The Borough of Shaftesbury

To all Constables, ~~Tythingmen, and others of his Majesty's Officers of the Peace, whom these may Concern.~~

THESE are in his Majesty's Name, to will and require you, on Sight hereof, to Summon John Rutter of the said Borough Printer

personally to be and appear before me, or such other of his Majesty's Justices of the Peace, for the said Borough, as shall be present at the GROSVENOR ARMS, in the said Borough, on Monday the 14th Day of Augt Inst at the hour of 10 in the forenoon to answer the complaint ~~of~~ and Information of William Swyer for that he the said John Rutter did on the 2nd day of August Inst print a certain paper intended to be published and dispersed purporting to be a Letter from one Thomas James Bardouleau to the said William Swyer without having printed the name and place of abode of him the said John Rutter in legible Characters upon the front of such paper the said paper not being within any exception enumerated and set forth in and by any act or acts of parliament contrary to the Statute in that case made and provided

AND you are to make due return hereof. Given under my Hand this 10th day of August 1826

Chas Bowles

Copy

John Rutter, Summons of 10 August 1826 (S&DHS, D.H.C., D-SHS/Box 41.3017)

The Mayor, William Swyer, brought the prosecution which was heard on 14 August 1826 by the Shaftesbury magistrates, who were Richard Buckland and Charles Bowles. Rutter had prepared a defence, a long one of eleven written pages, but his speech was curtailed by the magistrates. Through his printing and publishing interests, Rutter had contacts with the media in London and arranged for *The Times* to publish his own account of the proceedings. The newspaper reported the story on 16 August under the heading 'Caution to Printers'. It wrote that Rutter had claimed that

> It was the custom of the trade to print notes without putting the printer's name to them: that he had scarcely seen the manuscript: that the author's name was attached to it; and that it was disgraceful to the town of Shaftesbury that its mayor should condescend to turn common informer.[447]

Philip Chitty, who was a practising attorney in partnership with Charles Bowles, one of the two magistrates, acted as prosecuting counsel for the Mayor. Chitty 'urged that the note contained matter offensive to Mr. Swyer, and that it was necessary to check the licentiousness of the press. If Mr. Rutter would express his contrition for his conduct in printing the note, Mr. Swyer would be satisfied, and many other informations would be put a stop to'.[448] Rutter refused and was fined £5.[449]

John Rutter reacted angrily to this as he believed he had been unfairly treated. He felt that he had been the victim of a conspiracy and the subject of discrimination by the ruling elite. He had both the education and the money to continue the fight.[450] So, on 9 September, he published in full the written defence that he had prepared on 14 August. This document *The Defence of John Rutter* began with two classical quotations demonstrating his knowledge of literature

> Things lawfully and mildly requested, exact performance; but if harshly and illegally commanded, produce dislike, and sometimes refusal and resistance — *Claudian.*
>
> If a man be improperly or maliciously attacked, there is nothing like arrogance in his asserting his innocence, or that rank in society which he has fairly earned, and still feels himself qualified to sustain — *Horace.*[451]

The Defence was indeed long and rather rambling. The magistrates would have wished to shorten the proceedings as they did not care for any of the views expressed by Rutter and desired a speedy conviction. Rutter began by pointing out that the present chief magistrate of the town (William Swyer) was also a deputy or sub-agent to Lord Grosvenor. In the case of the complainant (Bardouleau) Rutter argued that any man has a right to demand an explanation from someone who has insulted him and that sending a letter to the Mayor (Swyer) was the least confrontational as well as a 'legal and honourable' manner of dealing with this, even if some of the language used had been 'strong'. Rutter explained that Bardouleau, a trainee lawyer, had been dismissed from his employment in the law firm, Bowles, Chitty & Chitty, which was punishment enough for him, his wife and three children. Rutter pleaded that the omission of the printer's name was purely accidental and that printers acted as agents, thus they should not be prosecuted. He pointed out that his actions did not imply any opposition to Lord Grosvenor who 'has not more warm and "disinterested" friend in this Borough than myself'. But he advised, in an attempt to demonstrate prejudice among the leaders in the town that, 'It is also stated that I am a troublesome fellow. I acknowledge it, but I am troublesome only to evil doers; and it is added, I must be quieted and taught my right place as a tradesman'. But then, in a less than conciliatory or cautious note, he laid into the Mayor. The following words would have assured his conviction and would also lead to a greater charge. In his *Defence* he wrote

> And who is this dignified personage that forces me into the comparison? Is he not a tradesman himself? He is indeed the magistrate, but has he not other titles also? He is William Swyer the mayor and the alderman, but he is also William Swyer the sub agent of Lord Grosvenor, and the receiver of his Lordship's rents; William Swyer the brick and tile maker; William Swyer the reputed common brewer, and William Swyer the half pay officer. These, Gentlemen, are titles and appellatives sufficient to satisfy the ambition of a moderate man, and occupations sufficient to fill the time of an industrious one, without adding thereto the odious one of an Informer.[452]

At the age of 30, Rutter was eloquent but he had not yet learnt to curb his tongue. He said what he thought and he wrote what he believed. This was not the optimum way of achieving an acquittal or a small fine. There was no hint of conciliation. Quite the opposite, he had some points to make and the hearing at the Magistrate's Court gave him a platform. His messianic zeal did not stop there for, on 2 October 1826, he printed and published the first of four issues of a satirical periodical, *The Shastonian*, which was priced at 3d. (£1 in 2018 prices). It was dedicated to Earl Grosvenor as 'Patron of the Borough of Shaftesbury'.

With much input from Rutter, *The Shastonian* was edited by another reformer, author and political agitator, James Acland. It was an early 19th century version of today's *Private Eye* – critical of people and organisations, and seeking to expose corruption, nepotism, conflicts of interest and other forms of anti-social behaviour. The motto on the title page of *The Shastonian* was taken from Seneca and translated as 'Bow to no patron's influence; rely on no frail hopes, in freedom live and die'.[453]

Cartoon from James Acland article about John Rutter (enemyofcorporatedespots.files.wordpress.com/2010/03/1826)

The first issue of *The Shastonian* contained a report of proceedings of the Corporation to elect Philip Chitty as Mayor. It pointed out that

> The Chief Magistrate is elected by a majority of the corporation of the Borough, comprising, the Mayor, Recorder, and twelve capital burgesses. Of these the Mayor for the current year, with the Recorder, and the Mayor for the past year, form the magisterial bench for the Borough.

There then followed a satirical account of the proceedings, including the following imaginary dialogue, intended to ridicule the political clique in the Corporation and to expose its petty nature and nepotism

> Mr. P.M. Chitty – We are all here except Mr. Hurd
> Mr. (Charles) Hannen – He was just now seen to go to the Ship Inn
> Mr. P.M. Chitty – We had perhaps better send one of the mace-bearers there, and another to his residence, with our compliments and to request his immediate attendance

> Mr. Bowles – I protest against that proceeding. Pray, Mr. Chitty, if Mr. Gillingham was absent, would you send to his residence at Cann? Because if you would not, it will be equally incorrect to send for Mr. Hurd.

The Shastonian gave a sarcastic account of the building materials which might be used for facing the front of the new Town Hall which was the gift of Earl Grosvenor[454]; a criticism of the state of Shaftesbury's paving 'causing tender feet and hard corns'[455] and of the poor water supply in the borough; and the inadequate street lighting, commenting that 'men whose deeds are evil love darkness rather than light'.[456]

A second court hearing, for which Rutter was given three hours' notice, took place before the magistrates (Charles Bowles and Richard Buckland) at 18.00 on 26 September 1826.[457] Not unnaturally, Rutter sought an adjournment, on account of lack of time to prepare.

A third hearing was held on 2 October.[458] Rutter questioned the jurisdiction of the court. On this occasion, Chitty asked for an adjournment.

A fourth hearing was held on 5 October. Rutter again questioned the competence of Buckland to act as magistrate as he had 'prejudged the question at issue'. Reading from a pre-prepared letter, he also protested against Bowles judging the case since he was one of Lord Grosvenor's agents. The normally mild mannered Recorder was indignant offering the following rebuke 'Oh, John, I want no compliments; you address me with words sweeter than honey, whilst you advance charges that stab me to the heart'.[459] Rutter's protests were overruled and, after retiring for just ten minutes, the magistrates fined him a further £5.[460]

The case was reported in the *Dorset County Chronicle* on 12 October 1826 and included the following

> Mr Rutter defended his own cause. Several objections were raised by Mr Rutter, as to the competency of the court to try the information, and also to the manner in which the information was drawn, which, however, were all overruled.[461]

The *Dorset Chronicle* went a step further by writing

> A great deal of time was lost in discussing points, which to a practising lawyer would have occupied by a few minutes. The greatest credit however is due to Mr. Rutter for having conducted his cause as temperately and judiciously as he did, against Mr. Chitty' but also added

'no magistrate could have pursued a more honourable and upright course than that which Mr. Bowles adopted.[462]

At the end of the hearing, John Rutter announced his intention of appealing to the Quarter Sessions of the Court of King's Bench in Dorchester. But, prior to that, on 2 October, he had been served with a writ for libel against William Swyer in connection with content in the first issue of *The Shastonian.* This writ lapsed and another was issued on 25 May 1827 and served on 15 June[463], leading to the case being listed for hearing at Dorchester Assizes in August 1827.[464]

Meanwhile, a second issue of *The Shastonian* appeared on 10 October 1826, priced 6d. In the light of the charges being brought against Rutter, Acland was careful to point out that he was the editor, so shielding John Rutter, as much as he could, from the clique who sought to punish Rutter for his actions. The second issue contained articles about the removal of the Quarter Sessions from Shaftesbury. There were attacks on the agents, the magistrates and the Corporation. The former Mayor, William Swyer, was criticised for lack of dignity and that he had stooped to being a 'Common Informer'. The conflicts of interest were highlighted: that one of the magistrates was the Grosvenor's chief agent in Shaftesbury, that another agent had been the prosecuting counsel and that the chief witness was the Town Clerk, brother of the second magistrate and brother-in-law of the prosecutor, and that in the mayoral year of 1826/7 all three of Lord Grosvenor's local agents were magistrates. The Editor, James Acland, was outspoken about the 'persecution' of John Rutter commenting that Earl Grosvenor 'who personally has manifested nothing but kindness and favor towards the inhabitants of Shaftesbury has within the past six months lost considerable ground in the estimation of the Shastonians'. Acland blamed Grosvenor's agents for this, referring to them as 'a "trio juncta in uno" of Magistrate, Agent and Solicitor'.[465] *The Shastonian* offered a warning to the inhabitants of Shaftesbury

> Have a care, Shastonians! ye who value your money, or ye who have it not. Offend not the high aristocracy of magisterial agents – thwart not the personal views they may happen to entertain – question not the authority they may please to exercise over you lest ye provoke another mayor (if unhappily he be an agent) to become informer ! a second of the trio to argue points of law against his professional partner!! and the third to adjudge your conviction on questionable evidence, unquestionably obtained !!![466]

A third issue of *The Shastonian* was published on 1 November 1826, also priced 6d. This reiterated some of the previous complaints and scandals. It gave examples of magisterial injustice, Corporation inefficiency and corruption. It contained satirical letters, real or concocted, about affairs in Shaftesbury and about the individuals running the close corporation. There were also scathing articles on the lack of integrity of charity trustees and commentary on generous, as well as selfish, inhabitants in the financial support of the Shaftesbury Mendicity Society.[467]

A fourth issue had been printed and was ready for sale on 1 December 1826. However, negotiations had been taking place with Swyer about the libel action he sought to bring and, so, on 4 December, Rutter issued an apology for words used in *The Defence* and in the second issue of *The Shastonian*, of which he was the printer and publisher. Discussions continued in the first half of 1827 to resolve the matter. Swyer would not, however, let up and his demands kept increasing, leading to the second writ being served on 15 June 1827.[468]

Early in July, Rutter approached Lord Grosvenor and met him at Grosvenor House in London with a view to settling the dispute. On 10 July, Lord Grosvenor transmitted to his Shaftesbury agents an apology which Rutter had prepared. In it, Rutter wrote

> John Rutter being anxious to allay the irritation which has too long subsisted between William Swyer and himself, and the more effectually to restore harmony and good fellowship, hereby acknowledges himself to have been actuated by unchristian feeling, and that he regrets having printed any accusation charging Lord Grosvenor's agents with oppressive conduct; and that he also regrets having written or printed anything to injure William Swyer's character as a gentleman or to hurt his feelings as a neighbour.[469]

Swyer responded with conditions that John Rutter could not accept. Following this Rutter wrote to Grosvenor explaining why he could not abide by the terms proposed by Swyer. He begged Grosvenor to 'give him credit for the feeling of deep regret at this failure'.[470]

On 21 July, Rutter was served with notice of the trial in Dorchester and, on the same day, a subpoena was issued requiring the attendance of Lord Grosvenor. Rutter wrote again to the Earl on 22 July with the following message 'John Rutter regrets this necessity, as it may probably prove personally unpleasant to the Earl, and it would much grieve John Rutter to wound the Earl's feelings in any way, after the kind reception which he experienced at Grosvenor House'.[471]

In the event, his Lordship's presence was not required at the trial at the Quarter Sessions which was scheduled to take place on 2 August 1827. In court, at the commencement of the proceedings, Swyer's counsel announced that his client had accepted the written apology from John Rutter. The case therefore never came to trial but, on the instructions of the judge, Lord Chief Justice Best, the jury found in favour of the plaintiff and damages of 40 shillings were assessed against the defendant.[472] In addition, Court costs and other legal fees were awarded against Rutter who had to bear these and other expenses, resulting in total expenditure estimated to be around £300 (£28,000 in 2018 prices).

In a further move to ruin John Rutter, the ruling clique encouraged a rival bookseller and stationer to set up in town in competition.[473]

After this, no further issues of *The Shastonian* were published. In a later reminiscence, James Acland, praised John Rutter as

> A true patriot, many considered him progressive and certainly he was energetic. He was a good man and a staunch friend. Although John was originally apprentice to a linen draper, nonetheless, he later became a printer, a profession in which he could use his fine education and vent his stated belief that the great panacea is publicity.[474]

He also described how he and Rutter worked together and concluded 'it is true to say that many of the principles that I carried through life were nurtured by the good John Rutter'. Acland also related a conversation with Rutter's brother Samuel who regarded him as someone who 'would not tell ought but truth' and who 'is not on to be led by any man'.[475]

The Shastonian was well received by the public in Shaftesbury and the three issues generated a strong feeling in favour of Rutter, whose reputation was enhanced as a champion of the oppressed.

The Recorder, Charles Bowles, who held that office from 1804 to 1827, was no longer willing to accept the dominance of the clique and was concerned at the injustices. As a result he dissolved his partnership with the Chitty brothers and then resigned his position as Recorder. A petition was drawn up by Rutter and others to agree 'an address to Charles Bowles....and to address the Corporation upon his rumoured resignation of that office'. Fractious meetings were held in January 1828 over whether the resignation was effective and over the form and substance of the address. John Rutter later printed two accounts of the story so that the public could understand the circumstances of Bowles' departure.

Rutter also continued to attack the political elite and their performance in managing the town's Corporation. In April 1828 he printed a number of papers which were critical of the highways and the street lighting. In February 1829 he wrote to Philip Chitty, as Grosvenor's agent, requesting use of the Town Hall for a lecture on Astronomy by John Bird, a teacher at Eton and Westminster. In an explanatory note to Earl Grosvenor, which accompanied his letter, Rutter wrote that the old Town Hall had been for the use of the inhabitants generally and not just for the private meetings of the Corporation, whereas the new Town Hall, built by Lord Grosvenor in 1827, had been kept exclusively for the latter purpose. He pointed out that no public meeting had been permitted to be held in it and that the inhabitants at large were not permitted to enter the Town Hall without the consent of Edward Buckland who 'keeps one of the keys and who being the most unpopular mayor'.[476] Just two weeks later Rutter wrote another letter of complaint, this time to Mayor Buckland reprimanding him for a 'calumny' he committed against Rutter's former employer, John Shipley. According to Rutter, the Mayor had advised William Swyer (the next Mayor) that Shipley had charged '7 to 9 pounds more for the blue-coat clothing' than another draper.[477] In 1829 and 1830 he pressed for transparency in relation to Corporation accounts.[478] In October 1829 he led the attempt to invalidate the re-election of William Swyer as Mayor on the grounds that he had served in the same office within the previous three years.[479] None of these actions can have endeared him to the political clique of Buckland, Chitty and Swyer.

Indeed, in May 1829, Rutter received an anonymous spoof letter challenging him to redress a wrong and even challenging him to a dual. It refers to a 'Mr Saddlebags', the sobriquet given to Lord Grosvenor's London agent, John Jones.[480] The letter read as follows

> For the Gross insult, you offered yesterday, to my respectable and very dear Friend, Mr Saddlebags, I now call upon you to give him that satisfaction which as a Gentleman, he is bound to demand, and which you cannot refuse him, without incurring the disgrace of Cowardice. I therefore request that you will immediately appoint Time, Place, Weapons &c. I suppose you will consult the radical lawyer[481], before you send an answer if so, and that you will nominate him Second – My Saddlebag Friend, with my assistance, will have the consolation of benefit to society, by sending two ______s out of the world in double quick time.[482]

Rutter was driven by the desire to bring about electoral reform and to achieve greater fairness in Shaftesbury. In his view, those who were entitled to vote should be able to do so without being frightened of being turned out of their homes. He was determined to challenge the ruling clique. In this he was joined by others: the attorney Charles Hannen, the brothers William and Robert Storey (who owned the Shaftesbury and Salisbury Bank), George Chitty (the brother of Philip Chitty), James Andrews (a cheese dealer), William Atchison (a glover and breeches maker), Henry Norton and Thomas Shirley (a pawnbroker).[483]

1830 General Election

THE SCENE OF the next most serious confrontation between John Rutter and the ruling clique was the election of 1830, triggered by the death of King George IV on 26 June 1830. The Duke of Wellington, the Prime Minister, announced the dissolution of Parliament on 23 July.[484]

Lord Grosvenor's candidates for Shaftesbury were announced: Edward Penrhyn and William Dugdale. Although Lord Grosvenor was a reformer and a Whig supporter, John Rutter and colleagues in Shaftesbury (including George Chitty, Charles Hannen and Robert Storey) sought a third candidate. They were introduced to Francis Knowles, who advocated Parliamentary reform, the abolition of slavery, repeal of the Corn Laws, legal reform and religious tolerance. They invited Knowles, the son of Admiral Sir Charles Henry Knowles, to stand against Penrhyn and Dugdale. Knowles agreed to offer financial support to any of Grosvenor's tenants who were evicted by his agents for voting the wrong way. No doubt with a tongue in his cheek, Rutter wrote to the Prime Minister, the Duke of Wellington, on 20 July 1830 asking him to guarantee this financial support. He described himself as a bookseller of Shaftesbury 'of some character, respectability and influence' in support of a candidate in the 1830 election. He wrote

> A gentleman named Francis Charles Knowles whose father Admiral Knowles of Old Windsor is represented to be a personal friend of thine, has made his appearance in this Borough as a parliamentary candidate under the auspices of several respectable gentlemen of the vicinity. He appears to have been most favourably received by the Inhabitants generally, but there is one obstacle to his election, viz that he must and will have several of the Earl Grosvenor's tenants to vote for him, and who will inevitably be turned out of their Cottage for doing so. It is absolutely essential that one thousand pounds should be lodged in the hands of some trustworthy inhabitant of the town to be hereafter divided amongst the sufferers as compensation.[485]

There is no evidence that Wellington replied.

Towards the end of July the candidates introduced themselves to Shaftesbury's electorate by publishing addresses. Over a period of ten days speeches were made in the town's market place, an area known as the Commons at the northern end of the High Street, and from the balcony of the Grosvenor Arms which overlooks the street.[486] The key issue was a free and fair election. The debates became more heated and the attacks became more personal as the campaigning progressed.

On Monday 26 July, the rival groups, supporting Penrhyn and Dugdale on the one hand and Knowles on the other, glared at each other from either side of the Commons. The Earl's London agent, John Jones, was booed and hissed, with cries of 'down with Jones' and 'Go back and play your tricks at Stockbridge'[487]. There were scuffles, with sticks used as well as attacks by horsemen representing the Earl's candidates. John Rutter spoke passionately and forcefully, calling on Dugdale to act constitutionally and calling for Jones to 'go home and tell the noble Lord that he is indebted to himself and those whom he employs, for his present unpopularity in Shaftesbury'[488]. Rutter invited the electors to vote for Knowles because he 'presents himself upon the true principles of independence and responsibility'.[489] The banker, Robert Storey, praised Rutter's eloquence and encouraged 'every man to give his vote according to his conscience'.[490] The crowd was clearly in support of Knowles and, after much verbal skirmishing, the Grosvenor faction slunk into the Grosvenor Arms, which was their base.[491] Knowles' friends had also hoped to dine at the inn but their application was refused by the landlord who intimated that he might 'run the risk of giving offence to the Earl Grosvenor's agent, which might lead to a notice to quit'.[492]

Tuesday 3 August was the day of nomination. The writ for the election was read and the oaths were administered. The Quaker banker, Robert Storey, formally proposed Francis Knowles, who was seconded by Charles Hannen, the solicitor. Knowles asked if the electors would be permitted to vote for their chosen candidate without intimidation and fear of retribution.[493] George Chitty called upon 'my Lord Grosvenor's agents to tell the electors, that those who vote freely shall not be turned out of their houses'.[494] Grosvenor's agents refused to give such pledges.[495]

At that time, according to the 1831 census, the population of Shaftesbury was 2,742 of whom only 315 were able to vote, per the 1830 Poll Book. Each voter was permitted to cast two votes. In some cases, only one vote was cast in order to try to secure the election of one of the candidates – these voters were known as 'plumpers'.

The polling took place over four days at the new Town Hall which had been completed in 1827, as a gift from Lord Grosvenor. William Swyer was the Mayor and acted as Returning Officer despite the fact that he was one Grosvenor's agents. The election was stormy. Rutter and George Chitty complained about the control by the Grosvenor faction of the parish lists, which detailed the names of registered electors. They argued against the rejection by Swyer, the Returning Officer, of some votes which had been cast in favour of Knowles. Rutter gave a political speech at the hustings complaining about inequality in the country, the lack of pensions for widows of officers and soldiers, and the reforms required in Parliament as a result of corrupt practices and the rotten and pocket boroughs.[496]

At the end of the third day (Thursday 5 August), the Mayor announced the results thus far, showing Knowles trailing in third place. That evening, it was reported that a huge crowd of 'over 10,000 people' assembled in the market place.[497] Knowles addressed them 'expressing confidence in the final triumph of the cause of liberty'.[498] After this, the crowd dispersed, with the exception of 200 to 300 people, mostly women and boys, who went to Rutter's house on the Commons, where he addressed them outside, requesting them to retire quietly to their homes. Many, particularly the young men, paraded through the streets, accompanied by a band, and carried on drinking. About ten in the evening some threw stones at the windows of inhabitants known to favour the Grosvenor candidates and a carriage was destroyed. Grosvenor's agents were lodged at the Grosvenor Arms, where they were regaling themselves at a sumptuous dinner. It was reported that 'a blaze of light was sent into the street as in an illumination for a great victory, or in feast of Belshazzar'[499]. Rutter thought this revelry of self-satisfaction was provocative to the young men and went into the Grosvenor Arms to suggest to the landlord that he shut the gates, thus endeavouring to avert a breach of the peace. Towards eleven o'clock the gates of the inn were rushed and more than 50 men got into the yard. Windows were broken and the doors were kicked in. It has been alleged that no harm was done to anyone, although at the subsequent Petty Sessions in Shaftesbury, one witness, Robert Burridge, stated in court that in going past the Grosvenor Arms after twelve o'clock on the night of the riot 'he was called a spy, knocked down twice, and had his collar broken'.[500] By daybreak peace had been restored. That morning the scene on the Commons was one of utter devastation. Then, under the command of Captain Fawcett, 44 men of the 2nd Dragoons arrived, dusty after their march from Blandford. Ostensibly they were brought in to restore order but by this time there was hardly anyone about. The Mayor had summoned them in case of trouble when the final declaration of the result was made. The Earl's London agent, John

Jones, left the town escorted by two soldiers. Knowles had retired knowing that he was likely to come third albeit with a respectable 150 votes, including those rejected by Swyer. In the event, the official results were: Penrhyn: 169; Dugdale: 145; and Knowles: 121. The huge crowd inside and outside the Town Hall cried 'No! No!' and 'Knowles is our member'[501]. Rutter spoke about intimidation and the rigging of the results. Of the 313 votes that were polled, 43 were rejected by Mayor Swyer, who was one of Lord Grosvenor's agents. If all the votes in favour of Knowles had been allowed, his total would have been 146.[502]

Penrhyn and Dugdale left town soon after the results were announced. *The Evening Mail* of 9 August 1830 reported the electoral proceedings, as described above and concluded that

> It cannot be doubted that Lord Grosvenor has lost all moral power in Shaftesbury, and that henceforth the electors will send two independent men to Parliament, to represent themselves and the country rather than his Lordship, or any other individual to whom he will sell his houses!!![503]

On the same day, Monday 9 August, the Shaftesbury Petty Sessions examined witnesses in relation to the alleged riot on the evening which closed the Parliamentary election. Several inhabitants were charged with disturbing the peace and affray. The Mayor, William Swyer, was now wearing a different hat as magistrate, together with the two Bucklands. Philip Chitty was the prosecutor. Thus the same old gang of Corporation burgesses, who were also Grosvenor's agents, tried the cases. The innkeeper of the Grosvenor Arms, Mr Edwards, stated that an attack was made on his house between ten and eleven in the evening which continued till between two and three in the morning. He reported that the gates were forced open by the mob and over a hundred panes of glass in his windows had been broken. He said that 'he did not hear any improper language applied to Mr. Rutter' and he stated that 'Mr Rutter advised him to remove the lights to the back of the house, and shut the gates'. Rutter had endeavoured to avert a breach of the peace. But, Mr Walter Swyer, brother of the Mayor called Rutter 'a blackguard, who would willingly assassinate any of the Grosvenor interest'. The magistrates refused to hear all the witnesses for the defence and presided over the committal of four of the accused to Dorchester prison for trial at the next Assizes.[504]

John Rutter wrote about the mistreatment of the electors in *History of the Shaftesbury Election 1830* and in a letter dated 23 August to *The Times*. He reiterated his concern about William Swyer's conflict of interests by responding to Swyer's letter to *The Times* of 10 August

> I am surprised at William Swyer's attempt to deny a bias in favour of his employer's nominees, whilst acting in the capacity of returning officer, it being notorious that on one occasion when a voter unexpectedly polled for them, Wm. Swyer cried out 'we had put him down against us;' thus expressly declaring himself to be a party man, and identifying his two characters of agent and returning officer.[505]

John Rutter claimed that 'Had justice been done us, Mr Knowles would have been returned as the successful candidate'.[506] In a letter to the 'Free and Independent Electors of Shaftesbury', Knowles claimed that he had lost 'through a mass of corrupt influence'. He went on to thank 'your eloquent and enlightened townsman and fellow-elector, Mr. John Rutter, for the very valuable support he afforded me during the late contest'.[507]

Meanwhile, on Tuesday 17 August, a public dinner was given for Knowles by 250 of his friends and supporters in a tent on a field near Cann Church in Salisbury Street, overlooking the Dorset countryside. Apparently it

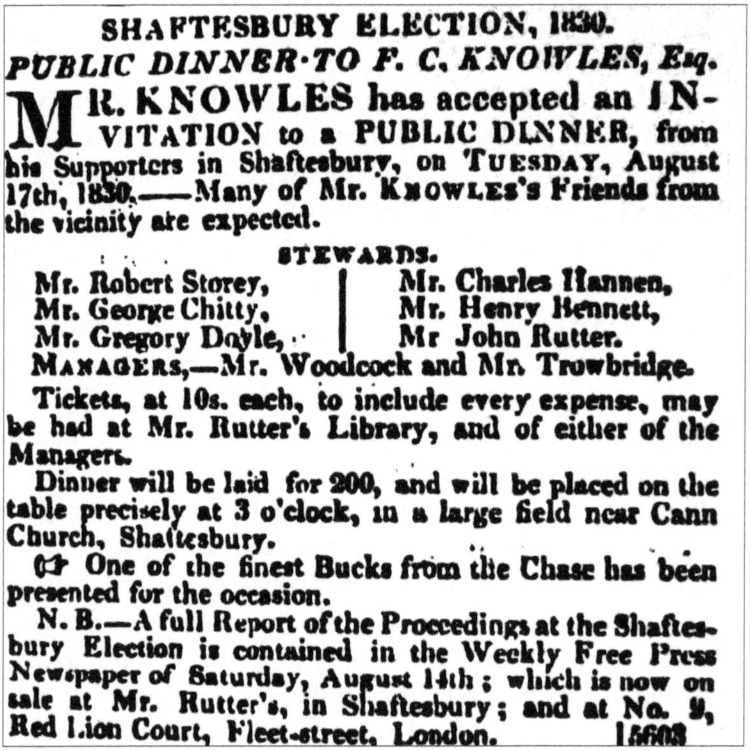

SHAFTESBURY ELECTION, 1830.

PUBLIC DINNER TO F. C. KNOWLES, Esq.

MR. KNOWLES has accepted an INVITATION to a PUBLIC DINNER, from his Supporters in Shaftesbury, on TUESDAY, August 17th, 1830.—Many of Mr. KNOWLES's Friends from the vicinity are expected.

STEWARDS.

Mr. Robert Storey,	Mr. Charles Hannen,
Mr. George Chitty,	Mr. Henry Bennett,
Mr. Gregory Doyle,	Mr John Rutter.

MANAGERS,—Mr. Woodcock and Mr. Trowbridge.

Tickets, at 10s. each, to include every expense, may be had at Mr. Rutter's Library, and of either of the Managers.

Dinner will be laid for 200, and will be placed on the table precisely at 3 o'clock, in a large field near Cann Church, Shaftesbury.

☞ One of the finest Bucks from the Chase has been presented for the occasion.

N. B.—A full Report of the Proceedings at the Shaftesbury Election is contained in the Weekly Free Press Newspaper of Saturday, August 14th; which is now on sale at Mr. Rutter's, in Shaftesbury; and at No. 9, Red Lion Court, Fleet-street, London. 15608

Notice of dinner for Knowles on 17 August 1830, Salisbury and Winchester Journal, 16 August 1830, p. 3, Newspaper image © The British Library Board. All rights reserved. With thanks to The British Newspaper Archive (www.britishnewspaperarchive.co.uk)

rained very hard and the tent leaked. After dinner others forced their way in and it is estimated that around 2,000 came to express their thanks to Knowles but mainly to partake of the refreshments. It was reported that many voters and supporters got little to drink while 'many who had no right to be there got more than enough'. When the intruders were finally persuaded to leave, the formal proceedings began and the toasts and speeches followed. John Rutter spoke in praise of the efforts of Knowles and those who voted for him saying 'Their enemies felt and acknowledged, that corruption in Shaftesbury had received a blow from which it would not recover'. Rutter was also thanked for his contribution and a toast to his health was proposed. Although Knowles had not been elected, the evening was one of celebration, with much merriment, including a song of three verses which had been specially penned for the occasion.[508]

The celebrations didn't end there. The ladies who had been supporting Knowles gathered together, on Wednesday 18 August, for a tea party in the same field opposite George Chitty's house, Cann Rectory[509], in Salisbury Street. About 2,000 residents of Shaftesbury attended. They enjoyed it so much that they returned on the following day, the Thursday, for a repeat celebration. On both days a band played and there was dancing which 'was kept up with great spirit', continuing on the Thursday evening until twelve o'clock. Knowles, Storey and Chitty attended and many voters dined together that evening at several inns in the town.[510]

Then, on Wednesday 1 September, the men who had been sent to Dorchester Gaol, prior to being tried, were released on the instructions of Lord Tenterden. They were brought back to Shaftesbury in a carriage and four. As they passed through Blandford the church bells were rung and in Iwerne they were accompanied by a band and plenty of flag waving. Finally on reaching Shaftesbury their carriage was halted at the Half Moon Inn, on the eastern edge of the town, and then hauled by enthusiastic residents to the market place. There they were met by a huge crowd with more music and more flag waving. John Rutter reported that their return was regarded as a 'triumph over injustice, oppression and partiality'.[511]

The following day, Thursday 2 September, the two elected Members of Parliament, Penrhyn and Dugdale arrived in town, accompanied by a posse of Lord Grosvenor's representatives and some of his tenants from Gillingham and Motcombe. A triumphant entry was made involving 36 horsemen four-a-breast, several men and women walking or in carts, a band and many 'handsome flags'. They were greeted by the inhabitants of Shaftesbury with loud cries of 'no Dugdale, Knowles for ever' and 'Fair play is a Jewel' and 'No twenty guinea dolls'. There were scuffles. John Rutter was asked to intervene to calm the public and responded 'it was indiscreet to attempt a parade this day, because the inhabitants will never acknowledge Messrs. Penrhyn and Dugdale to be their representatives' and 'if they had wanted to dine with their friends, they should have done so quietly'. Offering no concession and adding salt into an already festering wound, he concluded 'finally, if the magistrates authorise me to interfere, I will do so most readily, and shall be most willing to act as peace officer with some other respectable inhabitants'. Later in the afternoon, protected by nearly 100 special constables who had been drafted in to help keep the peace, Penrhyn and Dugdale set off for the Grosvenor Arms where they intended to dine. There were further scuffles in the market place and blows were exchanged. Rutter together with colleagues, including the banker Robert Storey, tried to intervene to separate the contending parties. The Riot Act was read by the Town Clerk from the balcony of the Grosvenor Arms but, in the commotion, this could not be heard. Finally the Grosvenor party was driven into the inn and the mob dispersed but not before breaking more of the hostelry's windows.[512]

The 19th century industrialist, Parliamentarian and social reformer, William E. Forster (1818–1886) attended the Friends Monthly Meeting at Shaftesbury on 7 September 1830. Aged twelve, he recorded in his diary some most perceptive comments about John Rutter

> We went to monthly meeting at Shaftesbury. We dined and slept at Sarah Mullet's, but I drank tea at John Rutter's, whom I like very much. There has lately been an election at Shaftesbury, in which he has been very much engaged. He is, I think, a complete picture of an independent, public-spirited man. Frank, noble, generous, and talented, he has by his abilities and exertions been the chief and almost successful means of spiriting up the people to a resistance of the immense influence of Lord ------------[513], whose agents have, by their harsh and tyrannical mode of procedure, strongly and deservedly excited the people against them. John Rutter has been blamed for rendering them more excited. But was he to be blamed for telling the truth and nothing but the truth; for exposing the practises of men who — as one instance out of many — have ordered every one of their tenants who have voted against them to be turned out of their houses in at least three months? Was he to be blamed because the lowest of the mob, who care not on whose side they are, have happened to commit excesses on his? Was he to be blamed because that by a few of the true words he had said he had further excited the people? No; John Rutter has done nothing but what every true-born Englishman ought to admire and applaud.[514]

Forster's biographer, T. Wemyss Reid, added *'Very juvenile, no doubt, this outburst in honour of the village Hampden of Shaftesbury, but striking, too, as showing that in the case of Mr. Forster also, the child was father of the man'.*[515]

In the autumn of 1830, Lord Grosvenor's agent, Philip Chitty, issued eviction notices to 33 of Grosvenor's Shaftesbury tenants, who were given between three and six months to leave their houses[516]. Inspired and led by John Rutter, the tenants put their names to an address to the peer, to be presented by Knowles. In the address[517], most likely drafted by Rutter, they argued that 'in moral rights there are no contracts to bind man to be the subject of his neighbour, whatever may be his station or degree of rank'. They suggested that his lordship had not given his agents authority to 'inflict on us, and our dependant families, such serious and irretrievable evils'. They added 'we deeply lament that your Lordship's public reputation should be so insultingly injured' and concluded that 'we cannot but believe that your Lordship would rather act as a man, and be virtuous, than as a Peer, and be oppressive'. Rutter and Knowles kept up the pressure. Petitions were made over the next six months to the Commons by the Radical MP, Joseph Hume.[518] These bore fruit and Lord Grosvenor agreed to abandon all evictions.

In October 1830, some of Shaftesbury's residents were summoned to appear at the Quarter Sessions at Dorchester. They were charged with riot, assembly and assault in connection with the disturbances on 5 August and 2 September. Twelve of these were found guilty and were sentenced to prison for terms of between one and four months. Although John Rutter had sought to keep the peace during the storming of the Grosvenor Arms on 5 August, by suggesting that the gates should be closed, nonetheless it was alleged that he had incited a riot by speaking against the Grosvenor political clique, accusing them of malpractice. He was charged with 'unlawfully, riotously, and tumultuously.... assembling.... making a great noise, disturbance, and riot.... outrageously, cast and throw stones, bricks and other missiles' etc. Rutter pleaded that he had 'no doubt of proving to the satisfaction of a Jury of my countrymen, that so far committing any breach of the laws, I have no single act derogatory to my character as a man, and Englishman, and above all, as a Christian'. He was accordingly granted leave, with sureties, to be tried at a future date, together with others, at the Assize Court in Dorchester which heard the more serious cases.

The next Assize for Dorset was due to take place in March 1831. In the meantime, the latter half of 1830 proved to be a very turbulent time in the country's history. The Swing Riots, as they became known, took the southern counties by storm. So named after threatening letters that were sent under the anonymous name of 'Captain Swing', the riots took the form of arson, destruction of farm machinery, demands for higher wages and extortion for money to buy food.

The background to this was dire rural poverty and the unemployment or underemployment of labourers in the countryside. After the Battle of Waterloo in 1815, up to 250,000 men from the British armed forces returned home and swamped the agricultural labour market.[519] The harvest had been poor in 1828 and had failed in 1829. Mechanised threshing machines had begun to be introduced which reduced the need for manual threshing in the winter months. Lower corn prices after the end of the Napoleonic Wars made farmers reduce costs where they could. Thus agricultural labourers were increasingly being hired on a weekly or even daily or hourly basis. Particularly in winter, with the reduced extent of manual threshing, they found themselves out of work and were forced to rely on the parishes for poor relief. There were also some external, non-economic, factors. In France, King Charles X, the Bourbon monarch, had been overthrown in a peaceful revolution.[520] In England, William IV had acceded to the throne and was thought to be supportive of the plight of the rural poor.[521] With the Whigs in the ascendancy, there was a feeling that change was in the air. Indeed it was. The farm labourer had nothing to lose. He did not own land. The traditional feudal system had broken down. He was a day labourer with no job security.

Starting in the autumn of 1830 this dispossessed and alienated group of farm labourers went on the rampage for the next six months. They burnt hay ricks and barns; they destroyed threshing machines; and they made demands for higher wages and greater financial security. Initially, the courts were lenient. Some tenant farmers even acquiesced in the destruction of their machines to prevent damage to their farms. There was also a widespread belief that mechanisation was destroying the established social order. But, by November, with the riots reaching a peak and with the new Home Secretary, Lord Melbourne, giving directions, magistrates became tougher in their sentences. There was one amusing moment in Dorset when Walter Snook made some arrests for machine smashing at Stour Provost. He escorted his prisoners to Shaftesbury where 'the keys of the lock-up house could not be found'. Those arrested easily made their escape. There were similar such incidents where the tenant farmers felt sympathy for the rioters. But retribution was to follow.

The special judicial commission tried 992 cases, of which 378 were dismissed, 35 offenders were sentenced to transportation and three were executed. The trials continued into 1831 and were more lenient, although out of 1,976 cases, 482 offenders were transported, of whom 330 were sent to Van Diemen's Land (today's Tasmania).[522] But sentencing varied throughout the country, depending on the ferocity of the Swing rioters. In Dorset, unlike neighbouring Wiltshire where John Benett of Pyt House in the parish of Tisbury had been singled out for special treatment by the rioters because of ill treatment to his cottagers, the extent of riot and damage was limited.[523] The judiciary was more inclined to seek to calm things down. This was the background to the March Assizes in Dorchester in March 1831 when John Rutter and others from Shaftesbury were tried for riotous assembly and criminal damage.

There were three trials. Rutter paid for a transcript to be made by John Sydenham, for a fee of £14.9s.6d. (£1,500 in 2018 prices). In the first two trials, 21 defendants were found guilty of assault and fourteen were given prison sentences of between one and four months. Eight were acquitted. In his summing up, Mr Justice Parks remarked that he had never seen so many individuals brought forward in one case before and that he was sure 'that if Earl Grosvenor had known of these transactions, he never would have sanctioned such a net, such a dragnet being thrown over the whole of Shaftesbury'.[524]

In the third trial, Mr Justice Park, criticised Grosvenor's agents and suggested that arrangements should be made to bring the prosecution against 36 inhabitants of Shaftesbury to a speedy conclusion. He suggested this in order to prevent the occupation of much Court time, to ensure that Election offences should be forgiven and forgotten, and to prevent local excitement. Having conferred with the prosecutors, he proposed that, if every defendant were to plead guilty, then they would be given a nominal fine and discharged. Every defendant except Rutter agreed. He objected strongly, saying that if the prosecutors were to exclude him from the proposed arrangements, then he would stand as the only defendant and try the merits of the case. The foreman of the Jury announced a guilty verdict, on the instructions of the Judge, so that the other accused could be discharged without a full trial. All the defendants, except Rutter, were fined one shilling and bound over to keep the peace for twelve months.[525] Rutter refused to accept an admission of guilt saying that, as he was innocent, it would 'stamp him with infamy' and lead to his expulsion from the Society of Friends. The Judge was offended by his determination and did all he could to frighten Rutter and to secure his conviction. During the course of the trial, as ever, Rutter was forthright in his views, telling the judge that he was thankful that there were 'twelve honest men between me and thee, and in their hands I do not fear the result'. The court was startled and Rutter left the Court room feeling that he had maintained his rights and obtained a great moral victory. His trial was postponed until the next Assize[526] but, in the end, the charge against him was allowed to lapse.[527]

1831 General Election

THE MINORITY TORY government, led by the Duke of Wellington, suffered a number of defeats in Parliament in the autumn of 1830 and the Whigs under Lord Grey formed another minority government. Grey pushed ahead with the Reform Bill but, realising that he could not get it passed, requested the Monarch to dissolve Parliament. Another election was called for May 1831.[528]

This was the last election before the Parliamentary Reform Act of 1832 which altered the franchise and the distribution of seats. There had been glaring anomalies in the country. The larger, and growing, cities such as Manchester and Birmingham were underrepresented while others such as Shaftesbury were overrepresented with two Parliamentary seats. There was increasing pressure for electoral reform and the Whigs had sought for nearly 40 years to bring this about. There was a clamour for change, to make the distribution of voters more equitable, to ensure that the vote was given to more people and to put an end to corruption. Prior to this, those who were elected would provide political support for the government of the day in return for titles, pensions, sinecures and jobs. There was a sense of injustice across the country with passionate speeches and periodic violence. Shaftesbury had experienced riots in 1830 but change had not yet come to the town. The old rules still applied, albeit for just one more year.

On this occasion, the Grosvenor 'candidates' in Shaftesbury were Edward Penrhyn and William Maberly, who had replaced Dugdale following his falling out with Grosvenor over the Reform Bill.[529] Rutter and Knowles encouraged a fourth candidate, William Trant, to stand in Shaftesbury. The results were as follows: Penrhyn: 171; Maberly: 168; Knowles: 133; and Trant: 123, with the total votes counted: 595, based on the 359 people who voted.[530]

John Rutter was less involved in these 1831 elections in Shaftesbury as he was mainly assisting the Whigs in the Dorset county contest. He was known throughout the county as an accomplished electioneer and it was hoped that he would help to defeat the Tory incumbent, Henry Bankes. With his usual enthusiasm he threw all his efforts into the fight, addressing public meetings in Dorchester and villages and towns throughout Dorset.[531] During this time, his wife Anne managed the businesses in Shaftesbury. In the county elections, a Whig, John Calcraft, was returned as an MP in place of Bankes. After the election and despite this success, Rutter thought that his efforts had not been fully appreciated by the Whigs. Despite all his hard work he was not permitted to send in a bill for expenses incurred let alone for time spent. He was even approached by the Tory Party who had observed his political insight and persuasive powers. Rutter was given to understand that any official position in the county would be offered to him if he fought for the Tories in future. True to his beliefs, he did not pursue the suggestion. But the attitude of the Whig Party in not recognising his efforts lessened his enthusiasm for them. He began to feel that his duties as a husband and father should claim greater attention in the future.[532] Despite this feeling of disappointment, Rutter was to continue the fight in 1832, as is recorded below. He was also listed as a possible Whig candidate for Poole at the 1832 election but this never materialised as Sir John Byng (later the Earl of Stafford) was chosen and won the seat.[533]

In the 1831 election, at a national level there was a landslide win for those who supported electoral reform. The Whigs won 370 seats with the Tories just 235, resulting in Earl Grey continuing as Prime Minister and enabling his government to pass the Great Reform Act in June 1832.

The passage of the Bill was not straightforward. A minority in the House of Lords endeavoured to defeat it. As ever, John Rutter was active encouraging challenge from Shaftesbury. He was one of 200 'Householders and Electors' who put their names to a Petition convening a meeting, held on 22 May 1832, in support of Earl Grey's Bill for Parliamentary Reform.[534]

The passing of the Act disenfranchised 56 boroughs in England and Wales and reduced another 30 to just one MP. It created 67 new constituencies and broadened the property qualification for electors to include small landowners, tenant farmers and shopkeepers. In boroughs such as Shaftesbury the vote was given to all householders who owned or occupied property worth at least £10 (about £1,000 in 2018 prices) per annum.[535] It did not however eliminate bribing and treating of voters and pocket boroughs still continued.[536] Voting continued to be transparent and votes were not cast in secret until after 1872.[537]

1832–33 General Election

IN SHAFTESBURY, THE 1832 Act reduced the number of MPs from two to one, although the borough was extended, embracing the three town parishes (St Peter, St James and Trinity) and ten other adjoining parishes. This increased the population in the constituency from 2,742 to 8,518 and the new electorate increased slightly to 634. In the 1832 national election, bought about to introduce the Reform Act, Penrhyn, who came first in the 1831 election, decided to stand again. Maberly stood for Chatham and was elected for that constituency. Francis Knowles had acceded to a baronetcy on the death of his father in November 1831 and claimed that he had incurred expenses amounting to £1,115 (about £120,000 in 2018 prices) in seeking election in 1830 and £500 deposited (£55,000 in 2018 prices) in 1831. Although he had been warmly welcomed and supported as an independent candidate in Shaftesbury, he was not happy about the conduct of the elections, particularly the former, and he was concerned about the continuing weight of Grosvenor's support for Penrhyn. So, he decided not to stand in the 1832 election.[538]

As he had done before, as soon as the election was called, in June 1832, Rutter set off to London in search of a candidate who would take on and match Penrhyn. John Farley Rutter recorded that his father made three separate visits before identifying John Sayer Poulter, a liberal, a rising London barrister and an excellent speaker. On 26 June 1832, John Rutter wrote to Grosvenor, by now further ennobled in the Coronation Honours of 1831 as the Marquess of Westminster, although the anticipated award of a ducal coronet was postponed until later. It has been variously suggested that the delay in the award of a dukedom was his opposition to the 'Bill of Pains and Penalties', described earlier in chapter three above or because of the problems created in Shaftesbury during the 1830 election. In his letter to the Marquess, Rutter explained that he was in London interviewing prospective candidates and he wrote 'the whole of Sir Francis Knowles' former supporters will adhere to their determined opposition to yourself and I think it more honest and manly to say so'.[539]

Perhaps as a result of his recent honour, or perhaps as a result of the unpleasantness of the 1830 and 1831 elections, or possibly even as a result of Rutter's letter, the Marquess decided not to put forward his own candidate in the Shaftesbury 1832 election. William Swyer had died in 1831 and Philip Chitty's agency for Grosvenor had been terminated. Unlike his agents, Westminster was a reformer.[540]

There was a certain amount of euphoria in the town, even prior to the election. John Rutter was fast becoming a hero and a much respected citizen who had encouraged and brought about reform. To buoy support for Rutter's candidate and to praise the reformer, a sixteen verse song was written, entitled *Election 1832 – A Song for the Merry Men of Shaston. Old Voters, New Voters, Voters Altogether'.* Six of the verses are repeated below

There is a man in our town,
His name is Johnny R---r,
A clever fellow is he
For making such a splutter.

A great reformer John would be
And make a mighty bustle,

Because he saw no reason he,
Should be outdone by Russell.

At length to London Johnny went
To seek a man of metal,
Who'd find the Cash that must be spent.
To tinker Johnny's kettle.

A learned Lawyer eke was he
Known all through London City
Stupid or deaf that man must be,
Who knew not he was witty

But Shaston men too well can see,
The tricks of Johnny R---r,
To quarrel with their own M.P
And eke their bread and butter.

Resolv'd by their united voice,
When polling in December,
To make a wise, consistent choice,
THEIR OLD & HONEST MEMBER[541]

In the election at the end of 1832, the Shaftesbury seat was won by John Poulter, who defeated Penrhyn by 108 votes (318 to 210). Nationally the Whigs won 441 seats out of 658, enabling the Prime Minister, Earl Grey, to push through Parliamentary reform. Rutter and the electoral reformers at both national and local level had won. After this success, John Rutter reduced, but did not entirely cease, his political activity at General Elections.[542]

There was an interesting sequel to the 1830 and 1831 General Elections when the solicitor, George Chitty (Rutter's companion in arms), sought to recover 'various sums of money for professional assistance' which he had incurred in support of Knowles (now Sir Francis Knowles Bt. following the death of his father). He claimed that these expenses, amounting to £1,056, (£115,000 in 2018 prices) related to both elections and to assisting the defence of the Shaftesbury rioters after the 1831 election. The case was heard before the Dorset Assizes in March 1834. Despite his friendship with George Chitty, John Rutter spoke in support of Sir Francis. As a steward of Knowles' Election Committee, Rutter told the Court that Chitty had told him that in the event of Knowles' failure to get elected 'he would only have to pay for the band and the beer' and that 'his own services were to be gratuitous'. At the time of the trial in 1834, Rutter was training as a solicitor. William Hannen, a future partner of Rutter's in the firm of Hannen & Rutter, also spoke in Sir Francis' defence, advising members of the jury that he remembered George Chitty saying at a dinner party that, in connection with the election 'he acted gratuitously'. At the end of the trial, after just ten minutes' consideration, the jury returned a verdict in favour of Sir Francis Knowles.[543]

ELECTORS

OF

SHAFTESBURY!!

Reports having been circulated, that the Politics of the Most Noble the MARQUIS OF WESTMINSTER, agree with those of Mr. POULTER, and are decidedly OPPOSED TO THE TORY PRINCIPLES OF Mr. BEST; those Electors who wish to be satisfied with the truth of these reports, and who also wish to be confirmed in the report, that his Lordship's Tenants may vote as they please, but will not oblige his Lordship by giving their votes to Mr. BEST, a Tory, but are more likely to please their Noble Landlord by voting for Mr. POULTER, the True Reformer; may apply at Coward Shoot, where a letter has just been received from his Lordship.

(Signed) **WESTMINSTER.**

(Dated) Eaton Hall, January 2nd, 1835.

Bastable, Printer, &c. Bell-Street, Shaftesbury.

Open letter from the Marquis (sic) of Westminster to Electors of Shaftesbury supporting John Poulter in the 1835 General Election, 2 January 1835 (Thomas Shirley's Scrapbooks, S&DHS, D.H.C., D-SHS/Box 44.2645)

1835 General Election

THE SHAPE OF English politics was beginning to change at this time and, over a period of nine months, there were three different Prime Ministers, Viscount Melbourne (Whig), the Duke of Wellington (Tory) and Sir Robert Peel (Conservative). Peel could not maintain a minority Government in power and Parliament was dissolved in December 1834.

In Shaftesbury, Lord Grosvenor did not put forward a candidate and confirmed that electors could vote as they wished.[544] But he did write to the town's electors confirming that the politics of Poulter, who had won the 1832 election, were 'in unison with his'[545]. He voiced his opposition to the 'Tory principles' of Poulter's opponent, the Hon W.S. Best. With this support, John Poulter won the election, held on 9 January 1835, with 237 votes compared to 148 for Best. At a national level, the Tories gained ground but not enough to prevent Melbourne from becoming Prime Minister and continuing in that office for most of the next seven years.

1837 General Election

JOHN POULTER STOOD again for the Whigs in the 1837 election, assisted as before by John Rutter. Poulter was initially declared to be the winner but, on a petition and after a scrutiny of votes, his election was declared null and void. His opponent, George Mathew, who was a Tory, was duly elected.

It was about this time that John Rutter started to tire of politics. Although others encouraged him to continue and even harsh words were said of him for not doing so, he stated that he wished to devote more time to his family and to his work.[546]

By this stage Rutter had almost completed his legal training and would shortly become a qualified solicitor.

Municipal government reform

MEANWHILE, AT BOROUGH level, the end was nearing for Edward Buckland's domination. In the wake of the passage of the Reform Act, an enquiry was launched, in 1834, into the municipal government in England and Wales. A public meeting was held in Shaftesbury on 27 March 1834 when one of the visiting commissioners, Edward Gambier QC, asked for information about the governance of the borough. Although evidence was given by Charles Edward Buckland who had been Town Clerk since 1816, the Mayor and Corporation had passed a motion that 'it is the unanimous opinion of this meeting that such enquiries are illegal and unconstitutional'. Rutter kept a copy of the handbill and carefully bracketed the 'il' of 'illegal' and the 'un' of 'unconstitutional'. He took his own minutes of the meeting and drew the attention of the commissioner to the clique which had developed as a result of the traditional constitution. He claimed that the same group controlled the magistracy and that there were inadequate records kept of the Corporation's income and expenditure.[547] The subsequent report of the commissioners dated March 1835 documents the governance arrangements in Shaftesbury. There is special mention of 'Family Interests' with the following observation

> The members of the corporation seem to be all of them among the principal inhabitants of the town, but it has been objected that the selection has been too much confined to particular families, and that family interests prevail to a great degree in the choice of head officer of the corporation to the exclusion of those members of the body who stand in a more isolated condition. And it certainly appears that out of the thirteen mayors who have been elected since 1820, six have borne the name of Buckland, four that of Chitty, two of Swyer, and the thirteenth is closely connected with one of the former families.[548]

In a sad comment on the 'State of the Town', the report contains the following 'The Town of Shaftesbury is not in an improving state. No manufactures are now carried on there, and the parishes within which it lies are greatly burdened with poor'.[549]

The resulting Municipal Corporation Act of 1835 reformed Shaftesbury's close corporation and introduced a democratic form of governance. A new Town Council was appointed, comprising four aldermen and twelve councillors who were to be elected by the ratepayers.[550] The self-perpetuating oligarchy of the Shaftesbury mafia was finished and the Buckland era was over. Recognising that the end had come, in December 1835, the retiring Council agreed that a piece of plate to the value of ten guineas should be given to C E Buckland 'as a small but sincere mark of the respect and approbation of the Corporate Body' for twenty years' service as Town Clerk.[551]

And, as noted earlier, in a final gesture perhaps seeking to leave a favourable impression, the members of the Court of Common Council provided £400 (£50,000 in 2018 prices) for the rebuilding of Chubb's Almshouse (for women) and a similar amount to the trustees of the Spiller's Almshouse for the same purpose.[552]

Opposition to the Establishment

JOHN RUTTER NEVER stopped fighting against nepotism, corruption and special interests. Indeed, John Farley Rutter later recorded that his father never swerved from the position of an advanced Radical reformer and an enemy to political serfdom

> He advocated the views that are now recognised by the Radical party though at times such advocacy was unpopular and dangerous. Throughout the years 1821–1832 there was a continuance of this political strife, my father was heavily out of pocket on account of the Grosvenor faction concocting various charges which necessitated appearance at with invariable heavy fines against him; one case[553] cost my father £402 and it was estimated that during this period it cost him at least £1,500 (about £165,000) to adhere to his principles and fight for political freedom of the Shaftesbury borough. At this juncture my father felt that he was politically handicapped in his struggle for political freedom; he was a mere tradesman and his position was taken every advantage of: consequently he determined that this should be altered; the only solution was to become a lawyer.[554]

John Rutter also never stopped questioning the status quo and challenging the political elite and the established church. In common with other Quakers, he refused to pay church rates and tithes. This resulted in one of the local Shaftesbury magistrates, often one of the political clique of Bowles, Buckland or Swyer, issuing a warrant for distraint. Two local constables would then seize cash or goods, which could be sold, often by auction, for an amount which exceeded the unpaid tax and the '*damages*'. The *Account of Sufferings* maintained by the Society of Friends contains details of distraints against John Rutter for tithes or church rates not paid by him, as follows:

Date	*Amount not paid*	*Charges*	*Goods seized*	*Value of goods*
July 1822	£2.16s.	£1	Writing paper	£4.10s.
October 1825	£2.8s.	12s.6d.	Books and paper	£6.4s.6d.
April 1827	£2.10s.	£1.5s.6d.	Stationary	£5.17s.3d.
October 1829	£1.7s.	5s.	Paper and quills	£2.11s.6d.
November 1830	£1.10s.	10s.	Cash from till	£2.1s.
October 1832	£1.4s.	8s.	Cash from till	£2.9s.
July 1835	12s.	8s.	Reams of paper	£1.7s.[555]

Sometimes, these distraints were reported in the Press. For example, in 1842, Rutter did not pay tithes amounting to 11s.3d (about £55 in 2018 prices) to the Reverend Sanderson. As a result, a 'handsome engraving worth several guineas was seized from him and sold at public auction for the sum of £1'. He published, as a result of this, a pamphlet entitled '*A State Church inconsistent with the New Testament*'.[556] There was a report in the *Salisbury and Winchester Journal* of March 1840 that he had objected to the church rate of the parish of St Peter being raised to fund the churchwardens' estimate of expenditure relating to the salaries of the organist and organ-blower and the expense of lighting the church for evening service on Sundays. An amendment was proposed to reduce the rate, in support of Rutter's objections, but was defeated by 66 to 56.[557] John Rutter was a consummate agitator and the conscience of the community. When it came to restraining the powers of the established church, despite its Christian purpose, he was particularly driven.

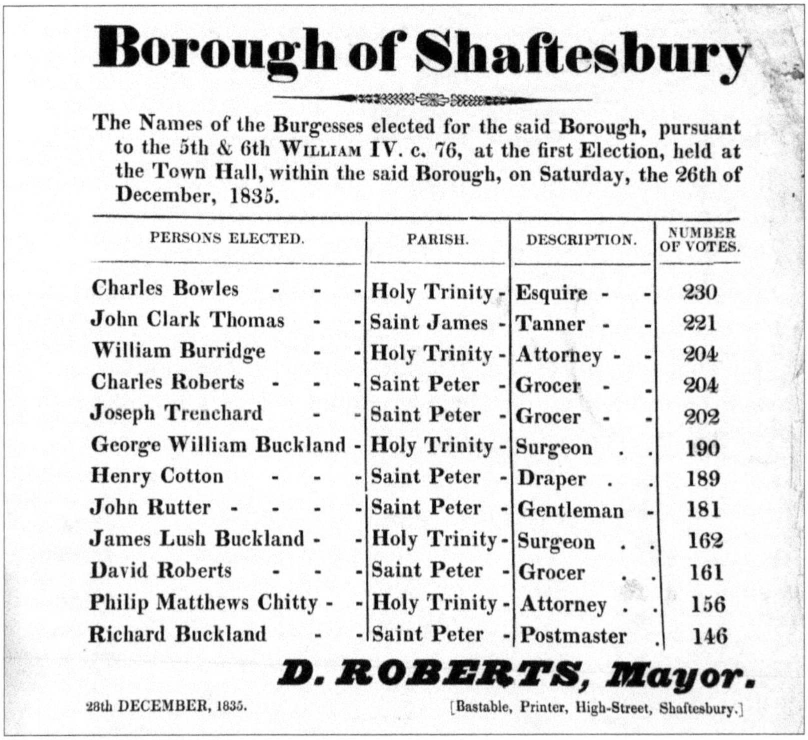

Borough of Shaftesbury

The Names of the Burgesses elected for the said Borough, pursuant to the 5th & 6th William IV. c. 76, at the first Election, held at the Town Hall, within the said Borough, on Saturday, the 26th of December, 1835.

PERSONS ELECTED.	PARISH.	DESCRIPTION.	NUMBER OF VOTES.
Charles Bowles - - -	Holy Trinity -	Esquire - -	230
John Clark Thomas - -	Saint James -	Tanner - -	221
William Burridge - -	Holy Trinity -	Attorney - -	204
Charles Roberts - - -	Saint Peter -	Grocer - -	204
Joseph Trenchard - -	Saint Peter -	Grocer - -	202
George William Buckland -	Holy Trinity -	Surgeon . .	190
Henry Cotton - - -	Saint Peter -	Draper . .	189
John Rutter - - - -	Saint Peter -	Gentleman -	181
James Lush Buckland - -	Holy Trinity -	Surgeon . .	162
David Roberts - - -	Saint Peter -	Grocer . .	161
Philip Matthews Chitty - -	Holy Trinity -	Attorney . .	156
Richard Buckland - -	Saint Peter -	Postmaster .	146

D. ROBERTS, Mayor.

28th DECEMBER, 1835. [Bastable, Printer, High-Street, Shaftesbury.]

Results of Borough Elections on 26 December 1835, printed by Bastable, Shaftesbury (S&DHS, D.H.C., D-SHS/Box 44.2645)

7
Public Servant and Philanthropist

In keeping with his Quaker beliefs, John Rutter was always seeking ways of enhancing the quality of life of the residents of Shaftesbury. His remit and his energy showed no bounds.

In February 1829 he wrote to the Prime Minister drawing attention to certain inhabitants of Shaftesbury who wished to avail themselves of 'an opportunity of emigrating to the new Settlement on the Western coast of New Holland' (Australia) and to 'go out as articled labourers'. Rutter sought Government help in identifying masters to whom they could become attached.[558] As might be expected, the reply from No 10 was polite but stated 'it is not in the power of the Secretary of State to further the views of the persons attended to in your Communication'.[559]

Rutter on the new Town Council

Then, after the passage of the Reform Act of 1832 and the Municipal Corporation Act of 1835, Rutter concluded that he had achieved what he wished in the field of electoral reform. With the abolition in 1828 of the Corporation and Test Acts, he was no longer constrained by not being permitted, by his Quaker faith, to swear an oath.

So on 26 December 1835 he stood as a candidate in the local government elections. After receiving 181 votes, thus coming 8th in the poll, he was elected as one of the first twelve councillors of the town's new Corporation. At the first meeting of the new Council on 31 December 1835, Rutter 'being one of the people called Quakers took and subscribed the Declaration of Fidelity instead of the Oaths of allegiance and supremacy'.[560]

During his time on the Council John Rutter served on a number of committees. In 1836 he was one of four councillors, together with the Mayor, Charles Bowles, who examined the expenses of the previous Mayor, David Roberts, who was the last incumbent of that office under the old regime. Many items of expenditure were disallowed, particularly those which were incurred after Roberts left office. In the same year, Rutter was appointed a member of the committee that approved proposals for lighting the town using gas. This led to a local company being established, of which Rutter became a founder shareholder, subscribing £5, for the construction of a gas works in Bimport to make gas for public and private lighting for Shaftesbury. Rutter remained on the committee, effectively the board of directors, of the Shaftesbury Gas Company from 1836 to 1850[561], when it is believed that he retired through ill health.

Rutter was re-elected as a councillor in November 1837. Then, a year later in November 1838, he was elected as an Alderman.[562] However, in the same month, he tended his resignation from the Council. In a letter dated 28 November he wrote 'I have long been anxious gradually to retire from active and prominent participation in the public and political proceedings connected with his Borough'.[563] It appears that Rutter was disgruntled over proceedings of the Council. The last Mayor of the old Borough Council, David Roberts, had been elected to the new Town Council and Rutter's criticism of his election expenses in 1836 cannot have made for an easy relationship. In addition, the Council's decision to support a proposal to establish a National School for Boys and Girls 'in accordance with the principles of the established Church' would not have accorded with his dissenting nonconformist views. As described below, he sought to establish a rival non-denominational school.

During the four years as a councillor Rutter witnessed many fractious exchanges on the Council and disagreements over the choice of Mayor. It is clear from the Council minutes that Shaftesbury's local government had not lost its reputation for controversy and dissent.[564] However he remained on the Council until August 1840.[565]

From that time onwards he devoted more of his time to doing good works, outside the Shaftesbury Corporation, as well as practising as a lawyer, described further in chapter eight.

The Shaftesbury Union

In 1818, Rutter had researched the plight of the poor in Shaftesbury and published his findings and recommendations in his book *A Brief Sketch of the State of the Poor in Shaftesbury* in 1819. The movement to reform the Poor Law gathered pace and, under a Whig Government, the Poor Law Amendment Act was passed in 1834. This led in turn to the Shaftesbury Poor Law Union being formed in 1835, comprising nineteen parishes.

Rutter had been instrumental in the Union being established following his sketch on the poor of Shaftesbury, with his recommendations for a House of Industry. He was elected by the Parish of St Peter, Shaftesbury, to be one of their two representative guardians under the Poor Law Amendment Act.[566]

He was then appointed Vice-Chairman and reported to his fellow parishioners in March 1837 that the establishment of the Union had been a great success. The annual expenditure of the parish, on account of the poor, had been reduced from an average of £893 (in the three years prior to the

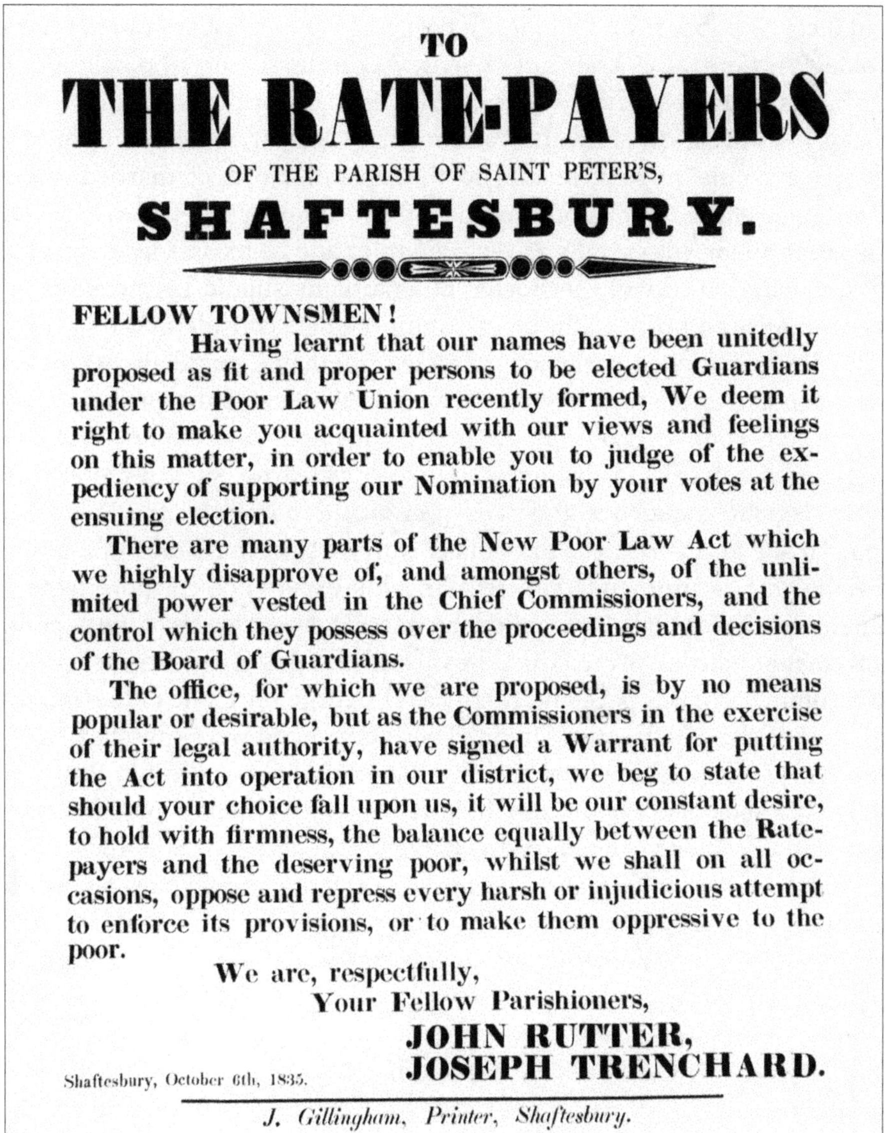

TO

THE RATE-PAYERS

OF THE PARISH OF SAINT PETER'S,

SHAFTESBURY.

FELLOW TOWNSMEN!

Having learnt that our names have been unitedly proposed as fit and proper persons to be elected Guardians under the Poor Law Union recently formed, We deem it right to make you acquainted with our views and feelings on this matter, in order to enable you to judge of the expediency of supporting our Nomination by your votes at the ensuing election.

There are many parts of the New Poor Law Act which we highly disapprove of, and amongst others, of the unlimited power vested in the Chief Commissioners, and the control which they possess over the proceedings and decisions of the Board of Guardians.

The office, for which we are proposed, is by no means popular or desirable, but as the Commissioners in the exercise of their legal authority, have signed a Warrant for putting the Act into operation in our district, we beg to state that should your choice fall upon us, it will be our constant desire, to hold with firmness, the balance equally between the Rate-payers and the deserving poor, whilst we shall on all occasions, oppose and repress every harsh or injudicious attempt to enforce its provisions, or to make them oppressive to the poor.

We are, respectfully,
Your Fellow Parishioners,
JOHN RUTTER,
JOSEPH TRENCHARD.

Shaftesbury, October 6th, 1835.

J. Gillingham, Printer, Shaftesbury.

Election leaflet to Shaftesbury ratepayers regarding the Shaftesbury Union, 6 October 1835, printed by J. Gillingham, Shaftesbury (S&DHS, D.H.C., D-SHS/Box 44.2645)

Union's formation) to £413 in the year ended Christmas 1836. For the nineteen parishes in and around Shaftesbury forming the Union, the expenditure had reduced from £8,882 to £5,111, a saving of £3,771 in the same period. He claimed that there had been no reduction in the comforts of the destitute and of the aged poor, while at the same time benefiting the ratepayers.[567] However, he was scathing about the national chief commissioners who determined and dictated policy from London. In particular, he did not see eye to eye with Colonel A' Court, the Assistant Poor Law Commissioner, who believed that husbands and wives should be separated in the workhouse because it was cheaper.[568] Rutter expected the Parliamentary Enquiry, then taking place in 1837, to examine the rules relating to 'the separation of aged married couples; illegitimate children; religious instruction and out-door relief'. As always with Rutter, he abhorred centrally driven rigid rules and he recommended that 'the discretionary powers of the Boards of Guardians should be increased, and the legislative authority of the chief Commissioners considerably lessened'.[569]

He encouraged parishioners to select suitable guardians who would represent parishioners' interests and would be 'liberal to the aged, deserving, and invalid poor, - encourage the industrious and independent, and check the idle, dissolute, and dishonest'. He also called for such representatives to 'by regular attendance and care, prevent the powers of the Board from being made an instrument for sinister purposes, in the hands of a few'. In making this recommendation, recalling his experiences of governance in Shaftesbury's Borough Corporation, he was all too well aware of the nepotistic and corrupt practices which can develop in the hands of few who are not held to account.[570] He was particularly critical of George Burt, one of the 'relieving officers' of the Shaftesbury Union. These criticisms were investigated by a Poor Law Commissioner and found to be groundless. As result, Rutter was obliged to apologise to Burt and, in a public letter of September 1837, stated that 'The allegations which I made against Mr. George Burt now appear to me not to be founded in fact; and I deeply lament that I should have put forward assertions seriously reflecting on his character without more mature enquiry on the subject'.[571] As demonstrated by this episode, forever zealous, Rutter did not always get it right.

Education

FROM THE VERY foundation of the Society, the Friends have been committed to education. Joseph Lancaster was a London Quaker who opened his first school in Borough Road, Southwark in 1798 to provide education to the poorer classes. His system of education was based on teaching older pupils who, as monitors, would then pass on what they had learnt to the younger ones. This enabled the number of paid teachers to be reduced; thus the cost of operating the school was lower. In 1803 he wrote about these principles of education in *Improvements in Education as it respects the Industrious Classes of the Community*. In 1808, the management of the school was taken over by the Royal Lancaster Society which changed its name in 1818 to the punchier (!) *The British and Foreign School Society for the Education of the Labouring and Manufacturing Classes of Society of Every Religious Persuasion* or, for short, *The British and Foreign School Society*. During the 19th century, the Society established a number of 'British Schools', which complemented the 'National Schools' of the Church of England, and also many schools abroad.[572] When he heard about the society, John Rutter was inspired to follow Lancaster's example and he became a great advocate of education and learning.

In 1825 he was a founder member of 'The Shaftesbury Instructive Institution', whose objectives were to employ 'the leisure hours of those persons residing in the Town and its Vicinity, who may be desirous of availing themselves of its advantages, and also of promoting the mental and moral improvement of the rising generation'. Its main aim was to establish a library but excluding 'all Works on controversial divinity, on party politics, and of infidel or immoral tendency'. Rutter was asked to find subscribers and to draft its rules, which he diligently completed. However, the Institution had a short life.[573] At the same time John Rutter became secretary of 'The Shaftesbury Reading Society' which had been founded in 1780. Its purpose was to encourage reading in the town by acting as a lending library. But it, too, never developed into a thriving organisation.[574] So, as described earlier, in 1827 he established his own library, 'The Shaftesbury Subscription Library' with a Reading Room for newspapers, reviews and magazines, and a collection of over 2,000 volumes. This continued for many years under his, and later under his son Clarence's, management.

In 1839 Rutter promoted the establishment of 'The Shaftesbury Sunday Infant and Day School'. He persuaded the Marquess of Westminster to sell to him, for £20, a small plot of land in St James on which Rutter proposed to build a school. The transaction comprised two parts, a lease for five shillings with an annual rent of a peppercorn followed by a release, on the following day, of the landlord's interest in the property for a sum of £20.[575] This method of transferring ownership of property was common in England until the Conveyance by Release Act of 1841, after which land could be conveyed by a single transaction. In April 1839, Rutter issued a notice soliciting donations to found the school. The notice stated that the most populous district of Shaftesbury 'ShastonSaintJames has been destitute of any such means of moral and religious instruction, except the Parish Church and the Friends Meeting House'. The cost of land, buildings and fittings was estimated to be £350 (£37,000 in 2018 prices).[576] Subscriptions were forthcoming and, with funds also provided by John Rutter, the school opened in January 1840 as a non-denominational school for poor children. Rutter delivered an inaugural address on National Education in the presence of Lord (Richard) Grosvenor, son of the 1st Marquess and a resident of nearby Motcombe House. Both the Marquess and Lord Grosvenor were among the subscribers as was the Shaftesbury MP, Captain George Mathew. In his address, Rutter commented favourably on the state of education in Prussia, Germany, Holland and France. He criticised the English system which was based around the Established Church and did not cater for dissenters.[577] Initially John Rutter bore the entire cost of salaries and repairs of the new non-denominational school.[578]

In October 1841, Rutter conducted the second public examination of 140 pupils, with reference to the children's proficiency in reading, writing, arithmetic, mental calculations, geography and the Holy Scriptures. He concluded that there had been a marked improvement since the last examination. Attended by 200 of the friends of the Infant Sunday School, several ministers of various denominations spoke on 'the subject of scriptural education uncontaminated with sectarianism'.[579] In its third annual report, printed by Clarence in August 1842, the School was described as 'healthy and prosperous'. At that time, there were 21 teachers and 120 children of parents 'belonging to various denominations'; and the average attendance was between 80 and 90. However, the report also advised that the income received from scholars had proved inadequate to fund the school's expenditure and to pay off the considerable debt on the building. Rutter continued to fund the deficit but appealed to 'the liberality of the friends of Scriptural Education, irrespective of denominational distinctions' to contribute to its support.[580]

In September 1840, he was the guest speaker at the opening of a new school at Downton, near Salisbury. It was reported that he spoke eloquently on the 'beauties of the Government plan of Education' and also on 'the advantages which belong to the latitudinarian system of the British and Foreign Society'.[581]

According to his granddaughter, Elizabeth Rutter, John Rutter was also the prime mover behind the formation of thirteen other schools in the surrounding area. At the St James' Street Sunday school, he drew on the resources of no fewer than twenty teachers from six different denominations. He met with considerable opposition from the established clergy in carrying out this broadminded design of giving education to the children of the working

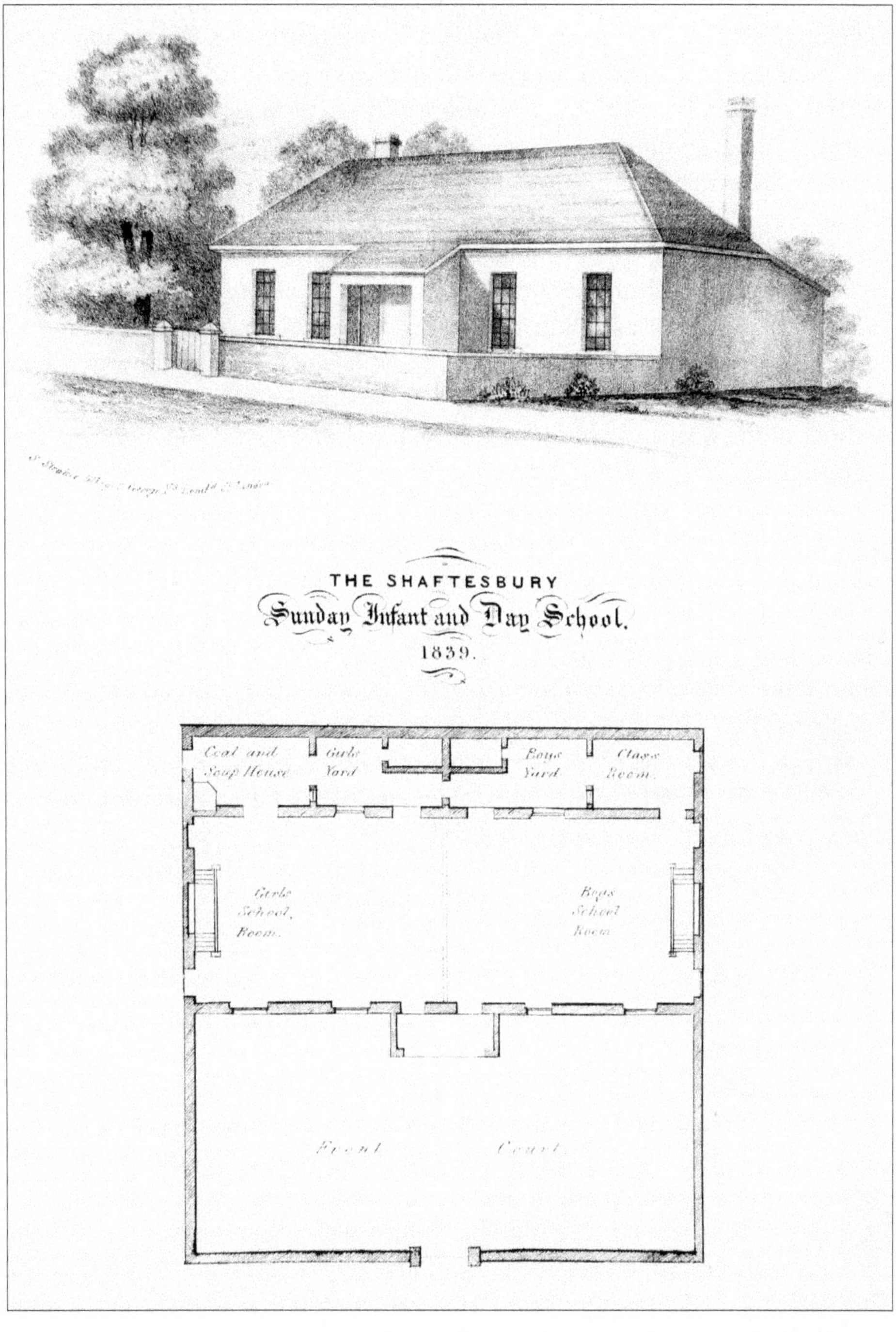

Sunday Infant and Day School - Sketch and Plans, 1839 (S&DHS, D.H.C., D-SHS/Box 44.2719)

classes. One Shaftesbury resident even remarked to him 'Mr Rutter, another school! What a dangerous man you are. You quite frighten the parsons'.[582]

John Rutter's Infant School in St James closed in 1848[583] following the establishment of a National School built in 1847 on Abbey Walk. One also suspects that the donations from Shaftesbury residents were not sufficient to keep the school going. In 1894, the building was sold for £200 by John Farley Rutter and Anne Elizabeth Rutter[584] for use by the St James Primitive Methodist Church.[585] It continued as an educational establishment for many years as well as a church hall[586]. The property is recorded in the Ordnance Survey map of 1901 as 'Meth. Chap. Prim.' and of 1929 as 'Institute'[587]. At some stage the building was acquired by St James' Church and was used as church hall and for social gatherings. It was sold when St James Primary School, at the west end of St James' Street, was enlarged[588]. It is now a private house, comprising three separate dwellings.

In a letter dated 21 August 1850 to the *Manchester Times*, Rutter wrote that, for the last seven years, he had endeavoured to educate 'at my own expense' children in the agricultural districts in the West of England who are 'in a most degraded state, as are their parents, who have to support themselves and a family on 7s. or 8s. a week' (£42 to £48 in 2018 prices). In a dig at the established system he went on to write 'The children are sent into the fields at an early age, and if they go to the National School, or the Sunday-school connected therewith, they learn very little reading, but a great deal of catechism'. He finishes by writing 'The fact is, the agricultural labourers in the south of England are serfs attached to the soil'.[589]

Road and railway infrastructure

JOHN RUTTER TOOK a great interest in seeking to enhance the economy of Shaftesbury and the lives of its inhabitants through improved transport communications.

The state of the roads in the early part of the 19th century was not good. Trade was increasing but without the infrastructure to support it. In 1827, he wrote to 'The Commissioners of the Shaftesbury District of Turnpike Roads', with detailed recommendations as to changes which could be made to improve the roads connecting Shaftesbury with other towns.[590]

The invention of the steam locomotive, the construction of the Stockton and Darlington Railway (in 1825) and the London and Manchester Railway (in 1830) changed the debate. The 1830s and 1840s heralded a boom in the construction of railways across the United Kingdom. Many local railway companies were formed to promote and seek finance for railway lines in their region. The benefits to communities arising from small towns being linked with the major cities were significant. Agricultural produce could be transported to the larger urban areas much faster and at lower cost.

In the West Country, there was fierce competition between Great Western Railways (GWR) with its broad gauge (7 feet) and London and South Western Railways (L&SWR) with its standard gauge (4 feet 8½ inches). Both wished to extend their network so as to control traffic from London to the South Coast and also west to Exeter. Several routes were contemplated and it took some years of Parliamentary debate before Acts were passed enabling local train companies to be established, with investment from GWR or L&SWR, before London could finally be joined up with Exeter.

Already, in 1834, Royal Assent had been given for a railway line to run west from London via Basingstoke to Southampton. The line was constructed between 1834 and 1840 by the London and Southampton Railway (L&SR) which changed its name in 1839 to the L&SWR. Discussions had taken place about a link from Basingstoke to Salisbury, which was finally joined to London in 1847.

John Rutter played a part in encouraging these developments. In November 1838 a meeting was held in the Council Chamber at Salisbury to discuss the advantages to Salisbury of a link to London by the L&SWR. He moved a resolution to this effect which was approved unanimously. In a passionate speech, Rutter advised that

> It was his opinion that the formation of a railroad from Salisbury to London was no longer a matter of policy, since Salisbury and the surrounding country would be ruined unless a direct communication was opened with London.' He 'pointed out the advantageous situation of Salisbury as the centre of communication in that part of the country.[591]

Rutter could be imaginative and amusing, as well as eloquent, in his speeches in order to gain support. The *Salisbury and Winchester Journal* reported that while some had objected to railroads that they were unsightly objects. The newspaper continued

> So far from that being the case, however, Rutter regarded them with a very different feeling, and thought that few things could produce more interest or animation than the sight of the trains passing along them with the velocity of a rocket. – a velocity which we understood Mr Rutter to say had enabled a friend of his to proceed fifty miles before breakfast![592]

Rutter argued that 'cattle would be sent to Salisbury from all parts of the West, and might from thence be easily and cheaply forwarded to the metropolis.' He then highlighted 'the importance of the proposed railroad to Shaftesbury, Dorchester, Sherborne, Yeovil, and all the neighbouring towns, which would thus be compelled to depend upon Salisbury at once for a market, and for a safe and rapid mode of communication with London. Thus it was evident that nothing could so far promote the prosperity of Salisbury as a railroad to London.' At which there were loud cheers.[593]

Being a hill-top town, 705 feet above sea level, Shaftesbury was never going to be directly on a railway line. However, in the valley three miles to the north lay the village of Semley, almost directly en route from Salisbury to Gillingham, Sherborne and Yeovil.

John Rutter promoted the idea of a railway in the area of South Wiltshire and North Dorset linking the towns east to Salisbury and west to Exeter. At a special general meeting of the proprietors of the Exeter, Yeovil and Dorchester Railway (EY&DR) on 20 November 1845 in Exeter, he pointed out that the area possessed a population of 25,000 which was 'as far as railway communication was concerned, entirely neglected'.[594] He advised that

> No less than 25 tons of agricultural produce were sent every week from Shaftesbury to London, of which the greater part was conveyed to the Andover-road station, and to the Bath station of the Great Western Railway; and the great delay which continually occurred was a serious drawback to that branch of business. In conclusion, the Meeting would permit him to say, as a shareholder of the London Salisbury and Yeovil Company (LS&YC), that he had been at work for several days in London with the Committee...and all the plans, maps and books of reference of that Company were finally corrected by him on the previous night; and like those of the Exeter Yeovil and Dorchester Company would be deposited on Saturday; and he hoped soon to see the amalgamation of the Companies, so as to concentrate the powers of management, and he wished to see the opening of the direct line.[595]

The *Exeter & Plymouth Gazette* reported that 'The Hon. Gentleman sat down amid much applause'.[596]

In February 1846, during a visit to London, John Rutter wrote to his son John Farley

> We have been in attendance the whole of the day in the cloisters of the House of Commons waiting for our turn, which did not arrive, but we expect it tomorrow morning and we just dismissed. My patience is rapidly evaporating. The Court Report in favour of the Narrow Guage (sic) is thought to be much in our favor (sic) and to be a severe blow to Great Western whose shares have fallen 10£ per Share. There is a negotiation going on with them, by which it is possible that their opposition to us on the standing orders may be withdrawn. I hope this will prove to be the case tomorrow. Our men at Headquarters seem sure of our getting either the line from Basingstoke to Yeovil or Salisbury to Yeovil – Two Bills, destined at 10 per cent paid up on both and deposited. We are in good spirits - but it is very tiresome, so noisy and full of interruption that I cannot write or do anything.

Then, in November 1846, a special meeting was held in London to agree a proposal to be put to Parliament for a narrow (standard) gauge all the way from London to Land's End and to provide for the eventual amalgamation of the companies involved, namely the EY&DR, the LS&YC and the L&SWR, with the aim of raising share capital to bring this about.[597]

By December 1846, John Rutter had been appointed Local Agent in North Dorset and West Wiltshire for the L&SWR. In this capacity he hosted a dinner, shortly before Christmas, at the Grosvenor Arms, attended by landowners in the area who had 'shown him and the surveyors of the Company personal civilities whilst preparing the Parliamentary plans and books of reference'. Rutter pointed out the superiority of the L&SWR scheme compared to the GWR who had not fulfilled their promise to place Shaftesbury on a main line from London to Exeter. It was reported that 'several glees were sung with great taste and effect' and that 'the Cornopean Band, from Blandford, played with their accustomed ability'. It was further reported that a Mr R.B. Sheridan of Frampton House (north-west of Dorchester) presented 50 shillings for the poor of Shaftesbury which resulted in 'The poor old almswomen' being made 'right merrie on the day when peace and mercy were announced to this nether world'. Their Christmas fare had been 'a sumptuous one, prime beef, excellent plum-pudding, and the best of bread, with a washing down (and a glass or two to spare) of prime old strong beer'. The newspaper finished its account of the evening with a biblical quote 'He that giveth to the poor, lendeth to the Lord'.[598]

Rutter campaigned passionately and effectively for the West Country line to pass through North Dorset en route from Salisbury to Exeter. In April 1847, he appeared before a committee of the House of Commons considering

Railway Bills and, in particular, 'The Exeter Direct Line'. It is reported that he gave detailed and important evidence about the area between Salisbury and Yeovil. He listed the amount of agricultural produce transported out of the district within five miles north and south of the proposed line, namely '14,084 tons of butter, cheese, veal, and pork; 241,200 sheep; 9,300 cattle; 6,000 hogsheads of cider; and 50,000 tons of produce, including the manufacturing tonnage in the vicinity of Gillingham'. He argued against a break of gauge at Salisbury (which would result from the GWR proposal), thus favouring the L&SWR option. He added that the L&SWR's Salisbury to Yeovil line would accommodate and serve a much larger population than that proposed by the GWR, especially the seven manufacturers 'employing 1,500 hands at and near Gillingham'.[599]

In May 1847 the South-Western Railway Company held a hearing of evidence in favour of various options for the lines being proposed. The *Salisbury and Winchester Journal* gave a very full account of the hearing. The paper reported that

> Mr. John Rutter, of Shaftesbury, gave long and very important evidence as to the district between Salisbury and Yeovil, and put in a table of traffic which showed the amounts of tonnage sent out of that district within five miles north and south of the line: viz., 14,681 tons of butter, cheese, veal, and pork; 241,200 sheep; 9,300 cattle; 6,000 hogshead of cider; and 50,000 tons of other produce, including the manufacturing tonnage in the vicinity of Gillingham, but not including corn, potatoes, malt, hay, straw, or grass seed, which he was unable to estimate, being in great quantities. Nearly the whole of the traffic passed through Salisbury to London, and into Essex, Sussex, &c. A break of gauge at Salisbury on this great stream of traffic would be far more injurious and important than breaks of gauge on cross lines, running north and south below Bruton, or elsewhere in directions where a small amount of traffic existed. There were 25 flour-mills in 17 miles of the intended line from Salisbury to Yeovil, with ample water-power to do twice or thrice their present amount of business, confined, as it is, for want of a railroad outlet. Mr. Rutter also showed that the Salisbury and Yeovil Line would accommodate a much larger amount of population and traffic than the Wilton and Compton Line of the Great Western, especially the seven manufacturers employing 1,500 hands at and near Gillingham.

As ever, Rutter had an eye for detail and was persuasive in his argument. He was mindful of the benefits to Shaftesbury and Gillingham of promoting a route that took the L&SWR West Country line from Salisbury to Exeter as close as possible to the two towns.

Then, in July 1847, John Rutter was able to write to his son, John Farley 'Saturday. The news of Railway victory came this morning: Salisbury and Yeovil – proved'. [600]

John Rutter was fast becoming a leader in the local community. When appropriate, he could make compelling and amusing speeches. On 1 February 1848, a public meeting was held at the Grosvenor Hotel, organised by the L&SWR, at which the Chairman of the company and other officials were present, to discuss the L&SWR's proposals. Those attending included the 2nd Marquess of Westminster, Lord Rivers, the Earl of Pembroke and the High Sheriff of Dorset who was elected to take the chair. The plan for a railway line between Salisbury and Yeovil, thence to Exeter, as proposed by the L&SWR was favoured, compared to that put forward by the GWR who regarded a line between Salisbury and Yeovil as being unnecessary. At the end of the meeting Rutter stated that

> They, in the town, felt much obliged to the gentlemen who attended from a distance, for their support and assistance. He trusted when they met again they would meet to celebrate the passing of the bill for the direct railroad from Salisbury to Yeovil, from Yeovil to Exeter, with great benefit to all in that room, from the peer to the peasant, from the landowner, the agriculturalist, and the shopkeeper, even down to them, "poor" professional men. At this, a local newspaper reported that there was 'laughter and cheering'.[601]

Between 1847 and 1854, L&SWR sought permission to construct new lines to the West Country and various Acts were passed enabling it to complete its network from London to Exeter via investments in the local train companies. The line from Salisbury to Semley and onward to Gillingham was opened in May 1859 and the line from London to Exeter, covering 171 miles, was completed by L&SWR in June 1860.

But all this took some time and required local help. It appears that John Rutter's evidence, as their agent, impressed L&SWR and the Parliamentarians whom they sought to influence. In August 1848 Rutter's contribution to their efforts was recognised by the presentation of a silver salver.

The *Sherborne Mercury* recorded the inscription on the salver as

> Presented to John Rutter, Es., by the inhabitants of Gillingham and its vicinity, as a testimonial of their high esteem for his unwearied attention

to the interests of this district, whilst discharging his professional duties as an agent of the South-Western Railway Company in their scheme for direct Railway communication between London and Exeter. August 10, 1848.[602]

The salver is, today, in the possession of the Gold Hill Museum, Shaftesbury. The current route of the South Western Railways line, which runs from London to Exeter, via Salisbury, Semley and Gillingham, owes something to the facts presented by Rutter and to his advocacy. Sadly, as he died in 1851, Rutter did not live long enough to see the completion of the project, for which he campaigned so vigorously and successfully.

Silver Salver presented by inhabitants of Gillingham to John Rutter, agent of SWRC, 10 August 1848 (S&DHS, D.H.C., D-SHS/Box 44.2623)

Commencement of the Salisbury & Yeovil Railway - Cutting of the First Sod in Gillingham, 12 April 1856, p. 381 © Illustrated London News Ltd/Mary Evans

Civic responsibilities

THE YEAR 1848 was a turbulent one in Europe with revolutions taking place in very many continental countries against the established monarchies. Discontent amongst the rural poor and the growing urban workers spilled over in almost every country. Demands were being made for political reforms, greater democracy and freedom of the Press. These revolutions were put down with great force, in some cases causing thousands of deaths. The outcome was that the absolute power of some monarchies was reduced and some borders were altered to create independent national states.

Fortunately, Great Britain escaped the worst of this social upheaval, mainly because of the constraints placed on the monarchy after the Civil War and because of fundamental political and social changes which had been made in the 1830s and 1840s. During these two decades many liberal reforms had been introduced into Great Britain, including the Factories Acts (1831, 1833, 1844 and 1847), the Great Reform Act (1832), the Abolition of Slavery Act (1833), the Poor Law Amendment Act (1834), the Chimney Sweeps Acts (1834 and 1840), the Mines and Collieries Act (1842) and the repeal of the Corn Laws (1846). In 1838, the working class Chartist movement began with its aims of introducing universal suffrage, equal electoral districts, election by secret ballot, removal of property qualifications for MPs, payment of MPs and parliaments elected every year. There were periodic riots across the country in the 1840s and support for the Chartists was greater at times of failed harvests and economic depression. The Chartists put forward three petitions to Parliament, in 1839, 1842 and 1848. It was claimed that the last of these was supported by six million signatures, a statistic later fiercely challenged as many signatures were found to be faked. On 10 April 1848, the final petition was to be presented to Parliament after a demonstration on Kennington Common. The Government sent in 8,000 soldiers and special constables. Only 20,000 Chartists turned up as it was a cold and rainy day. The movement then collapsed. But the Government had been so concerned that Queen Victoria was asked to leave for the Isle of Wight for her safety.

Across the country messages of support were transmitted to Her Majesty and, in Shaftesbury, a Loyal Address was signed by the Mayor, David Roberts, on 27 April 1848. John Rutter, by then a leading member of the community as well as an accomplished writer and speaker, wrote and read the Address. He added that 'he thought every loyal and well-disposed inhabitant of the borough....could agree to, and he had prepared it so as to insure the unanimous approval of the present meeting'. He added that 'Although he sometimes differed in political sentiments with many of the gentlemen present, still it would not deter him from expressing his disapproval of any measures tending to bring anarchy and confusion into these realms, and he believed the same feeling actuated every one present'. The Marquess of Westminster had earlier promised to present the Address to the Queen.[603]

Public amenities in Shaftesbury

In 1845, on the death of his father, the Marquess of Westminster (Robert Grosvenor), Lord (Richard) Grosvenor inherited the Marquisate, including properties in Shaftesbury. The 2nd Marquess was interested in the town and was very approachable, with more amenable and friendly agents than had been the case under his father. He had lived at nearby Motcombe House since 1833 and therefore knew the area well. Accounts show that, in Shaftesbury, he was a prudent and generous landlord, with income matching expenditure. New property was built, including good working class housing to replace rundown accommodation in St James and also tradesmen's cottages and purpose built stables and workshops in Victoria Street.[604]

After receiving a request from the 2nd Marquess for ideas for improving the town, John Rutter wrote to him in December 1849 with the following suggestions: a market place or piazza under which farmer, millers and dealers could be sheltered from the weather; a waterworks, powered by steam or a windmill, to raise water to an open reservoir on Castle Hill with pipes to bring it to the upper town for the supply to almost every house; and the erection of public pumps in Bimport, the Commons and Angel Square, for 'the deficiency of water is a fruitful source of evil to the poor in Shaftesbury'.[605]

The Marquess responded by providing a deep well on Barton Hill with a steam engine to pump free water to all parts of the town. A fine grain store was erected in front of the pumping station. The traders needed a market hall, which the Marquess provided, with a corn market at the High Street end of town and a produce market at the other end, in Bell Street. He also provided an open cattle market which has, today, become the Bell Street car park. The produce market building survives as the Shaftesbury Arts Centre's theatre.[606]

Richard Grosvenor, 2nd Marquess of Westminster (1795-1869)

PROPERTY PROTECTION SOCIETY.

5 GUINEAS REWARD!!

Whereas on Friday night or Saturday morning last, some evil-disposed person or persons entered the Orchard of **Mr. JOHN CURTIS of MERE,** in the County of Wilts, (a member of this Society,) and STOLE therefrom

A quantity of Apples.

A Reward of TWO GUINEAS will be paid by Mr. CURTIS, and a further Reward of THREE GUINEAS by the PROPERTY PROTECTION SOCIETY, to any person who will give such information as may lead to the conviction of the offender or offenders.

RUTTER & SON,

SHAFTESBURY, October 2nd, 1850. AGENTS TO THE SOCIETY.

Terms of Subscription to the

Property Protection Society.

For an annual subscription of 20*s.* the Society will superintend, at its own cost, by its Solicitors, the prosecution of criminal offenders against the property of its Subscribers.

It will also make good the loss sustained by theft, (excepting money, notes, and bills,) to the amount of £50; one half to be paid upon satisfactory proof of the theft and value of the property stolen, (although the offenders may not have been apprehended,) and the remaining half immediately after the trial of the offender.

For further terms, apply to the Agents, as above.

THOMAS JOYCE, Secretary.

C. RUTTER, Bookseller & Printer, Shaftesbury.

Property Protection Society Reward, 2 October 1850, printed by C. Rutter, Shaftesbury (S&DHS, D.H.C., D-SHS/Box 44.2802)

8
Lawyer

Until the Municipal Government Reform Act of 1835, the Mayor of Shaftesbury was chosen from among the Corporation's capital burgesses who could not be removed from office. Being a capital burgess was effectively a job for life. When there was a vacancy, a new capital burgess was chosen by the Mayor, the Recorder and a majority of the capital burgesses. The Recorder was chosen by the capital burgesses. Thus, the Corporation was effectively a self-perpetuating oligarchy. A capital burgess served as Mayor for a year and could not serve again in that office until two years had passed. From 1821 to 1833, all the Mayors came from three families, Bucklands, Swyers and Chittys, except one who was an attorney in the Buckland law firm.[607]

In addition to political power being concentrated in the hands of a small clique, so was the rule of law. The exercise of justice in Shaftesbury was undertaken by three magistrates who comprised the Mayor, the previous Mayor and the Recorder. Charles Bowles served as Recorder from 1804 to 1827. Both William Swyer and Philip Chitty, who was the son in law of Edward Buckland, were also agents of Lord Grosvenor. There was no separation between political governance, which was nepotistic and corrupt, and the magistracy. The small ruling clique of Buckland, Chitty and Swyer was able to control the town in every respect.[608]

There were quite a few attorneys in town, for example Buckland, Bowles, Burridge, the two Chitty brothers, Hannen and Swyer. But most were capital burgesses or magistrates or Grosvenor's agents. As a result, some (Edward Buckland, William Swyer and Philip Chitty) considered themselves above the law because of the positions they individually held. But they did not always act in unison. Even in the firm of Bowles, Chitty & Chitty, there was strife, with George Chitty siding with John Rutter from time to time against his brother Philip who was one of the Earl's agents. Charles Bowles, a gentlemanly character and more professional than his contemporaries, eventually fell out with Philip Chitty and the partnership split up. Philip Chitty's brother, George, was himself no role model for, in March 1822, he was fined £5 for horsewhipping a rival Shaftesbury attorney, William Burridge, who had written to Chitty in a rather forthright manner and refused to retract the words he used. John Rutter wrote in his manuscript notebook that it was reported that 'This case excited great interest amongst the gentlemen of the profession'.[609]

The legal environment in Shaftesbury in the early 19th century was still very much cowboy territory. Who you knew and who sided with you was more important than the strict rule of law, which was still administrative rather than judicial. But times were changing and the legal system in England was becoming more robust.

In 1826 and again in 1830, John Rutter had experienced unfortunate brushes with the judiciary. In both cases he felt aggrieved and unfairly treated. He sensed that if he were more knowledgeable about the laws of the land he could better protect himself, his family and those who were forever dominated and persecuted by the Grosvenor faction. After the passing of the Sacramental Test Act of 1828, which abolished the 1661 Corporation Act and the 1673 Test Act, it was no longer a requirement for a public officeholder or a lawyer to swear an oath of allegiance. Thus these careers became open to Quakers. So, in 1832, Rutter gave up his printing, stationery and chemists' businesses and began to study law, training for which would absorb the next five years.

He took up articles in 1832 with John Rowland, a solicitor who had recently settled in Shaftesbury.[610] It appears that Rutter and Rowland did not always see eye to eye. In a letter to a Mr Mullens of 21 August 1833, Rutter complained that legal work undertaken by him for the Semley Union had been inappropriately billed by Rowland and that Rutter was owed three guineas. He pulled no punches when writing about his principal

> I hope Mr Rowland will take immediate steps to bring his Bill of Costs against your Club into a Court of Justice so that the real truth may be made manifest, my character cleared from aspersion, and your Club made to pay what is just and reasonable for the work done.[611]

John Rutter's decision to train to become an attorney was commented upon by his son, John Farley Rutter who wrote

> It was a very bold move and required great care to secure the business in the family; As a solicitor was not allowed to carry on business apart from that profession it was essential, in order not to infringe this rule, that he secured his existing business in the family before he embarked on his new career; his next step was to be articled to a solicitor for five years. He overcame all the difficulties without much effort, but did not become admitted as an Attorney without very considerable trouble

> owing to underhand obstacles. When it became known that he intended to become an Attorney it struck his opponents with consternation and surprise. They felt their Day of Domination was over, from then all outward opposition ceased.[612]

On the other hand, Rutter's satirical and reforming colleague, James Acland, who assisted in the publication of *The Shastonian,* was less impressed. He wrote

> I shall always hold this man in the highest regard; but he made one great mistake in his mature age, for he turned lawyer; in the hope, doubtless of operating more effectually in the law Courts against his political persecutors. I do not think that in his case that circumstances made him a worse man; but it is dangerous for any man to seek even justice by threading the intricate maze of the law and devote himself to the study of a tortuous system for circumventing an opponent. How many men have I known or thought to be great and good, but that they were lawyers by profession, their judgements warped and their sense of right perverted! How many lawyers in the City of Bristol and Hull have I unearthed and denounced and denuded of this moral garb of seeming respectability![613]

But John Rutter's interest in becoming a lawyer was stimulated by his desire to protect the unprotected, the poor agricultural labourers who were suffering from land enclosure, lack of security of tenure and low wages. In 1834, the arrest, trial and transportation of the Tolpuddle Martyrs who had sought to form a trade union (the Friendly Society of Agricultural Labourers) in the village of Tolpuddle twenty miles to the south would not have gone unnoticed. There was a huge outcry. They became popular heroes, political marches were organised, there were debates in Parliament and 800,000 signatures were collected for their release. In 1836 all were given full and free pardons.[614] This episode may have further strengthened Rutter's desire to become proficient in the law.

John Rutter completed five years of training to become a solicitor towards the end of 1837 and is recorded, in the *Legal Observer* of 1838, as being admitted as an attorney in the Hilary Term (January to March) 1838. In the same journal, he is shown as having been 'articled' to John Rowland but then 'assigned' to William Hannen, the son of Charles Hannen, suggesting that Rowland had left Shaftesbury before Rutter had finished his training or that Rutter had changed employer.[615] Either way, he formed a partnership in 1837 with Charles and William Hannen, practising as Hannen & Rutter. Charles Hannen was twenty years older than John Rutter and they had formed a bond together when opposing the Grosvenor clique, together with George Chitty and Robert Storey. Charles rose to prominence in Dorset when he was appointed County Coroner. On his death in 1847[616], his son William was elected to this office[617] having served as Deputy Coroner[618] and also, in 1840, as Mayor of Shaftesbury.[619]

In Robson's Directory of 1839 Hannen & Rutter is recorded as having an office in the High Street, from which they also acted as agents to the West of England Fire and Life assurance.[620] As a solicitor in a country town, John Rutter had a broad range of clients including the 11th Baron Arundell, who inherited the title from his brother, whose mansion Rutter had earlier described in his book *An Historical and Descriptive Sketch of Wardour Castle.* In a letter dated 19 April 1839 from Rutter's daughter, Ann Elizabeth, to her brother Clarence, she wrote 'Papa went to Donhead and as Lord Arundell's deputy steward held the first manor court'.[621]

Hannen & Rutter is also recorded in Pigot & Co's Directory of 1842.[622] Then, in February 1845, a notice in the *Salisbury and Winchester Journal* announced that 'the practice of Attorneys-at-Law and Solicitors, carried on in Shaftesbury by William Hannen and John Rutter was dissolved, with each practising separately after this date'.[623]

The Tithe Map of 1846 shows Rutter operating as a sole legal professional from Church Lane, just off the High Street.[624] As a solicitor, he was engaged in conveyancing, preparation of legal agreements and wills.[625]

He also sought to defend the poor, where he could. In one case, in the Shaftesbury Small Debts Court, in 1847, John Rutter acted for a defendant who owed £6 and one shilling for some pigs which he had purchased and told the Court that he had a sick wife and nine children and earned just seven shillings a week. The judge was astonished at the paucity of the sum, asking 'was that all?' Rutter advised that it was so and that in the parish of Stour Provost seven shillings was the weekly wage. His Honour made an order for one shilling a week observing that it would take a long while to pay it off at that rate, but it was useless ordering a higher sum to be paid.[626]

In Kelly's Post Office Directory of 1849, John Rutter is listed, for the first time, under the category 'Gentry', shown as living at Layton Cottage. He is also listed as a conveyancer and solicitor operating from premises in the High Street, as well as the insurance agent for the Property Protection Society.[627] This Society was established in London with the twofold purpose of bringing about 'the prosecution of offenders by theft against the property of subscribers, and, with certain exceptions, of making good their losses sustained thereby.'[628] As agent for Shaftesbury, Gillingham and Mere, he collected and recorded subscriptions, typically £1 or 10s per year, and offered rewards for information leading to convictions of offenders.[629]

By 1851, John Farley Rutter (1824–1899) had joined his father, having qualified as a solicitor, and they were operating under the name Rutter & Son, solicitors, in the High Street.[630]

After John Rutter's death in 1851, the legal practice in Shaftesbury was taken on by John Farley Rutter, who moved to Dewes House, his widowed mother-in-law's home, in nearby Mere.[631] There he opened his firm's second solicitors' office.

John Farley Rutter, 1885, reproduced by kind permission of Rutter & Rutter, Wincanton

The law firm was expanded further with new offices in Wincanton and Gillingham under the leadership of John Farley's sons (the third generation) who also qualified as solicitors:

John Kingsley Rutter (1855–1929) took responsibility for the Shaftesbury and Gillingham offices and was also Town Clerk of Shaftesbury from 1892 to 1926

Clarence Edwin Rutter (1859–1922) took responsibility for the Mere and Wincanton offices[632]

According to Peter Rutter, grandson of John Kingsley, the two brothers had a disagreement after Clarence wished to acquire a law firm in Gillingham, which would have competed directly with his brother.[633] Thus, two separate firms of solicitors emerged[634]:

Rutters in Shaftesbury and Gillingham
Fourth generation:
William Farley Rutter (1888–1991), also Town Clerk of Shaftesbury (1926–1945)
Arthur Kingsley Rutter (1895–1986)
And their sons, comprising a fifth generation, who opened offices in Sturminster Newton and Tisbury (now closed):
Peter Tregelles Rutter (1923-)
Stephen Rutter (1927–2009)

Rutter & Rutter in Wincanton and Mere (the latter now closed)
Fourth generation:
Clarence Leslie Rutter (1894–1963)
Joseph John Burchett Rutter (1899–1990)
And their sons, comprising a fifth generation:
Thomas Randle Leslie Rutter (1929-)
John Fenton Rutter (1922–2014)
Currently, John Fenton's son, Charles Foster Rutter (1951-) manages the Wincanton based firm as the sixth generation.

After 180 years, John Rutter's legacy as a solicitor lives on in the two separate law firms which bear his name: Rutters and Rutter & Rutter.

9
Life and Legacy

JOHN RUTTER WAS a Renaissance man, a polymath who turned his hand, knowledgeably and successfully, to a wide variety of activities. Printer, Author, Publisher, Social and Political Reformer, Public Servant, Philanthropist and Lawyer are all labels which cover the rich tapestry of this man's life, cruelly cut short at the age of 54.

Rutter lived through an era of significant political and social change in Great Britain. He was born in 1796, during the French Revolutionary Wars. By the time Rutter reached his 20th birthday, Napoleon had been defeated at Waterloo, in 1815, and the century of British Empire had commenced. But, on the domestic front, there were serious political and social injustices and there was rampant poverty. Soldiers returning from the Napoleonic Wars were given a hero's welcome but this was not accompanied by a job. The growing industrial revolution was causing disruption and new challenges, as well as great opportunities. In the Colonies, slavery had not yet been abolished. Rotten and pocket boroughs, and thus Parliamentary seats, were controlled by the landowning aristocracy and there was bribery, nepotism and corruption at local government level.

By the date of Rutter's death, in 1851, the world had changed. Largely as a result of Whig Government measures, the Great Reform Act had been passed, slavery had been abolished in the British Empire, various Industry Acts had been passed, with some protections for the workforce and children, and the Poor Laws had been amended. There was less discrimination in the country against Catholics and nonconformists. Jewish emancipation was taking longer to achieve but was on the horizon. Public spirited individuals, such as John Rutter, who were prepared to fight against injustice, against the established regime and against inequality, contributed greatly to the significant changes of the 1830s and 1840s.

It is something of a marvel that someone who lost his father when he was four years old and his mother at the age of ten should have been so learned. His Quaker school in Bath clearly gave him a good grounding in classics, literature and the scriptures. He was well-educated. His drive and ambition may well have stemmed from being left without parents from such an early age. But the Quaker upbringing from his older siblings and the Society of Friends must have had a crucial influence in his life. Rutter was driven by faith and was not to be distracted by hardship. As a boy at school, it is related that he asserted his innocence and refused to confess to a false accusation, despite three floggings. His determination to seek justice and fairness remained with him throughout his life.

Aged 21, he received a small, but not insignificant, legacy from his father's will of about £90,000 (in 2018 prices). With that he acquired a printing press. As a printer, publisher and author, he was entrepreneurial and soon developed a successful trade. He also acquired a chemists' business and dispensed *Rutter's Life Pills*. His guides to Cranborne Chase, Wardour Castle, Fonthill Abbey and the county, towns and villages of Somerset demonstrated his ability to research and write. His works were descriptive, well crafted, full of classical and learned quotations as well as amusing asides. They showed great sensitivity and an appreciation of, and empathy with, the subject matter, be it architecture, fine art, gardens or the countryside. His ability to print different editions of the same book enabled him to reach audiences paying different prices. He was commercially smart. He used his connections, for example with Sir Richard Colt Hoare, Bt. of Stourhead, Lord Arundell of Wardour Castle and John Nichols, the London printer and publisher, to good effect. If he had done no more in his life than publish the finely described and illustrated *Delineations of Fonthill and Its Abbey*, he would be lauded for this exceptional accomplishment alone.

But Rutter also knew the power of the Press and the ability to communicate through the written word. Believing in equality and fairness, Rutter engaged in political reform. He fought against nepotism and corruption. No doubt influenced by the Peterloo Massacre in Manchester in 1819, he championed Parliamentary reform. He introduced candidates to fight in the General Elections of 1820 and 1826 against the nominees of Lord Grosvenor who owned most of Shaftesbury and nearby estates. This pocket borough returned two MPs until the Great Reform Act of 1832. The costs and damages arising from his difficulties in 1826 and 1827, for printing a letter without showing his name as the printer, amounted to almost £30,000 (in 2018 prices). Yet, that did not deter him from campaigning further to introduce candidates to fight Earl Grosvenor's nominees at successive General Elections from 1830 to 1835 and from fighting his charge of riotous assembly at the Dorchester Assizes in March 1831. He will remembered, amusingly, for announcing to the judge that he was thankful that there were 'twelve honest men between me and thee, and in their hands I do not fear the result'.

John Rutter spoke against and was, in turn, hounded by members of Shaftesbury's political elite. As unelected councillors, magistrates and Grosvenor's agents, they ran the borough's corrupt and nepotistic 'close' corporation and controlled the town. Yet Rutter survived, witnessing the clique's demise following the Municipal Corporations Act of 1835.

His fight for social reform was equally impressive and successful. Starting in 1818 with his investigation into the conditions of the poor in Shaftesbury and the resultant *Sketch of the State of the Poor,* his voice contributed to changes implemented in the Poor Law Amendment Act. He was instrumental in the formation of the Shaftesbury Union, relieving poverty in the district, and in advocating champions who would be 'liberal to the aged, deserving, and invalid poor, - encourage the industrious and independent, and check the idle, dissolute, and dishonest'. He founded a subscription library in Shaftesbury, societies for the encouragement of reading and many schools in the district including The Shaftesbury Sunday Infant and Day School in St James. Yet, in many respects Rutter had more in common with the town curates, despite his different religion, than the working classes he sought to help.

John Rutter was elected to the new Shaftesbury Town Council in 1835, serving for almost five years, including championing proposals for the provision of gas to produce light for the town's streets and private houses. He reviewed and questioned the previous Mayor's expenses, demonstrating his continuing fight against corruption and excess. Then he promoted the construction of a railway line from Salisbury to Yeovil, via Tisbury, Semley, Gillingham and Sherborne. His accumulation of the facts and his presentation of the case was admired by a House of Commons Select Committee and, ultimately, led to the line being constructed in 1859 by the London & South Western Railway Company along the route advocated by Rutter. After battling against the agents of the 2nd Earl Grosvenor (later ennobled as the 1st Marquess of Westminster), he advised the 2nd Marquess on the provision of amenities in Shaftesbury.

Starting afresh and training as an attorney when he was almost 37 years of age cannot have been easy. Today, his most tangible legacy in the area of North Dorset and East Somerset are the two firms of solicitors, Rutters in Shaftesbury and Gillingham and Rutter & Rutter in Wincanton, which still practise and serve the community.

Rutter had strong moral principles. As a Quaker Christian he encouraged Bible reading, abstinence, relief of poverty and religious tolerance. He was engaged in movements to abolish capital punishment and to bring about peace. He had great conviction and was determined, holding true and fast to his ideals. Unrelenting, with boundless energy, he pushed the boundaries and was loathe to hold his tongue. He was, to some, abrasive and referred to as *The Turbulent Quaker*. His disownment by the Society of Friends is further evidence of Rutter maintaining his principles, in this case introducing the scriptures to the poor of Shaftesbury. He disliked what he believed to be hypocrisy and humbug. But this disownment did not prevent him and his family from continuing to pray at the Meeting House and from his being buried in the Quaker Burial Ground, albeit as 'not a member'.

He was a good friend and, as a family man, he was loving and caring. He was calm, strategic and thoughtful. Ever meticulous, he was a master of the written word and an eloquent, witty and convincing speaker. He was energetic and progressive. He was philanthropic and public-spirited.

John Rutter was, in many ways, ahead of his time and the town of Shaftesbury benefited from his foresight, his imagination, his determination and his success. He lived life to the full, using his gifts in the service of God and the community.

Appendix 1
Publications by John Rutter

1818

A Brief Sketch of The History of Cranborn Chace and of the Dispute concerning its Boundaries (note Rutter's spelling of the current name of Cranborne Chase)

1819

A Brief Sketch of the State of the Poor and of the Management of Houses of Industry; Recommended to the Consideration of the Inhabitants of the Town of Shaftesbury, and Other Places

1822

An Historical and Descriptive Sketch of Wardour Castle and Demesne, Wilts: The Seat of Everard Arundell, Lord Arundell of Wardour, with a Catalogue of the Celebrated Collection of Paintings. Intended as an Accurate and Pleasing Guide

A Description of Fonthill Abbey, and Demesne, Wilts; Seat of William Beckford, Including a List of its Numerous and Valuable Paintings, Cabinets, and Other Curiosities. Intended as a Guide to the Visitor ... later titled *A Description of Fonthill Abbey and Demesne, in the County of Wilts...* (six editions)

1823

An Historical and Descriptive Sketch of Wardour Castle and Demesne, Wilts: The Seat of Everard Arundell, Lord Arundell of Wardour, with a Catalogue of the Celebrated Collection of Paintings (second edition with more comprehensive catalogue and more illustrations)

A New Descriptive Guide to Fonthill Abbey and Demesne, for 1823: including a list of its paintings and curiosities

Delineations of Fonthill & Its Abbey

1826

The Defence of John Rutter, 'delivered on Monday the 14th August, 1826', with additional observations

The Shastonian, edited by James Acland, with significant input from John Rutter (four issues: the fourth was written but not published)

Swyer versus Rutter. A plain narration of Shastonian occurrences without comment (published anonymously. The author could be either John Rutter or James Acland or both.)

1827

An *Historical and Descriptive Account of the Town of Shaftesbury* (in six parts, written but not published and later typed, in 1972)

Extracts, &c. concerning the Prevalence of Vagrancy in some of the Western Counties of England, The Means of Correction, and the Necessary Relief of Distressed Travellers

A Letter to the Commissioners of the Shaftesbury District of Turnpike Roads

1829

Delineations of the North West Division of the County of Somerset

Delineations of the North Western Division of the County of Somerset and of its Antediluvian Bone-caverns

Thirteen views in the North Western division of Somersetshire, forming the original embellishments of the Delineations of that district

Illustrations to Rutter's Somersetshire (33 illustrations)

The Westonian Guide; intended as a visitor's companion to that favourite watering place, and its vicinity; including a descriptive account of Woodspring Priory, and of Brockley Hall and Combe

The Banwell and Cheddar Guide: including a descriptive account of the Antediluvian bone caverns on Banwell and Hutton hills; of Cheddar cliffs, and of the druidical temple at Stanton Dew, in Somersetshire

The Clevedon guide, with a descriptive account of Leigh Court: and of other objects of topographical interest within the hundred of Portbury, in Somersetshire: including a catalogue of Philip John Miles' celebrated collection of paintings

1830

History of the Shaftesbury election of 1830, containing a complete and correct account of the extraordinary contest for the liberty and independence of that borough. To which is prefixed a supplement, containing an account of the subsequent proceedings. (Published anonymously but described as being by 'a constitutional reformer' and known to be John Rutter)

1836

Letters in defence of the Bible Society to L. Neville, in reply to his accusations against the British and Foreign Bible Society and against Dissenters

1840

A new Guide to Weston-super-Mare

Appendix 2
Abbreviations

Beckford of Fonthill – *Beckford of Fonthill* by Brian Fothergill, Faber & Faber, 1979 and Nonsuch Publishing Limited, 2005

BMD – Record of Births, Marriages and Deaths, National Archives, Kew

Colt Hoare History – The Hundred of Dunworth by James Everard, Baron Arundell, and Sir R. C. Hoare, Bt, *The Modern History of South Wiltshire,* Volume IV, Part I, by Sir Richard Colt Hoare, Bt., initially published as *The History of Modern Wiltshire. Hundred of Dunworth and Vale of Noddre,* by James Everard, Baron Arundell of Wardour Castle, Count of the Roman Empire, and Sir Richard Colt Hoare, Bart., printed by and for John Bowyer Nichols and Son, 25 Parliament Street, 1829

Corruption and Reform – *Corruption and Reform: Municipal Government in the Borough of Shaftesbury (1750–1835)* by F.C. Hopton, S&DHS Publication No 5, 1975

Defence of Rutter – *The Defence of John Rutter, 1826,* Shaftesbury Library

Delineations of Fonthill – *Delineations of Fonthill & Its Abbey,* by John Rutter, 1823

Delineations of Somerset – *Delineations of the North Western Division of the County of Somerset and of its Antediluvian Bone Caverns, with a Geological Sketch of the District,* by John Rutter, 1829

D.H.C. – Dorset History Centre

Gold Hill – Gold Hill Museum, Shaftesbury & District Historical Society

Hopton 1830 Election – The 1830 Parliamentary Election by F.C. Hopton, The Mansel-Pleydell Prize Essay, Dorset Natural History and Archaeological Society, 1988

Le Roter – *The Family of Le Roter or Rutter,* compiled and edited by W Huggins Wingate, 1966

Life at Fonthill – *Life at Fonthill 1807–1822: From the correspondence of William Beckford,* translated and edited by Boyd Alexander, Rupert Hart-Davis, London, 1957 and Nonsuch Publishing, 2006

Parliament History Shaftesbury, 1754–1790 website – *Shaftesbury Double Member Borough, The History of Parliament: the House of Commons 1754–1790,* Cannon, J.A., ed. Namier, L., Brooke. J., 1964, Cambridge University Press, © Crown copyright and The History of Parliament Trust 1964–2017

Parliament History Shaftesbury, 1790–1820 website – *Shaftesbury Borough, The History of Parliament: the House of Commons 1790–1820,* Thorne, R.G., 1986, Cambridge University Press, © Crown copyright and The History of Parliament Trust 1964–2017

Parliament History Shaftesbury, 1820–1832 website – *Shaftesbury Borough, The History of Parliament: the House of Commons 1820–1832,* Farrell, S., ed. D.R. Fisher,

2009, Cambridge University Press, © Crown copyright and The History of Parliament Trust 1964–2017

Rex versus Rutter – *Rex v Rutter, Trial Transcript, March 1831*, MS Rex v Rutter and Others, Knowles' Election Bills, Miscellaneous, 1830–31, S&DHS, D.H.C., D-SHS/Box 40.3023.

Rutter Family – *The Rutter Family*, edited by Elizabeth Beaven Rutter, from a manuscript journal written by her father John Farley Rutter in the 19th century, with additional memories by Elizabeth Beaven Rutter, typed in the 20th century

Rutter 1830 Election – *History of the Shaftesbury Election 1830*, John Rutter, 1830

S&DHS – Shaftesbury & District Historical Society

Shaftesbury Poor – *A Brief Sketch of the State of the Poor and of the Management of Houses of Industry; Recommended to the Consideration of the Inhabitants of the Town of Shaftesbury and Other Places*, John Rutter, 1819, from a facsimile copy, Shaftesbury Library

Shaftesbury Sale - Auction Sale particulars of *The major portion of the Town of Shaftesbury, Dorsetshire*, by Messrs. Fox & Sons of Properties for Sale in Shaftesbury, May 27th, 28th & 29th 1919

Souvenirs of Fonthill – *Souvenirs of Fonthill Abbey* by Jon Millington, Bath Preservation Trust, 1994

Swyer versus Rutter – *Swyer versus Rutter: A Plain Narration of Shastonian Occurrences, without comment*, printed by John Rutter, 1826–7, S&DHS, D.H.C., D-SHS/Box 40.3022

The British Newspaper Archive - The British Newspaper Archive (www.britishnewspaperarchive.co.uk)

Wardour Castle – *An Historical and Descriptive Sketch of Wardour Castle and Demesne, Wilts*, by John Rutter. 1822

Appendix 3
Rutter Ancestors and Children of John Rutter

Abbreviated descriptions have been taken from Le Roter and the Rutter Family

1. Hugh Lupus came to England with William the Conqueror. Made an Earl
2. Richard Lupus was made Earl of Chester in about 1101. Died without issue
3. Robert Fitzhugh was the supposed natural son of Earl Hugh Lupus. Became Baron Malpas. No male heir.
4. Daughter Mabilia married William Belwarde
5. William Belwarde became Lord of Moeity of Malpas
6. David de Malpas, alias le Clerc, was Lord of a Moeity of Malpas, Justice of Chester
7. Peter le Clerc, alias Le Roter, was Secretary to the Palatine Earl of Chester, from whom he obtained the township of Thornton en le Mores, Chester
8. Sir Ranulph le Roter, alias Randle, assumed the name Le Roter, Lord of Thornton
9. Sir Peter le Roter, knight, enjoyed the privileges of the manor of Thornton. Died 1280
10. Richard le Roter obtained a share of the manor Thornton, Kingsley
11. Richard le Roter owned land in Kingsley, Crowton and Newton, all near Chester
12. Randle le Roter of Kingsley. Died 1363
13. Sir Ranulph le Roter of Kingsley. Died 1365
14. William le Roter of Kingsley. Died about 1421
15. Richard Rutter of Kingsley assumed the name Rutter. Died 1424
16. William Rutter of Kingsley (1410–1484)
17. Thomas Rutter of Kingsley (1447–1520)
18. William Rutter of Kingsley (1480–1546)
19. Thomas Rutter of Kingsley (1517–1579)
20. Thomas Rutter of Kingsley. Died 1594
21. George Rutter of Kingsley (1561–1623)
22. John Rutter of Kingsley Hall (1592–1648)
23. John Rutter of Kingsley Hall (1613–1663)
24. Richard Rutter of Kingsley Hall (1644/5-?)
25. Thomas Rutter of Kingsley Hall (about 1661–1717) was disinherited in consequence of joining the Quakers
26. Benjamin Rutter (1699–1768) was the fourth child of Thomas and Rachell (nee Ashbrooke). Went to Bristol aged 21. Bellows and brush maker
27. Thomas Rutter (1741–1800) was the fourth child of Benjamin and Jane (nee Rutty). Bellows and brush maker in Bristol. Became an active Quaker Minister

28. John Rutter (1796–1851) was the youngest child of Thomas and Hester (nee Farley). Orphaned at the age of 10. Apprenticed in Shaftesbury in 1811. Married Anne (nee Clarance) in 1818. Their children were:
    a. Thomas (1819–1823). Died in childhood
    b. Clarence (1820–1855). Unmarried
    c. John (1822–1822). Died in infancy
    d. John Farley (1824–1899). Married Hannah Turner and had eleven children, seven of whom had children
    e. Elizabeth Anne (1828–1828). Died in infancy
    f. Ann Elizabeth (1829–1915). Unmarried
    g. Llewellyn (1832–1857). Unmarried

Appendix 4
Amplification – The Grosvenors

THE NAMES LORD Grosvenor, Earl Grosvenor and the Marquess of Westminster are mentioned on many occasions in this book. In order to avoid misunderstanding as the person being referred to, the following may be helpful. Information about the Grosvenors has been précised so that it relates mainly to John Rutter's life and activities in Shaftesbury.

Robert Grosvenor (1767–1845)
Eldest son of Sir Richard Grosvenor Bt., who was ennobled as Baron Grosvenor in 1761 and who was advanced to Viscount Belgrave and Earl Grosvenor in 1784
Known as Viscount Belgrave from 1784 to 1802
Became the 2nd Earl Grosvenor on the death of his father in 1802
Acquired property and estates in Shaftesbury from Lord Rosebery in 1819
Known as Lord Grosvenor from 1820 until 1831
Acquired property and estates in Motcombe and Gillingham in 1822 and 1828
Further ennobled as the 1st Marquess of Westminster in 1831

Richard Grosvenor (1795–1869)
Eldest son of Robert Grosvenor (1767–1845)
Known as Viscount Belgrave from 1802 to 1831
Became the 3rd Earl Grosvenor in 1831 when his father was made a Marquess
In 1831 was given Motcombe House by his father and moved there in 1833
Became the 2nd Marquess of Westminster on the death of his father in 1845

Robert Grosvenor (1801–1893)
Third and youngest son of Robert Grosvenor (1767–1845)
Member of Parliament for Shaftesbury from 1822 to 1826 (in his father's gift)
Known as Lord Robert Grosvenor from 1831 when his father was made a Marquess
Ennobled as Baron Ebury in 1857

Hugh Grosvenor (1825–1899)
Second and eldest surviving son of Richard Grosvenor (1795–1845)
Known as Viscount Belgrave from 1831 to 1845 and the 4th Earl Grosvenor between 1845 and 1869
Member of Parliament for Chester from 1847 to 1869
Became the 3rd Marquess of Westminster on the death of his father in 1869
Created the 1st Duke of Westminster in 1874

Richard Grosvenor (1837–1912)
Fourth but second surviving son of Richard Grosvenor (1795–1845)
Known as Lord Richard Grosvenor after the death of his father in 1845
Raised to the peerage as Baron Stalbridge in 1886
Inherited most of the properties in Shaftesbury, neighbouring estates and Motcombe House in 1891 on the death of his mother, the Dowager Marchioness
In 1918 sold property in Shaftesbury and the neighbouring estates

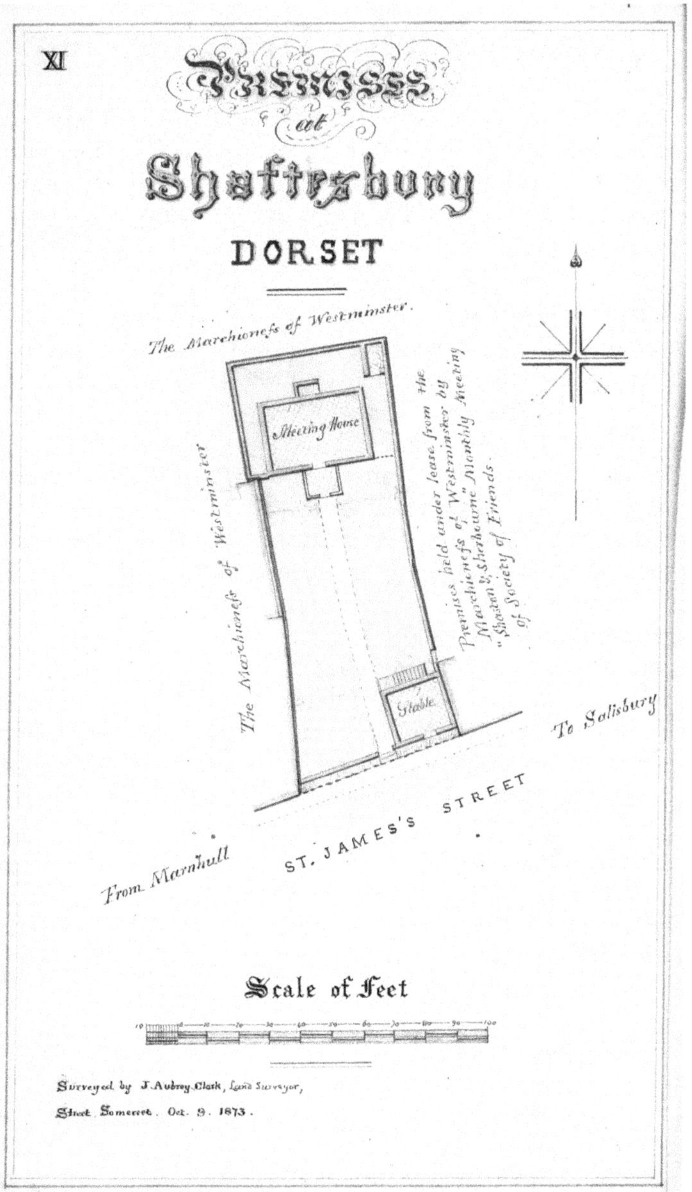

Plan of Shaftesbury Quaker meeting house from a volume of plans of estates belonging to Shaftesbury and Sherborne Monthly Meeting Society of Friends, 1873

Appendix 5
Illustrations

MANY OF THE illustrations in this book have been photographed by Pete Jenkins of PDMS Photography who also improved the quality of many others.

Front cover and Frontispiece

Oil painting of John Rutter (1796–1851) by Monsieur Jacqueline, reproduced by kind permission of Rutters Solicitors and members of the Rutter family.

Preliminaries

Quotation from Advices & Queries
John Rutter's Book Plate (S&DHS, D.H.C., D-SHS/Box 41.3387)

Chapter 1

Alderman William Beckford, (1709-1770) by John Dixon, printed for Carington Bowles, mezzotint, published 1770, NPG D19348, © National Portrait Gallery, London

William Beckford, of Fonthill Abbey, (1760–1844) by T. A. Dean after the portrait by Joshua Reynolds which forms the frontispiece to Beckford's *Recollections of an Excursion to the Monasteries of Alcobaca and Batalha* (1835) (Sidney Blackmore)

Chapter 2

An Account of the Rutter Family (S&DHS, D.H.C., D-SHS/Box 41.3387)
Wesley's New Room Chapel at Bristol (The New Room)
John Wesley preaching outside a church (Wellcome Collection V0006868, Wellcome Images, Creative Commons Attribution (CC-BY-4.0) licence
Kingswood School, Bristol (The New Room)
Felix Farley's Bristol Journal (Allen, L., *Jane Austen's London*, Shire Publications)
Felix Farley, publisher to the Wesleys, 1743

Chapter 3

Gold Hill, Shaftesbury, showing the rear of the 1827 Town Hall, St Peter's Church and, top right, the second of Shaftesbury's Quaker Meeting Houses from 1904, with a working men's club and replacing the old poor house, formerly the Lamb Inn. It is now St Peter's Parish Hall, with an antique shop and church office on the ground floor (Gold Hill)

Shaftesbury High Street, 1840, published by Clarence Rutter (Gold Hill)

John Rutter's shop in the Commons, High Street, Shaftesbury (Gold Hill)
Marriage certificate of John Rutter and Ann Clarance, 7 July 1818 (BMD)
John Rutter, drawn by Samuel Pearce, Bath, 1829, reproduced by kind permission of Rutter & Rutter, Wincanton
Anne Rutter, drawn by Samuel Pearce, Bath, 1829, reproduced by kind permission of Rutter & Rutter, Wincanton
The Dandy Horse, 1819 (Glasgow City Council, Libraries Information and Learning)
Selection of Discourses by Quaker Ministers, © Religious Society of Friends (Quakers) in Britain, (LSF tract box 204_49)
Rutter's Life Pills (S&DHS, D.H.C., D-SHS/Box 44.2645)
Notice of Shaftesbury Subscription Library, 1827 (Gold Hill)
Clarence Rutter, Notice of September 1839 (S&DHS, D.H.C., D-SHS/Box 44.2645)
Penny Postage, Notice of 9 May 1840 (S&DHS, D.H.C., D-SHS/Box 44.2645)
Layton House, 1919 (Shaftesbury Auction Sale, Gold Hill)
John Rutter's Burial Note (Burial Notes of the Shaftesbury and Sherborne Monthly Meeting, Volume 50, 1838 to 1851, D.H.C.)

Chapter 4

James Everard, 10th Baron Arundell of Wardour (1785-1834) (Wiltshire & Swindon History Centre)
Sir Richard Colt Hoare, 2nd Baronet (1758-1838), oil painting by Henry Hoppner Meyer (Public Domain via Wikimedia Commons)
Advert for Rutter's shop in Wincanton, printed on silk (Audrey Hart-Roy)
A Brief Sketch of the State of the Poor, 1819 (Shaftesbury Library)
Old Wardour Castle, drawn by P. Crocker, engraved by G. Hollis, Plate XII, taken from Sir Richard Colt Hoare's The History of Modern Wiltshire. Hundred of Dunworth and Vale of Noddre, 1829 (Wiltshire and Swindon Archives, Chippenham)
New Wardour Castle, drawn by J. Rutter, engraved by T. Higham, 1822 (DZSWS 1983.1503)
Fonthill Abbey – South West View, 1823, drawn by J. Rutter, engraved by T. Higham, 1823 (DZSWS 1983.2653)
Fonthill Abbey – Interior of the Great Western Hall, 1823, drawn by Geo. Cattermole, engraved by J.C. Varrall, published by J. Rutter, Shaftesbury (S&DHS, D.H.C., D-SHS/Box 43.3363)
Fonthill Abbey in Ruins, 1825, drawn on stone by William Westall, after a drawing by John Buckler, engraved by William Westall, printed by C.J. Hullmandel (Fonthill Estate Archives)
Brockley Hall, 1829, drawn by J.C. Buckler, published in Lithography by J. Rutter, Shaftesbury (S&DHS, D.H.C., D-SHS/Box 42.3016)
Weston Super Mare, with bathing machines, 1829, drawn by J.W. Brett, Bristol, engraved by Thomas Higham, published by John Rutter (S&DHS, D.H.C., D-SHS/Box 42.3016)
Banwell Church, 1829, drawn by J.C. Buckler, engraved by Thomas Higham, published by John Rutter (S&DHS, D.H.C., D-SHS/Box 42.3016)

Chapter 5

George Fox, (1624-1691) by Thomas Fairland, printed by Darton 1822, © Religious Society of Friends (Quakers) in Britain, (LSF 94_AXL 33)
Bible Society Notice – Salisbury & Winchester Journal, 16 July 1838. With thanks to The British Newspaper Archive (www.britishnewspaperarchive.co.uk)
Notice about a Total Abstinence Society Meeting, 12 March 1841, printed by C. Rutter, Shaftesbury (S&DHS, D.H.C., D-SHS/Box 44.2645)
Notice of reward for wine stolen, 5 January 1837, printed by C. Rutter and Wallbridge, Shaftesbury (S&DHS, D.H.C., D-SHS/Box 44.2645)
Notice of Meeting on 27 February 1838 about Negro Slavery, printed by C. Rutter and Wallbridge, Shaftesbury (S&DHS, D.H.C., D-SHS/Box 2645)
The first Friends Meeting House in Shaftesbury, built 1746, in dilapidated state in the 1970s. Photo reproduced with the kind permission of Peter Rutter

Chapter 6

Tickets for drink at different public houses given away as bribes in Shaftesbury Election. Ticket No 112 on the right is for '2 Quarts best Beer – Plough' (Gold Hill)
The Shaftesbury Election or the Humours of Punch (Gold Hill)
Robert Grosvenor, 2nd Earl Grosvenor and 1st Marquess of Westminster (1767-1845), oil painting by John Jackson (Public Domain via Wikimedia Commons)
John Rutter, Summons of 10 August 1826 (S&DHS, D.H.C., D-SHS/Box 41.3017)
Cartoon from James Acland article about John Rutter
(enemyofcorporatedespots.files.wordpress.com/2010/03/1826)
Notice of dinner for Knowles on 17 August 1830, Salisbury and Winchester Journal, 16 August 1830, p. 3, Newspaper image © The British Library Board. All rights reserved. With thanks to The British Newspaper Archive (www.britishnewspaperarchive.co.uk)
Open letter from the Marquis (sic) of Westminster to Electors of Shaftesbury supporting John Poulter in the 1835 General Election, 2 January 1835 (Thomas Shirley's Scrapbooks, S&DHS, D.H.C., D-SHS/Box 44.2645)

Chapter 7

Results of Borough Elections on 26 December 1835, printed by Bastable, Shaftesbury (S&DHS, D.H.C., D-SHS/Box 44.2645)
Election leaflet to Shaftesbury ratepayers regarding the Shaftesbury Union, 6 October 1835, printed by J. Gillingham, Shaftesbury (S&DHS, D.H.C., D-SHS/Box 44.2645)
Sunday Infant and Day School - Sketch and Plans, 1839 (S&DHS, D.H.C., D-SHS/Box 44.2719)
Silver Salver presented by inhabitants of Gillingham to John Rutter, agent of SWRC, 10 August 1848 (S&DHS, D.H.C., D-SHS/Box 44.2623)
Commencement of the Salisbury & Yeovil Railway - Cutting of the First Sod in Gillingham, 12 April 1856, p. 381 © Illustrated London News Ltd/Mary Evans
Richard Grosvenor, 2nd Marquess of Westminster (1795-1869), oil painting by Henry William Pickersgill (Public Domain via Wikimedia Commons)

Chapter 8

Property Protection Society Reward, 2 October 1850, printed by C. Rutter, Shaftesbury (S&DHS, D.H.C., D-SHS/Box 44.2802)

John Farley Rutter, 1885, reproduced by kind permission of Rutter & Rutter, Wincanton

Appendix 4

Plan of Shaftesbury Quaker meeting house from a volume of plans of estates belonging to Shaftesbury and Sherborne Monthly Meeting Society of Friends, 1873. Photo reproduced with the kind permission of Simon Rutter

End

Sir John Stuttard

Appendix 6
Bibliography

Printed books, booklets, theses, dissertations, articles and websites

Acland, J., 'John Rutter' from *Enemy of Corporate Despots, Memoirs and Correspondences of a Ghost*, James Acland, 1827, facsimile copy, Wordpress, 2010

Acland, J., *The Shastonian*, John Rutter, Shaftesbury, 1826

Adams, T., *A history of the ancient town of Shaftesbury*, T. Adams of Shaftesbury, 1808

Aldrich, M., Chapter VII, 'Fonthill Abbey', in *William Beckford 1760 – 1844: An Eye for the Magnificent*, edited by Derek E Ostergard, Yale University Press, New Haven and London for The Bard Graduate Center for Studies in the Decorative Arts, Design and Culture, 2001

Aldrich, Professor R., *Joseph Lancaster and Improvements in Education*, an invited lecture given on 22nd May 1998 at the University of London Institute of Education

Alexander, B., *Life at Fonthill 1807–1822: From the correspondence of William Beckford*, translated and edited by Boyd Alexander, Rupert Hart-Davis, London, 1957 and Nonsuch Publishing, 2006

Atterbury, P. (ed.), *A.W.N. Pugin Master of Gothic Revival*, The Bard Graduate Center for Studies in the Decorative Arts, New York, by Yale University Press, 1995

Aviva Group website, 2018

Barclays Bank website, 2018

Barlow, A., *He is our cousin, Cousin - A Quaker Family's History from 1660 to the Present Day*, Quacks Books, York, 2015

Barry, J. and Morgan, K., *Reformation and Revival in Eighteenth-century Bristol*, Bristol Record Society, 1994

Berry, S., Chapter on 'Tourism in Somerset', from *Maritime History of Somerset*, edited by Dr Adrian Webb, The Somerset Archaeological and Natural History Society, 2014

Besse, J., *A Collection of the Sufferings of the People called Quakers for the Testimony of a Good Conscience*, L. Hinde, London, 1753

Best, G.M., *The Cradle of Methodism, 1739–2017: A History of the New Room and of Methodism in Bristol and Kingswood in the Time of John and Charles Wesley and the Subsequent History of the Building*, Tangent Books, 2017

Bleiler, E.F. (ed.), *Three Gothic Novels*, Dover Publications, 1966

Bowles, C., *An Account of the Proceedings at Shaftesbury in consequence of the Resignation of the Recordership by Charles Bowles Esq.; with Explanatory Notes and Remarks*, Second Edition, February 1828, facsimile copy, Shaftesbury Library

Braithwaite, W.C., *Second Period of Quakerism*, Macmillan, 1919
Brinton, H., *Friends for 300 Years*, Pendle Hill Publications, 1964
British and Foreign School Society website, 2018
Bristol Radical History Group website, 2016
Brougham, H., 1st Baron Brougham and Vaux, '*Speech in the case of Queen Caroline*', *Speeches of Henry Lord Brougham*, Volume I, Adam and Charles Black, Edinburgh, 1838,
Brundage, A., *The English Poor Laws, 1770–1930*, Palgrave, 2002
Burton-Page, A., 'Wealth, a martyr's bones and dissolution', *Dorset Life Magazine*, October 2008
Calvert, J.E., *Quaker Constitutionalism and the Political Thought of John Dickinson*, University of Kentucky
C&J Clark International website, 2018
Cannon, J.A., *Shaftesbury Double Member Borough, The History of Parliament: the House of Commons 1754–1790*, ed. Namier, L., Brooke. J., 1964, Cambridge University Press, © Crown copyright and The History of Parliament Trust 1964–2017
Carey, B., Plank, G., *Quakers & Abolition*, University of Illinois Press, 2004
Christianity Today website, 2018
Clarke, S., 'The Troubled Gestation of Britton's *Illustrations of Fonthill*', *The Beckford Journal*, Volume 6, Spring 2000, edited by Jon Millington, The Beckford Society
Cockburn, E.O., *The Almshouses of Dorset*, The Friary Press, Dorchester, 1970, p. 41
Defoe, D., *A Tour Thro' the Whole Island of Great Britain, divided into circuits or journeys* Volume 1, 1724
Delair, J.B., 'The Win Green Mosasaur', *Wiltshire Archaeological & Natural History Magazine*, Volume 101, 2008
Dickinson, J.R., 'Rutter, Samuel', *Oxford Dictionary of National Biography*, 2018
Dunning, R., *Introduction* to *Delineations of the North Western Division of the County of Somerset and of the Mendip Caverns* by John Rutter, 1829, from facsimile edition Amberley Publishing 2009
Evans, E.J., *The Great Reform Act of 1832*, Routledge, London, 1994
Everard, James, *The Hundred of Dunworth* by James Everard, Baron Arundell, and Sir R. C. Hoare Bt, *The Modern History of South Wiltshire*, Volume IV, Part I, John Bowyer Nichols and John Gough Nichols, London, initially published as *The History of Modern Wiltshire. Hundred of Dunworth and Vale of Noddre*, by James Everard, Baron Arundell of Wardour Castle, Count of the Roman Empire, and Sir Richard Colt Hoare, Bart., printed by and for John Bowyer Nichols and Son, 25 Parliament Street, 1829
Farrell, S., *Shaftesbury Borough, The History of Parliament: the House of Commons 1820–1832*, ed. Fisher, D.R., 2009, Cambridge University Press, © Crown copyright and The History of Parliament Trust 1964–2017
Fermor, P.L., *Between the Woods and the Water*, John Murray, 1986
Firth, C.H., revised by Worden, B., 'Edmund Ludlow', *Oxford Dictionary of National Biography*, 2004
Foster, J.J, *Wessex Worthies (Dorset)*, Dickinsons, London, 1920
Fothergill, B., *Beckford of Fonthill*, Faber & Faber, 1979 and Nonsuch Publishing Limited, 2005

Frenchay Village Museum Archives website, 2018

Grace's Guide website, British Industrial History, 2012

Granger, The Rev. J., *A Biographical History of England, From Egbert the Great to the Revolution,* Volume I, William Baynes and Son, Paternoster Row, London, 1824

Griffin, C.J., *Parish farms and the poor law: a response to unemployment in rural southern England, c.1815–35,* The Agricultural History Review, 2011

Handy, M., 'Shaftesbury: Pocket Borough', *Dorset Life Magazine,* July 2015

Hardy, T., *Jude the Obscure,* James R. Osgood, McIlvaine & Co, 1896

Hewat-Jaboor, P., Chapter III, 'Fonthill House', in *William Beckford 1760 – 1844: An Eye for the Magnificent,* edited by Derek E Ostergard, Yale University Press, New Haven and London for The Bard Graduate Center for Studies in the Decorative Arts, Design and Culture, 2001

Higginbotham, P., 'Shaftesbury, Dorset, The Workhouse', *Peter Higginbotham* website http://www.workhouses.org.uk, 2018; *Historic England* website, 2018

Hoare, Sir Richard Colt Bt., Letter, stating the true site of the ancient colony of Camulodunum, 1827, printed by John Rutter, Shaftesbury

Hoare, Sir Richard Colt Bt., *The Hundred of Dunworth* by James Everard, Baron Arundell, and Sir R. C. Hoare, Bt, *The Modern History of South Wiltshire,* Volume IV, Part I, John Bowyer Nichols and John Gough Nichols, London, initially published as *The History of Modern Wiltshire. Hundred of Dunworth and Vale of Noddre,* by James Everard, Baron Arundell of Wardour Castle, Count of the Roman Empire, and Sir Richard Colt Hoare, Bart., printed by and for John Bowyer Nichols and Son, 25 Parliament Street, 1829

Hopton, F.C., *Corruption and Reform: Municipal Government in the Borough of Shaftesbury, 1750–1835,* Shaftesbury, S&DHS Publication No 5, 1975

Hopton, F.C., *The 1830 Parliamentary Election,* The Mansel-Pleydell Prize Essay, Dorset Natural History and Archaeological Society, Volume 110 for 1988, edited by Jo Draper, issued 1989

Howarth, F. and Young, J.A., A brief history of the water supply of Shaftesbury, Dorset West Wilts Water Board and S&DHS, 1972

Hudson, T., *Temperance Pioneers of the West,* National Temperance Publication Depot, 1888

Huntley & Palmers website, 2018

Hutchins, J., *History and Antiquities of The County of Dorset:* Third Volume, John Bowyer Nichols and Sons, London, 1868

Innes, B., *Shaftesbury, An Illustrated History,* The Dovecote Press, 1992

Innes, B., 'Shaftesbury and the Grosvenors', *Dorset Life Magazine,* February 2007

Jervoise, E., *Notes on Shaftesbury Inns &c. from various sources,* 1951

Jones, R.M., *George Fox – An Autobiography,* Scriptura Press, 1909, Copyright at Scriptura Press, 2015

Kerr, B., *Bound to the soil. A social history of Dorset, 1750–1918,* by John Baker, Pall Mall, London, 1968

Klingaman, W.K., *The Year Without Summer,* St. Martin's Press, 2013

Lacock, R., 'Quakers in Gloucester: the first fifty years, 1655–1705', *Bristol and Gloucestershire Archaeological Society,* 2007

Lees-Milne, J., *William Beckford,* Michael Russell Publishing, 1976

Lloyds Banking Group website, 2018

Long, F.C., *Tales of Old Shaftesbury*, F.C. Long, Shaftesbury, 1979
Maggs, C., MBE., *A History of the Southern Railway*, Amberley Publishing, 2017
Martin, J., *Oratory, itinerant lecturing and Victorian popular politics: a case study of James Acland (1799–1876)*, Wiley Online Library, John Wiley & Sons, Inc, 2018
Masters, S., 'The Reformation and Friends – John Wesley', *The Friend*, 18 February 2018
Maxted, I., 'Farley Family', *Oxford Dictionary of National Biography* website, 2018
May, S.J., *Voyage of the Slave Ship, J.M.W. Turner's Masterpiece in Historical Context*, McFarland & Company, Inc, Jefferson, North Carolina, 2014
McDowell, A., 'Dorset Buttons', *Henry's Buttons'* website, 2018
Milligan, E.H., *Biographical Dictionary of British Quakers in Commerce & Industry 1775 -1920*, William Sessions Limited, York, 2007
Millington, J., *Souvenirs of Fonthill Abbey*, Bath Preservation Trust, 1994
Millington, J. (ed.), *Conversations with Beckford*, The Beckford Society, 2014
Minchinton, W.E., 'Agricultural Returns and the Government during the Napoleonic Wars', *Agricultural History Review*, Volume 1, 1953, The British Agricultural History Society
Minchinton, W.E., *The Trade of Bristol in the Eighteenth Century*, Bristol Record Society, 1957
Mitchell, B.R., *Abstract of British Historical Statistics*, Cambridge University Press, 1971
National Trust for Scotland, *Brodick Castle & Country Park*, 1987
O'Donnell, E.A., 'Quakers and Education', ed. Angell, S.W. and Dandelion, B.P., *The Oxford Handbook of Quaker Studies*, Oxford Handbooks Online, 2018
Oldfield, T.H.B., *The Representative History of Great Britain and Ireland: being a history of the House of Commons, and of the counties, cities, and boroughs of the United Kingdom*, Volume 1, Baldwin, Cradock & Joy, London, 1816
Omerod, G., King, D., Smith, W., and Webb, W., *The history of the county Palatine and city of Chester*, G. Routledge, 1819
Penny, J., *An Examination of the Eighteenth Century Newspapers of Bristol and Gloucester*, Bath Spa University College, 1996, *Fishponds Local History Society* website, 2018
Purdy, F., 'The Statistics of the English Poor Rate before and since the Passing of the Poor Law Amendment Act', *Journal of the Statistical Society of London*, Volume 23, No. 3 (Sep., 1860), Wiley for the Royal Statistical Society, 2013
Quaker Faith & Practice, Religious Society of Friends (Quakers)
Quakers in Britain, Britain Yearly Meeting of the Religious Society of Friends, website 2018
Quakers in the World website, 2018
Raistrick, A., *Quakers in Science and Industry*, The Bannisdale Press, London, 1950, Register Office, London
Reid, T. Wemyss, *Life of The Right Honourable William Edward Forster*, Volume I, Chapman and Hall, London, 1888. Taken from a digitised copy, made by Google, of an original third edition book held by Harvard University Library
Robins, J., *Rebel Queen: How the Trial of Caroline Brought England to the Brink of Revolution*, Simon & Schuster, 2006
Russell, Lord John, MP, *Memoirs, Journal, and Correspondence of Thomas Moore*, Volume II, D Appleton and Company, New York, 1857

Rutherford, L.M., 'John Wesley's Bristol Printer: Another W Gathering', *Bibliographical Society of Australia and New Zealand, Bulletin*, Volume 13 Number 4, 1989

Rutter, E.B., edited *The Rutter Family*, from a manuscript *Journal* written by her father John Farley Rutter in the 19th century, with additional memories by Elizabeth Beaven Rutter, typed in the 20th century

Rutter, F.C., *Descendants of John Farley Rutter*, after *The Rutter Family at 1984* by his father, J.J.B. Rutter, published privately, 2004

Rutter, H., *Some account of the Religious Experience and Gospel Labours of Thomas Rutter*, printed and sold by W. Phillips, Lombard Street, London, 1803

Rutter, J., *A Brief Sketch of The History of Cranborn Chace and of the Dispute concerning its Boundaries*, John Rutter, Shaftesbury, 1818, S&DHS, D.H.C., D-SHS/Box 42.3375

Rutter, J., *A Brief Sketch of the State of the Poor and of the Management of Houses of Industry; Recommended to the Consideration of the Inhabitants of the Town of Shaftesbury and Other Places*, John Rutter, Shaftesbury, 1819, facsimile copy , Shaftesbury Library

Rutter, J., *An Historical and Descriptive Sketch of Wardour Castle and Demesne, Wilts*, John Rutter, Shaftesbury, 1822, S&DHS, D.H.C., D-SHS/Box 43.3015

Rutter, J., *A Description of Fonthill Abbey, and Demesne, Wilts; Seat of William Beckford, Esq. Including a List of its Numerous and Valuable Paintings, Cabinets, and Other Curiosities*, 1st ed., John Rutter, Shaftesbury, 1822

Rutter, J., *A Description of Fonthill Abbey and Demesne, In the County of Wilts: Including a List of its Paintings, Cabinets, and Other Curiosities*, 2nd ed., John Rutter, Shaftesbury, 1822

Rutter, J., *A Description of Fonthill Abbey and Demesne, In the County of Wilts: Including a List of its Paintings, Cabinets, &c.*, 3rd–6th ed., John Rutter, Shaftesbury, 1822, 3rd ed., S&DHS, D.H.C., D-SHS/Box 43.3469

Rutter, J., *A New Descriptive Guide to Fonthill Abbey and Demesne*, John Rutter, Shaftesbury, 1823, S&DHS, D.H.C., D-SHS/Box 43.3365

Rutter, J., *Delineations of Fonthill & Its Abbey*, John Rutter, Shaftesbury, 1823, Rutter Archive Box 43.3363 and Box 43.3468

Rutter, J., *The Defence of John Rutter*, John Rutter, Shaftesbury, 1826, facsimile copy Shaftesbury Library. The author is anonymous but known to be John Rutter

Rutter, J., *Swyer versus Rutter. A plain narration of Shastonian occurrences without comment*, John Rutter, Shaftesbury, 1826, S&DHS, D.H.C., D-SHS/Box 40.3022 and facsimile copy Shaftesbury Library. The author is anonymous but could be either John Rutter or James Acland or both

Rutter, J., *An Historical and Descriptive Account of the Town of Shaftesbury*, in six parts, written but not published, MSS Rutter D-50/1, D.H.C; later typed, in 1972, typed copy S&DHS, Gold Hill Museum

Rutter, J., *Extracts, &c. concerning the Prevalence of Vagrancy in some of the Western Counties of England, The Means of its Correction, and the Necessary Relief of Distressed Travellers*, John Rutter, Shaftesbury, 1827, facsimile copy, Shaftesbury Library

Rutter, J., *A Letter to the Commissioners of the Shaftesbury District of Turnpike Roads*, 1827, S&DHS, D.H.C., D-SHS/Box 44.3396

Rutter, J., *Delineations of the North West Division of the County of Somerset*, John Rutter,

Shaftesbury, 1929
Rutter, J., *Delineations of the North Western Division of the County of Somerset and of its Antediluvian Bone Caverns, with a Geological Sketch of the District,* by John Rutter, Shaftesbury, 1829, S&DHS, D.H.C., D-SHS/Box 44.3018
Rutter, J., *Illustrations to Rutter's Somersetshire* (33 illustrations), John Rutter, Shaftesbury, 1829, S&DHS, D.H.C., D-SHS/Box 42.3016
Rutter, J., *Banwell and Cheddar Guide,* John Rutter, Shaftesbury, 1829
Rutter, J., *The Clevedon Guide,* John Rutter, Shaftesbury, 1829
Rutter, J., The Westonian Guide, John Rutter, Shaftesbury, 1829
Rutter, J., *The History of the Shaftesbury Election,* Shaftesbury, 1830, printed by George Adams, Shaftesbury. The author is anonymous but known to be John Rutter. Gold Hill Museum, S&DHS
Rutter, J., *Letters in defence of the Bible Society to L. Neville, in reply to his accusations against the British and Foreign Bible Society and against Dissenters,* James Dinnis, Paternoster Row, London, 1836
Rutter, J.F., *An Account of the Rutter Family* (S&DHS, D.H.C., D-SHS/Box 41.3387)
Rutter, S., Shaftesbury: Problem Politics and the Impact of Municipal Corporations Act, 1775–1845, a dissertation for the University of Gloucestershire, April 2014
Shaftesbury Quakers website, 2018
Slack, P., *The English poor law, 1531–1782,* Cambridge University Press, 1995
Smith, J., *A Descriptive Catalogue of Friends' Books,* Volume II, Joseph Smith, London, 1867, facsimile, Harvard College Library
Stephen, Sir Leslie, *Dictionary of National Biography,* Volume 20, 'Fry, Elizabeth', 1897
Stephen, Sir Leslie, *Dictionary of National Biography,* Volume 50, 'Rutter, John', 1897
Stockdale, P., *An Introduction: Poems by the late Mr Samuel Marsh Oram,* T. Cadell, Strand, 1794
The International Committee of the Red Cross website, October 2016
The National Archives website, 2018
The Yearly Meeting of the Religious Society of Friends (Quakers) in Britain, *Advices & Queries,* 1995
Thomas, A.B., 'The Beaconite Controversy', *Bulletin of Friends' Historical Society, (Philadelphia)* Volume IV, no. 2 (Third Month, 1912)
Thomas, R., *An Evening with Shaftesbury's (almost) Forgotten Poet: Samuel Marsh Oram (1765–1791),* Swans Trust, Shaftesbury
Thorne, R., *Shaftesbury Borough, The History of Parliament: the House of Commons 1790-1820,* 1986 Cambridge University Press, © Crown copyright and The History of Parliament Trust 1964–2017
Thurley, S., *Lost Buildings of Britain,* Penguin Books Limited, 2004
Turner, A., *Aspects of the Paleoecology of Large Predators, including Man, during the British Upper Pleistocene, with particular emphasis on Predator-Prey Relationships.* Thesis submitted for the degree of Doctor of Philosophy in the University of Sheffield, Department of Prehistory and Archaeology, May 1981
Wesley, The Rev. C., *Journal,* Volume I, Reprinted 1980 by Beacon Hill Press of Kansas City, Kansas City Missouri from the 1849 edition published by John Mason, 14 City Road, London
Wesley, The Rev. J., *The Works of the Rev. John Wesley, A.M.,* Volume 1, John Mason, 14 City Road, London, 1829

Wesley, The Rev. J., *Journal,* Volume II, ed. Nehemiah Curnock, Charles H. Kelly, City Road, London, 1909
Wilton, A., *Architectural Drawings for Commissions c.1797–1800*, subset, March 2013, in Brown, D.B. (ed.), *J.M.W. Turner: Sketchbooks, Drawings and Watercolours*, Tate Research Publication, April 2015 *Tate* website https://www.tate.org.uk/art/research-publications/jmw-turner/architectural-drawings-for-commissions-r1174078, accessed 21 May 2018
Wingate, W.H., *The Family of Le Roter or Rutter*, 1966
Wong, E.L., *Neither Fugitive nor Free" – Atlantic Slavery, Freedom Suits, and the Legal Culture of Travel*, New York University Press, New York and London, 2009

Newspapers, journals, official records, archival material and notices

Annual Report of the Poor Law Board, 1851
Anonymous letter annotated about May 1829 to John Rutter. John Rutter M.S. Miscellaneous
Antiques Trade Gazette
Auction Sale particulars of *The major portion of the Town of Shaftesbury, Dorsetshire*, by Messrs. Fox & Sons of Properties for Sale in Shaftesbury, May 27th, 28th & 29th 1919
Bath Chronicle & Weekly Gazette, The British Newspaper Archive
Bradshaw's Railway Gazette, 1845
Bristol Mercury, The British Newspaper Archive
Bristol & Somerset Monthly Meetings, Society of Friends (Quaker) Births 1578–1841
Bristol Times and Mirror, The British Newspaper Archive
Carey's Library of Choice Literature, Philadelphia, Princeton University, Annie Rhodes Gulick and Alexander Reading Gulick memorial Fund
Census Return, Holy Trinity, St Peter, St James, Shaftesbury, 1841 and 1851
Dorset County Chronicle, The British Newspaper Archive
Dorset Historic Towns Survey: Shaftesbury, 2011
Dorset Life Magazine
Dorset County Council
Evening Mail, The British Newspaper Archive
Exeter & Plymouth Gazette, The British Newspaper Archive
Gentleman's Magazine
Hansard
Independent Order of Rechabites, King Alfred Tent, DC-SYB/I/3, D.H.C.
Ipswich Journal, The British Newspaper Archive
John Bull, taken from the *Dorset Chronicle*, The British Newspaper Archive
Journal of the American Temperance Union
Kelly's Directory of Shaftesbury
Literary Gazette
Manchester Times, facsimile, Manchester Libraries, Information and Archives – Courtesy of Manchester Libraries, Information and Archives, Manchester City Council
Minutes of the Monthly Meetings of Friends of Shaftesbury and Sherborne
Norfolk Chronicle, The British Newspaper Archive

Notice of Election 1832 - A Song for the Merry Men of Shaston. Old Voters, New Voters, Voters Altogether, signed 'QUIN', printed by Neave of Gillingham

Notice to the Owners of Property and Rate-Payers of the Parish of St Peter, Shaftesbury, dated 12 October 1835, printed by Clarence Rutter

Oaths of loyalty to the Crown and Church of England, The National Archives, 2018

Ordnance Survey, 25 inch, England and Wales, Dorset IV.14, 1901 and 1929

Pigot & Co, Directory of Dorsetshire, 1823

Pigot & Co, Trade Directory of Shaftesbury & District, 1830 and 1842

Post Office Directory of Dorsetshire, Wiltshire, W Kelly and Co, Temple Bar, London, 1849

Quaker Births in Bristol, Public Record Office

Railway Times

Reform Act 1832, Parliamentary Archives, copyright © Parliamentary Archives

Report of the Commissioners appointed to enquire into the Municipal Corporations in England and Wales, 1835

Report of the Secretary of the Mendicity Society for the Shaftesbury District, 14 January 1828

Returns of Churchwardens and Overseers of the Parish of Shaftesbury St Peter, 1828 and 1829, D.H.C.

Robson's Directory, 1839, S&DHS, Gold Hill Museum

Rutter Archives: Manuscripts, letters, publications and other material relating to John Rutter, owned by the S&DHS, are stored in Dorchester at the D.H.C. which has the proper environmental conditions to look after historical material in a secure building staffed by professionally trained staff. During the preparation of this book these boxes have been brought to the Gold Hill Museum in Shaftesbury to facilitate the research and the preparation of this biography. The five boxes of archival material have been referred to in this book with the prefix S&DHS, D.H.C., D-SHS/Box

Rutter, J., Register of Subscribers and Payments, Property Protection Society, S&DHS, D.H.C., D-SHS/Box 44.2802

Rutter Scrapbooks, Mere Museum

Salisbury and Winchester Journal, The British Newspaper Archive

Shaftesbury Borough, Minutes and other papers, D.H.C.

Shaftesbury Branch Bible Society, North Dorset Press, printed by John Rutter, 1820 and 1821, facsimile copies S&DHS, Gold Hill Museum

Shaftesbury Corporation and Municipal Corporation Council Minutes, 1835–39, Shaftesbury & District Historical Society, Gold Hill Museum

Shaftesbury Heritage Trail

Shaftesbury Meeting House, Quaker Meeting Houses Heritage Project

Sherborne Mercury, The British Newspaper Archive

Statute law repeals: nineteenth report, draft Statute Law (Repeals) Bill, by Great Britain Law Commission

'Temperance, Longevity, Insurance. A Tract for the Times', Temperance and Life Assurance Company of North America, published by the *Canada Citizen*, Toronto, 1884

The Atlas, The British Newspaper Archive

The Baptist Register

The Beckford Society Journal

The British and Foreign Anti-slavery Reporter
The British Newspaper Archive (www.britishnewspaperarchive.co.uk); The British Library Board
The Church Magazine
The Dorset County Chronicle, The British Newspaper Archive
The Gardener's Magazine, September 1835
The Gentleman's Magazine: and Historical Chronicle
The Inquirer
The Ipswich Journal, The British Newspaper Archive
The Legal Observer
The London Literary Gazette
The New Monthly Magazine
The Parliamentary Gazetteer of England and Wales
The reliquary and illustrated archaeologist: a quarterly journal and review devoted to the study of the early pagan and Christian antiquities of Great Britain, Volume XII, 1871–72 edited by Jewitt, L., Bemrose & Sons and John Russell Smith, London, 1872
The Report of the Commissioners appointed to enquire into the Municipal Corporations in *England and Wales*, March 1835
The Shaftesbury Subscription Library for Circulation and Reference, John Rutter, 1827, facsimile copy, S&DHS, Gold Hill Museum
The Shastonian (Volumes I, II and III), anonymously written but ascribed to James Acland, printed and published by John Rutter, 1826, S&DHS, D.H.C., D-SHS/Box 40.3393
The Temperance Recorder
The Third Annual Report of The Shaftesbury Infant School, 11 August 1841, facsimile copy S&DHS, Gold Hill Museum
The Times
Tipperary Free Press, The British Newspaper Archive
Tithe Apportionment for Shaftesbury, 1846, D.H.C.; Shaftesbury & District Historical Society, Gold Hill Museum
Vindicator, The British Newspaper Archive
Wiltshire Archaeological and Natural History Society

Manuscripts and letters

Beckford, W., letter dated 3 October 1822 to John Rutter, MSS Beckford c27, fol. 15cv, Special Collections, Weston Library, Bodleian Libraries
Downing Street., letter dated 13 February 1829 to John Rutter. S&DHS, D.H.C., D-SHS/Box 41.3387
Grosvenor, Earl, letter dated 7 August 1825, S&DHS, D.H.C., D-SHS/Box 41.3421
Grosvenor, open letter dated 6 December 1834 to Electors of Shaftesbury, Thomas Shirley's Scrapbooks, S&DHS, D.H.C., D-SHS/Box 44.2646
Hannen, W.M., letter dated 12 February 1847 to the Freeholders of the County of Dorset, Sherborne Mercury, 6 March 1847
Hoare, Sir R.C., Bt., letter dated 1822 to the Reverend Lysons, Stourhead, DZSWS. MSS.751.33, The Wiltshire Museum, Devizes, The Wiltshire Archaeological

and Natural History Society

Keats, J., letter dated 27 April 1818 to John Hamilton Reynolds, Teignmouth Layton House, Architects' drawing 1847

Rutter, A.E., letter dated 16 June 1837 to her brother Clarence Rutter, MS Portfolio of Joseph Rutter

Rutter, A.E., letter dated 11 February 1839 to her brother, Clarence Rutter, MS Portfolio of Joseph Rutter

Rutter, A.E., letter dated 19 April 1839 to her brother, Clarence Rutter, MS Portfolio of Joseph Rutter

Rutter, C., letter dated 26 October 1840 to his brother, Llewellyn Rutter, MS Portfolio of Joseph Rutter

Rutter, J., letter dated 15 November 1822 to Nichols & Son, MSS Portfolio Volume 15. 64, Library, Society of Friends, followed by Undated note by Nichols & Son. MSS Portfolio Volume 15. 64, Library, Society of Friends

Rutter, J., letter dated December 1827 to Nichols & Son. MSS Portfolio Volume 15. 69, Library, Society of Friends

Rutter, J., letter dated 3 October 1828 to Nichols & Son. MSS Portfolio Volume 15. 70, Library, Society of Friends

Rutter, J., letter dated 2 February 1829 to The Prime Minister. John Rutter MS Miscellaneous Manuscripts 1829–1833, S&DHS, D.H.C., D-SHS/Box 41.3387

Rutter, J., letter dated 11 February 1829 to Philip Chitty. John Rutter MS Miscellaneous Manuscripts 1829–1833, S&DHS, D.H.C., D-SHS/Box 41.3387

Rutter, J., letter dated 26 February 1829 to Edward Buckland. John Rutter MS Miscellaneous Manuscripts 1829–1833, S&DHS, D.H.C., D-SHS/Box 41.3387

Rutter, J., letter dated 2 June 1829 to Nichols & Son. MSS Portfolio Volume 15.73, Library, Society of Friends

Rutter, J., letter dated 27 April 1830. John Rutter MS Miscellaneous Manuscripts 1829- 1833, S&DHS, D.H.C., D-SHS/Box 41.3387

Rutter, J., letter dated 20 July 1830 to the Prime Minister, D.H.C., D-50/3

Rutter, J., letter dated 23 August 1830 to the Editor of *The Times*

Rutter, J., letter dated 26 January 1832 to John Wallbridge. John Rutter MS Miscellaneous Manuscripts 1829–1833, S&DHS, D.H.C., D-SHS/Box 41.3387

Rutter, J., letter dated 26 June 1832 to The Most Honourable The (1st) Marquess of Westminster, MSS Grosvenor Estate Archives

Rutter, J., letter dated 21 August 1833 to Mr Mullens of Semley Union. John Rutter MS Miscellaneous Manuscripts 1829–1833, S&DHS, D.H.C., D-SHS/Box 41.3387

Rutter, J., letter dated 15 March 1837 to Fellow Parishioners in the Parish of St Peter, Shaftesbury, printed by Bastable of Shaftesbury, S&DHS, Gold Hill Museum

Rutter, J., letter dated 15 December 1849 to The Most Honourable The (2nd) Marquess of Westminster, Rutter Archives, S&DHS, Gold Hill Museum

Rutter, J., letter dated 21 August 1850, Manchester Libraries, Information and Archives, Courtesy of Manchester Libraries, Information and Archives, Manchester City Council

Rutter, J., D.H.C., MSS D-50

Rutter, J., MS *Rex v Rutter and Others, Knowles' Election Bills, Miscellaneous,* 1830–31,, S&DHS, D.H.C., D-SHS/Box 40.3023

Rutter, J., MSS *Mems on proceedings of the Shaftesbury Board of Guardians of Shaftesbury Poor Law Union by Rutter, Vice-Chairman from Nov 1835 to March 1837*, S&DHS, Gold Hill Museum;

Rutter, J., MSS Rutter 12, S&DHS, Gold Hill Museum

Rutter, J., letter dated 4 April 1836 to his son, John Farley Rutter, MS Portfolio of Joseph Rutter

Rutter, J., letter dated 2 July 1847 to his son, John Farley Rutter, MS Portfolio of Joseph Rutter

Rutter, J., letter dated 19 February 1846 to his son, John Farley Rutter, MS Portfolio of Joseph Rutter

Rutter, L., letter dated 1838 to his brother, Clarence, MS Portfolio of Joseph Rutter

Rutter, L., letter dated 23 February 1844 to his mother, MS Portfolio of Joseph Rutter

Rutter, L., letter dated 4 September 1847 to his father, John Rutter, MS Portfolio of Joseph Rutter

Rutter, L., letter dated 10 August 1848 to his mother, Anne Rutter, MS Portfolio of Joseph Rutter

Rutter, L., letter dated 11 September 1848 his mother, Anne Rutter, MS Portfolio of Joseph Rutter

Rutter Scrapbooks, Mere Museum

Wallbridge, J., letter dated 6 March 1832 to John Rutter. John Rutter M.S. Miscellaneous Manuscripts 1829–1833, S&DHS, D.H.C., D-SHS/Box 41.3387

Westminster, open letter dated 2 January 1835 to Electors of Shaftesbury, Thomas Shirley's Scrapbooks, S&DHS, D.H.C., D-SHS/Box 44.2646

Appendix 7
References

1 *Quakers in Britain,* Our Values, website, 2018
2 *Le Roter;* and *Rutter Family*
3 *Le Roter,* p. 24
4 Ibid, p. 25
5 Ibid, p. 28
6 Ibid, p. 26
7 John Rutter MSS Miscellaneous Manuscripts 1829–1833, S&DHS, D.H.C., D-SHS/Box 41.3421
8 Ibid; and Dickinson, J.R., '*Rutter, Samuel*', *Oxford Dictionary of National Biography*, 2018
9 *Rutter Family,* p. 2
10 *Le Roter,* p. 29
11 Ibid, p. 30
12 *Rutter Family,* p. 2
13 Raistrict, A., *Quakers in Science and Industry,* The Bannisdale Press, London, 1950, p. 37
14 Minchinton, W.E. (ed.), *The Trade of Bristol in the Eighteenth Century,* Bristol Record Society, 1957, p. ix
15 Barry, J., Morgan, K., (ed.), *Reformation and Revival in Eighteenth-century Bristol,* Bristol Record Society, 1994, p. 68
16 *Rutter Family,* p. 3
17 Ibid, p. 3
18 Best, G.M., *The Cradle of Methodism,* p. 211
19 Wesley, The Rev. J., *Journal,* Volume II, ed. Nehemiah Curnock, Charles H. Kelly, City Road, London, 1909, many entries
20 *Rutter Family,* p. 4
21 Wesley, The Rev. J., *Journal,* Volume II, ed. Nehemiah Curnock, Charles H. Kelly, City Road, London, 1909, entry of 2 July 1739, p. 233
22 Wesley, The Rev. J., *Journal,* Volume II, ed. Nehemiah Curnock, Charles H. Kelly, City Road, London, 1909, entry of 11 July 1739, p. 241
23 Best, G.M., *The Cradle of Methodism,* p. 65
24 Ibid, p. 81
25 *Rutter Family,* p. 4
26 Ibid, p. 4
27 Ibid, p. 4
28 Wesley, The Rev. J., *The Works of the Rev. John Wesley, A.M.,* Volume 1, John

Mason, 14 City Road, London, 1829, p. 383
29 Ibid, p. 383
30 Wesley, The Rev. C., *Journal*, Volume 1, Reprinted 1980 by Beacon Hill Press of Kansas City, Kansas City Missouri from the 1849 edition published by John Mason of London, p.166
31 *Ipswich Journal*, 26 June 1742, The British Newspaper Archive
32 *Rutter Family*, p. 3
33 *Christianity Today* website, 2018
34 Best, G.M., author of *The Cradle of Methodism*
35 *Rutter Family*, p 8; and Jewitt, L. (ed.), *The reliquary and illustrated archaeologist: a quarterly journal and review devoted to the study of the early pagan and Christian antiquities of Great Britain*, Volume XII, 1871–72, Bemrose & Sons and John Russell Smith, London, 1872. Note: by a post-nuptial agreement of 1754, Kingsley Hall had been settled on Mary Rutter and her issue after her marriage to John Helsby, who had been born there when his father was a lessee. Mary Rutter was Thomas Rutter's great aunt
36 *Some account of the Religious Experience and Gospel Labours of Thomas Rutter*, 1803, from a facsimile copy, Gold Hill, p. 4
37 *Rutter Family*, p. 4
38 Best, G.M., author of *The Cradle of Methodism* and former headmaster of Kingswood School
39 *Some account of the Religious Experience and Gospel Labours of Thomas Rutter*, 1803, from a facsimile copy, Gold Hill, p. 6
40 Ibid, p. 20
41 *Rutter Family*, p. 6
42 *Bath Chronicle & Weekly Gazette*, 31 January 1793, The British Newspaper Archive
43 *Rutter Family*, p. 6
44 Ibid, p. 7
45 Penny, J., *An Examination of the Eighteenth Century Newspapers of Bristol and Gloucester*, Bath Spa University College, 1996, *Fishponds Local History Society* website, 2018
46 Maxted, I., '*Farley Family*', *Oxford Dictionary of National Biography*, 2018
47 Rutherford, L.M., 'John Wesley's Bristol Printer: Another W Gathering', *Bibliographical Society of Australia and New Zealand, Bulletin*, Bulletin Volume 13 Number 4, 1989, p. 148
48 Penny, J., *An Examination of the Eighteenth Century Newspapers of Bristol and Gloucester*, Bath Spa University College, 1996, *Fishponds Local History Society* website, 2018
49 Rutherford, L.M., 'John Wesley's Bristol Printer: Another W Gathering', *Bibliographical Society of Australia and New Zealand, Bulletin*, Bulletin Volume 13 Number 4, 1989, p. 149
50 Best, G.M., author of *The Cradle of Methodism*
51 Brinton, H., *Friends for 300 Years*, Pendle Hill Publications, 1964, p. 32
52 *Rutter Family*, p. 8
53 Penny, J., *An Examination of the Eighteenth Century Newspapers of Bristol and Gloucester*, Bath Spa University College, 1996, *Fishponds Local History Society*

website, 2018
54 Frenchay Village Museum Archives website, 2018
55 *Rutter Family*, p. 8; and *Le Roter*, p. 39
56 Stephen, Sir L., *Dictionary of National Biography*, Volume 20, 'Fry, Elizabeth', 1897, p. 294; *Quakers in the World* website, 2018; *Christianity Today* website, 2018
57 Best, G.M., author of *The Cradle of Methodism*
58 Penny, J., *An Examination of the Eighteenth Century Newspapers of Bristol and Gloucester*, Bath Spa University College, 1996, *Fishponds Local History Society* website
59 *Sherborne Mercury*, 20 October, 1800, The British Newspaper Archive
60 *Rutter Family* p. 8
61 Bristol & Somerset Monthly Meeting, *Society of Friends (Quaker) Births 1578–1841*; and *Quaker Births in Bristol*, Public Record Office
62 *Rutter Family*, p. 9; and *Le Roter*, p. 40
63 Ibid, p. 9 and p.41
64 O'Donnell, E.A., *Quakers and Education*, ed. Angell, S.W. and Dandelion, B.P., The Oxford Handbook of Quaker Studies, Oxford Handbooks Online, 2018, p. 2
65 Minchinton, W.E. (ed.), *The Trade of Bristol in the Eighteenth Century*, Bristol Record Society, 1957, p. xi
66 *Rutter Family*, p. 9; and *Le Roter*, p. 41
67 *Dorset Historic Towns Survey: Shaftesbury*, 2011, p. 31
68 Burton-Page, A., 'Wealth, a martyr's bones and dissolution', *Dorset Life Magazine*, October 2008, *Dorset Life* website, 2018
69 Defoe, D., *A Tour Thro' the Whole Island of Great Britain, divided into circuits or journeys*, Volume 1, 1724, p. 218
70 St John's Church was built in the 13th century on St John's Hill, in the south west of Shaftesbury, with a view over the Blackmore Vale. After the merger of two parishes, St John's with St James in 1446, St John's Church was demolished, leaving the foundations visible with an adjacent church yard, as recorded by John Hutchins in The History and Antiquities of Dorset, Bower & Nicholls, London, 1774
71 Stockdale, P., *An Introduction: Poems by the late Mr Samuel Marsh Oram*, T. Cadell, Strand, 1794, p. 14
72 *Parliament History Shaftesbury, 1790–1820* website, 2018
73 *Report of the Commissioners appointed to enquire into the Municipal Corporations in England and Wales*, 1835, p. 1353
74 *Shaftesbury Quakers* website, 2018
75 *Dorset Historic Towns Survey: Shaftesbury*, 2011, p. 43
76 Hardy, T., *Jude the Obscure*, James R. Osgood, McIlvaine & Co, 1896, pp. 249, 250
77 *Le Roter*, p. 41
78 Minutes and Records of Friends, of the Monthly Meeting of Shaftesbury and Sherborne, from December 1804 to December 1818
79 Maxted, I., 'Farley Family', *Oxford Dictionary of National Biography* website, 2018

80 *Le Roter*, p. 41
81 Dunning, R., *Introduction to Delineations of the North Western Division of the County of Somerset and of the Mendip Caverns by John Rutter, 1829*, from a facsimile edition Amberley Publishing 2009, p. 1
82 *Rutter Family*, p. 9
83 Will of Thomas Rutter, Public Record Office
84 *Salisbury and Winchester Journal*, 7 July 1817, The British Newspaper Archive
85 Stephen, Sir L., *Dictionary of National Biography*, Volume 50, 'Rutter, John', 1897, p. 30
86 MSS 12, John Rutter, Gold Hill
87 Rutter, J., *A Brief Sketch of The History of Cranborn Chace and of the Dispute concerning its Boundaries*, Shaftesbury, 1818, S&DHS, D.H.C., D-SHS/Box 42.3375
88 Ibid
89 Delair, J.B., 'The Win Green Mosasaur', *Wiltshire Archaeological & Natural History Magazine* Volume 101, 2008, p. 6
90 *Salisbury and Winchester Journal*, 13 July 1818, The British Newspaper Archive
91 *Le Roter*, p. 40
92 *Norfolk Chronicle*, 3 May 1806, The British Newspaper Archive
93 Memoranda of Richard Clarence, containing marriage settlement and will of Charles Clarance (1761–1807), brother of Richard Clarance, S&DHS, D.H.C., D-SHS/Box 44.3400
94 Ibid
95 BMD
96 Ibid
97 *Rutter Family*, p. 10
98 *Rutter Family*, p. 25; *Le Roter*, p. 45
99 *Parliament History Shaftesbury, 1790–1820* website; and *Corruption and Reform*, p. 21
100 *Grace's Guide* website to British Industrial History, 2012
101 *Salisbury and Winchester Journal*, 3 May 1819, The British Newspaper Archive
102 *Rutter Family*, p. 19; and *Le Roter*, p. 44
103 *Salisbury and Winchester Journal*, 10 July 1820, The British Newspaper Archive
104 *The Times*, Weather Eye, 17 May 2018
105 Brougham, H., 1st Baron Brougham and Vaux, '*Speech in the case of Queen Caroline*', *Speeches of Henry Lord Brougham*, Volume I, Adam and Charles Black, Edinburgh, 1838, p. 134
106 Jenkins, T., *The Queen Caroline Affair, 1820, Hanoverians, The History of Parliament, © Crown copyright and The History of Parliament Trust 1964–2017; and* Robins, J., *Rebel Queen: How the Trial of Caroline Brought England to the Brink of Revolution*, Simon & Schuster, 2006
107 Notice entitled Bill of Pains and Penalties, dated 13 November 1820, printed by John Rutter
108 Shaftesbury Branch Bible Society, North Dorset Press, printed by John Rutter, 1820 and 1821, from a facsimile copy Gold Hill
109 Library, Society of Friends, tract box 204/49
110 *Rutter Family*, p. 11; and *Le Roter*, p. 42. Grosvenor Cottage is still standing, a

thatched cottage in Gillingham on the Shaftesbury side of the town, to the east of the River Stour

111 *Rutter Family*, p. 10

112 *Corruption and Reform*, p. 28

113 *Rutter Family*, p. 10

114 Ibid

115 Engraved illustration, Gold Hill

116 *Pigot & Co, Directory of Dorsetshire*, 1823

117 *Le Roter*, p. 42

118 *Rutter Family*, p. 11

119 Returns of Churchwardens and Overseers of the Parish of Shaftesbury St Peter, 1825 and 1829

120 *Rutter Family*, p. 12

121 *Le Roter*, p. 43

122 *The Shaftesbury Subscription Library for Circulation and Reference*, printed by John Rutter, 1827, from a facsimile copy, Gold Hill

123 Ibid; and *Rutter Family*, p.13

124 Rutter, J., *An Historical and Descriptive Account of the Town of Shaftesbury*, intended for publication in 1827 (Unfinished), D.H.C., D-50/1

125 *Rutter Family*, p. 14

126 *Salisbury and Winchester Journal*, 22 February 1830, The British Newspaper Archive

127 *Rutter Family*, p. 13

128 *Pigot & Co., Trade Directory for Shaftesbury & District*, 1830

129 *Oaths of loyalty to the Crown and Church of England, The National Archives* website, 2018

130 *Rutter Family*, p. 17

131 BMD

132 *Rutter Family*, p. 18

133 Ibid, p. 18

134 Letters dated 16 June 1837, 11 February 1839 and 19 April 1839 from Ann Elizabeth Rutter to her brother, Clarence

135 *Salisbury and Winchester Journal*, 4 November 1833, The British Newspaper Archive

136 *Salisbury and Winchester Journal*, 6 June 1832, The British Newspaper Archive

137 Letters to various clients from John Rutter. John Rutter MSS Miscellaneous Manuscripts 1829–1833, S&DHS, D.H.C., D-SHS/Box 41.3387

138 *Rutter Family*, p. 17

139 Ibid, p. 18

140 Letter dated 26 January 1832 from John Rutter to John Wallbridge. John Rutter MSS Miscellaneous Manuscripts 1829–1833, S&DHS, D.H.C., D-SHS/Box 41.3387

141 Ibid

142 Rutter Scrapbooks, Mere Museum

143 Notice printed by Clarence Rutter, Shaftesbury, September 1839, facsimile copy, Gold Hill

144 Leaflet describing Rutter's Life Pills, S&DHS, D.H.C., D-SHS/Box 44.2646

145 Innes, B., *Shaftesbury, An Illustrated History*, The Dovecote Press, Wimborne, 1992, p. 72
146 *The Musical Times*, 30 September 1864, Advertisement placed by Clarence Rutter
147 *Rutter Family*, p. 18
148 Letter dated 4 September 1847 from Llewellyn Rutter to his father, John Rutter, MS Portfolio of Joseph Rutter
149 Letters dated 16 June 1837, 11 February 1839 and 19 April 1839 from Ann Elizabeth Rutter to her brother, Clarence; and letters dated 10 August 1848 and 11 September 1848 from Llewellyn Rutter to his mother, Anne Rutter, MS Portfolio of Joseph Rutter
150 Letter dated 4 April 1836 from John Rutter to John Farley Rutter; letter dated 16 June 1837 from Ann Elizabeth Rutter to her brother, Clarence
151 Letter dated 1838 from Llewellyn Rutter to his brother, Clarence
152 Letter dated 11 February 1839 from Ann Elizabeth Rutter to her brother, Clarence
153 Letter dated 23 February 1844 from Llewellyn Rutter to his mother
154 Letter dated 10 August 1848 from Llewellyn Rutter to his mother; letter dated 11 September 1848 from Llewellyn Rutter to his mother; letter dated 26 October 1848 from Clarence Rutter to Llewellyn.
155 *Shaftesbury Corporation and Municipal Corporation Council Minutes*, Gold Hill
156 *Rutter Family*, p. 16
157 Ibid, p. 17
158 *Salisbury and Winchester Journal*, 13 April 1840, The British Newspaper Archive
159 *Robson's Directory*, 1839, Gold Hill; *London Gazette*, 4 February 1845, The Jurist, No. 422 Volume IX, 8 February 1845; and *Salisbury and Winchester Journal*, 1 February 1845
160 *Rutter Family*, p. 13
161 Ibid, p. 13
162 Ibid, p. 17
163 Census Return, 1841
164 Tithe Apportionment for Shaftesbury, 1846
165 There are 40 perches in a rood and four roods in an acre
166 Tithe Apportionment for Shaftesbury, 1846
167 Ibid
168 Architect's drawing of 1847 in the possession of Sir John & Lady Stuttard
169 Letter dated 26 October 1848 from Clarence Rutter to his brother, Llewellyn, MS Portfolio of Joseph Rutter
170 *Kelly's Directory*, 1895 and Ordnance Survey, 25 inch, England and Wales, Dorset IV.14, 1901 and Auction Sale particulars of The major portion of the Town of Shaftesbury, Dorsetshire, by Messrs. Fox & Sons of Properties for Sale in Shaftesbury, May 27th, 28th & 29th 1919
171 Letter dated 21 August 1850 from John Rutter, Manchester Libraries, Information and Archives - Courtesy of Manchester Libraries, Information and Archives, Manchester City Council
172 MS Diary of Llewellyn Rutter, Portfolio of Joseph Rutter
173 BMD

174 *Rutter Family*; and *Salisbury and Winchester Journal*, 5 April 1851, The British Newspaper Archive
175 Letter dated 4 April 1851 from Clarence Rutter to family and friends, MS Portfolio of Joseph Rutter
176 Burial Notes of the Shaftesbury and Sherborne Monthly Meeting, Volume 50, 1838 to 1851
177 Death notice, Dorset County Chronicle, 23 January 1879, The British Newspaper Archive
178 BMD
179 *Salisbury and Winchester Journal*, 8 September 1855, The British Newspaper Archive
180 *Rutter Family*
181 *Salisbury and Winchester Journal*, 29 March 1856, The British Newspaper Archive
182 *Report of Shaftesbury Branch Bible Society*, 1820 and 1821, printed by John Rutter, North Dorset Press, Gold Hill
183 *Rutter Family*, p. 10; and *Le Roter*, p. 42
184 *Shaftesbury Poor*
185 Slack, P., *The English poor law*, 1531–1782, Cambridge University Press, 1995, p. 34
186 Ibid, p. 22
187 Brundage, A., *The English Poor Laws*, 1770–1930, Palgrave, 2002, p. 25
188 Minchinton, W.E., 'Agricultural Returns and the Government during the Napoleonic Wars', *Agricultural History Review*, 1953, p. 29
189 Klingaman, W.K., *The Year Without Summer*, St Martin's Press, 2013
190 Slack, P., *The English poor law, 1531–1782*, Cambridge University Press, 1995, p. 22
191 Purdy, F., *The Statistics of the English Poor Rate before and since the Passing of the Poor Law Amendment Act*, Journal of the Statistical Society of London, Volume 23, No. 3 (Sep., 1860), Wiley for the Royal Statistical Society, 2013, p. 289
192 Adams, T., *A history of the ancient town of Shaftesbury*, 1808, p. 58
193 *Dorset Historic Towns Survey: Shaftesbury*, 2011, p. 38
194 *Statute law repeals: nineteenth report, draft Statute Law (Repeals) Bill*, by Great Britain Law Commission
195 *Dorset Historic Towns Survey: Shaftesbury*, 2011, p. 43
196 Kerr, B., *Bound to the Soil, A Social History of Dorset, 1750–1918*, John Baker, Pall Mall, 1968, p. 93
197 Griffin, C.J., 'Parish farms and the poor law: a response to unemployment in rural southern England, c.1815–35', *The Agricultural History Review*, 2011, p. 177
198 McDowell, A., *Dorset Buttons* website, 2018
199 *The parliamentary gazetteer of England and Wales, adapted to the new poor-law, franchise, municipal and ecclesiastical arrangements, and comp. with a special reference to the lines of railroad and canal communication, as existing in 1840–1844*
200 *Shaftesbury Poor*, p. *iv*
201 Ibid, p. 8
202 Ibid, p. 9
203 Ibid, p. 10

204 Ibid, p. 12
205 Slack., P., *The English poor law, 1531–1782*, Cambridge University Press, 1995, p. 28
206 *Shaftesbury Poor*, p. 12
207 Ibid, p. 17
208 Ibid, p. 18
209 Ibid, p. 19
210 Ibid, p. 28
211 Ibid, P. 29
212 Ibid, p. 29
213 Ibid, p. 35
214 Ibid, p. 36
215 *Annual Report of the Poor Law Board*, 1850, p. 118
216 Higginbotham, P., *Shaftesbury, Dorset, The Workhouse*, Peter Higginbotham website http://www.workhouses.org.uk, 2018; and *Dorset Historic Towns Survey: Shaftesbury*, 2011, p. 48
217 *Historic England* website, 2015
218 *The Gentleman's Magazine: and Historical Chronicle*, from July to December 1822, Volume 92 Part 2, printed by John Nichols, 1822, p. 258
219 Now Esztergom, in northern Hungary
220 Granger, The Rev. J., *A Biographical History of England*, From Egbert the Great to the Revolution, Volume I, William Baynes and Son, Paternoster Row, London, 1824, p. 246
221 *Hansard*, HL Deb 26 April 1993 Volume 545 cc1–4
222 Fermor, P.L., *Between the Woods and the Water*, John Murray, 1986, p. 33
223 *Wardour Castle*, p. 4
224 Ibid, p. 12
225 Ibid, p. 14
226 Firth, C.H., revised by Worden, B., 'Ludlow, Edmund', *Oxford Dictionary of National Biography*, 2004
227 *Wardour Castle*, p. 25
228 Ibid, p. 16
229 Ibid, p. 20
230 Ibid, p. 30–33
231 Ibid, p. 45
232 *Rutter Family*, p. 10; and *Le Roter*, p.42
233 *Historic England* website, 2018
234 *Life at Fonthill*, p. 295
235 *Delineations of Fonthill*, p. 107
236 Hewat-Jaboor, P., Chapter III, 'Fonthill House', in *William Beckford 1760 – 1844: An Eye for the Magnificent*, edited by Derek E Ostergard, Yale University Press, New Haven and London for The Bard Graduate Center for Studies in the Decorative Arts, Design and Culture, 2001, p. 67
237 Lees-Milne, J., *William Beckford*, Michael Russell Publishing, 1976, p. 60; *The Morning Post*, 22 September 1823; and Bleiler, E.F. (ed.), *Three Gothic Novels*, Dover Publications, 1966, preface
238 *Beckford of Fonthill*, p. 149

239 *Gentleman's Magazine*, March, April 1801, pp. 206–208, 297–298
240 *Beckford of Fonthill*, p. 277
241 Wilton, A., *Architectural Drawings for Commissions c.1797–1800*, subset, March 2013, in Brown, D.B. (ed.), *J.M.W. Turner: Sketchbooks, Drawings and Watercolours*, Tate Research Publication, April 2015, *Tate* website https://www.tate.org.uk/art/research-publications/jmw-turner/architectural-drawings-for-commissions-r1174078, accessed 21 May 2018
242 'Notes on Gardens and Country Seats, visited, from July 27 to September 16, 1833', by the Conductor, *The Gardener's Magazine*, Volume 11 (ed. Loudon, J.C.), Longman, Rees, Orme, Brown, Green, and Longman, Paternoster-Row, London, September 1835, p.448; and as also reported in '*The Literary Chronicle*', *Carey's Library of Choice Literature*, No. 7. – Part I. – Nov. 14, 1835
243 *The Gentleman's Magazine: and Historical Chronicle*, Volume XCII Part The Second, from July to December 1822, printed by John Nichols, 1822, p. 258
244 *Colt Hoare History, p. 23*
245 *Souvenirs of Fonthill*, p. 7; and *Antiques Trade Gazette*, 15 June 2012, *Antiques Trade Gazette* website, 2018
246 Stephen, Sir L., *Dictionary of National Biography*, Volume 50, '*Rutter, John*', 1897
247 Millington, J., 'John Rutter's *A History and Description of Fonthill Abbey and Demesne*, 1822', *The Beckford Journal*, Volume 13, Spring 2007, The Beckford Society, pp. 42–53.
248 Rutter, J., *A Description of Fonthill Abbey and Demesne*, Shaftesbury, 1822, Fifth Edition, S&DHS, D.H.C., D-SHS/Box 43.3365; and *Souvenirs of Fonthill*, p. 11
249 *Souvenirs of Fonthill*, p.7
250 *Souvenirs of Fonthill*, p. 7
251 *Colt Hoare History*, p. 27
252 *Souvenirs of Fonthill*, p. 7
253 Millington, J. (ed.), 'Recollections of the Author of Vathek', *The New Monthly Magazine*, 1844, Part The Second, incorporated into *Conversations with Beckford*, The Beckford Society, 2014, p. 155
254 *Souvenirs of Fonthill*, p. 8
255 Rutter, J., *A New Descriptive Guide to Fonthill Abbey and Demesne*, 1823, S&DHS, D.H.C., D-SHS/Box 43.3365
256 Unidentified Newspaper, British Newspaper Archive; Clarke, S., 'Serendipity in Tunbridge Wells', *The Beckford Journal*, Volume 23, 2017, p. 46
257 *Colt Hoare History*, p. 27
258 Aldrich, A., Chapter VII, 'Fonthill Abbey', in *William Beckford 1760 – 1844: An Eye for the Magnificent* (ed. Ostergard, D.E.), Yale University Press, New Haven and London for The Bard Graduate Center for Studies in the Decorative Arts, Design and Culture, 2001, p. 127; and *Beckford of Fonthill*, p. 309
259 'Notes on Gardens and Country Seats, visited, from July 27 to September 16, 1833', by the Conductor, *The Gardener's Magazine*, Volume 11 (ed. Loudon, J.C.), Longman, Rees, Orme, Brown, Green, and Longman, Paternoster-Row, London, September 1835, pp. 445, 446
260 Millington, J. (ed.), 'Recollections of the Author of Vathek', *The New Monthly Magazine*, 1844, Part The Second, incorporated into *Conversations with Beckford*,

The Beckford Society, 2014, p. 155
261 Thurley, S., *Lost Buildings of Britain*, Penguin Books Ltd, 2004, p. 70
262 *Life at Fonthill*, p. 173
263 Ibid, p. 173
264 Ibid, p. 180
265 Ibid, p. 180
266 Ibid, p. 188
267 Ibid, p. 219
268 *The Times*, 'Weather Eye', 15 March 2018
269 Letter dated 27 April 1818 from John Keats, Teignmouth, to John Hamilton Reynolds
270 Philip Proctor, April 2018
271 *Beckford of Fonthill*, p. 308
272 *Colt Hoare History*, p. 27
273 Dakers, C., *Fonthill Recovered*, UCL Press, 2018, p. 193
274 *Historic England* website, 2018
275 *Literary Gazette*, 6 October 1823, p. 639
276 *Delineations of Fonthill*, pp. 119–127
277 Letter dated 1822 (no exact date) from Sir Richard Colt Hoare, Bt to the Reverend Daniel Lysons, DZSWS MSS 751.33, Wiltshire Museum, Devizes
278 *Salisbury and Winchester Journal*, 30 September 1822, The British Newspaper Archive
279 Clarke, S., 'The Troubled Gestation of Britton's *Illustrations of Fonthill*', *The Beckford Journal*, Volume 6, Spring 2000, The Beckford Society, p. 60
280 *Life at Fonthill*, p. 229
281 Letter dated 3 October 1822 from William Beckford to John Britton, MSS. Beckford c27, fol. 15cv, Special Collections, Weston Library, Bodleian Libraries
282 Clarke, S., 'The Troubled Gestation of Britton's *Illustrations of Fonthill*', *The Beckford Journal*, Volume 6, Spring 2000, The Beckford Society, p. 64
283 *Souvenirs of Fonthill*, p. 8
284 Clarke, S., 'The Troubled Gestation of Britton's *Illustrations of Fonthill*', *The Beckford Journal*, Volume 6, Spring 2000, The Beckford Society, p. 65
285 BMD
286 Letter dated 15 November 1822 from John Rutter to J.B. Nichols & Son. MSS Portfolio Volume 15. 64, Library, Society of Friends
287 Undated note by Nichols & Son. MSS Portfolio Volume 15. 64, Library, Society of Friends
288 *The Literary Gazette*, No 301, 26 October 1822, p. 686
289 *Souvenirs of Fonthill*, p. 8
290 *The Gentleman's Magazine: and Historical Chronicle*, Volume XCIII, July to December 1823, Part the Second, printed by John Nichols, 1823, p. 346
291 Ibid, p. 345
292 Ibid, p. 345
293 Russell, Lord J. (ed.), *Memoirs, Journal, and Correspondence of Thomas Moore*, Volume II, D Appleton and Company, New York, 1857; and Stephen, Sir L., *Dictionary of National Biography, Volume 50, 'Rutter*, John', 1897, p. 30
294 Clarke, S., 'The Troubled Gestation of Britton's *Illustrations of Fonthill*', *The*

Beckford Journal, Volume 6, Spring 2000, The Beckford Society, p. 71

295 *Delineations of Fonthill*, p. *vii*

296 Ibid, pp. 2–65

297 Atterbury, P. (ed.), *A.W.N. Pugin Master of Gothic Revival*, Yale University Press, New York for The Bard Graduate Center for Studies in the Decorative Arts, 1995 Copyright © The Bard Graduate Center for Studies in the Decorative Arts; and *Delineations of Fonthill*, p. 20

298 *Delineations of Fonthill*, p. 61–63

299 Ibid, p. 63

300 Ibid, p. 63

301 *Le Roter*, p. 42

302 *Corruption and Reform*, p. 28

303 *Rutter Family*, p. 10

304 *Souvenirs of Fonthill*, p. 7

305 *Brodick Castle & Country Park*, National Trust for Scotland, 1987, p. 6

306 *Bristol Radical History Group* website, 2016; and Martin, J., *Oratory, itinerant lecturing and Victorian popular politics: a case study of James Acland (1799–1876)*, Wiley Online Library, John Wiley & Sons, Inc, 2018

307 *Swyer versus Rutter*, p. 90

308 Rutter D.H.C., D-50/1

309 Hardy, T., *Jude the Obscure*, James R. Osgood, McIlvaine & Co, 1896, p. 250

310 Letter dated 7 August 1825 from Lord Grosvenor, S&DHS, D.H.C., D-SHS/Box 41.3421

311 Howarth, F. and Young, J.A., *A brief history of the water supply of Shaftesbury, Dorset, West Wilts Water Board*, S&DHS, 1972, p. 17

312 Rutter, D.H.C., D50/1

313 Ibid

314 *Salisbury and Winchester Journal*, 14 October 1822, The British Newspaper Archive

315 Rutter, J., *Extracts, &c. concerning the Prevalence of Vagrancy in some of the Western Counties of England, The Means of its Correction, and the Necessary Relief of Distressed Travellers*, 1827, from a facsimile copy, Shaftesbury Library, p. 1

316 Report of the Secretary of the Mendicity Society for the Shaftesbury District, 14 January 1828, printed (gratis) by John Rutter

317 Letter dated December 1827 from John Rutter to Nichols & Son. MSS Portfolio Volume 15. 69, Library, Society of Friends

318 Letter dated 3 October 1828 from John Rutter to Nichols & Son. MSS Portfolio Volume 15. 70, Library, Society of Friends

319 Notice to potential subscribers printed by J. Rutter. Portfolio 15.70, Library, Society of Friends

320 Letter dated 2 June 1829 from John Rutter to Nichols & Son. MSS Portfolio Volume 15.73, Library, Society of Friends

321 *Delineations of Somerset*, included in the Advertisement

322 Foster, J.J., *Wessex Worthies (Dorset)*, Dickinsons, London, 1920, pp. 77–82; *William Barnes Society* website, 2018; *Dorset County Museum* website, 2018

323 Webb, Dr A, (ed.), Chapter on Tourism in Somerset by Sue Berry, from *Maritime History of Somerset*, The Somerset Archaeological and Natural History Society,

2014
324 *Rutter Family*, p. 14
325 Turner, A., *Aspects of the Paleoecology of Large Predators, including Man, during the British Upper Pleistocene, with particular emphasis on Predator-Prey Relationships*. This thesis was submitted for the degree of Doctor of Philosophy in the University of Sheffield, Department of Prehistory and Archaeology, May 1981, included in bibliography
326 *Delineations of Somerset*, p. 30
327 Ibid, p. 42
328 Ibid, pp. 277–333
329 Milligan, E.H., *Biographical Dictionary of British Quakers in Commerce & Industry 1775–1920*, William Sessions Limited, York, 2007, pp. 381–382
330 Rutter, J., *The Westonian Guide*, Shaftesbury, 1829, Introduction
331 Ibid, p. 25
332 Ibid, p. 87
333 *Delineations of Somerset*, p 267
334 *Quakers in Britain*, Britain Yearly Meeting of the Religious Society of Friends (Quakers), 2018
335 Jones, R.M. (ed.), *George Fox – An Autobiography*, Scriptura Press, 1909, Copyright at Scriptura Press, 2015, p. 62
336 *Quaker Faith & Practice,* Religious Society of Friends (Quakers), chapter 19, p. 32
337 Braithwaite, W.C., *Second Period of Quakerism*, Macmillan, 1919, p. 207
338 Besse, J., *A Collection of the Sufferings of the People called Quakers for the Testimony of a Good Conscience*, L. Hinde, London, 1753, pp. 539–638
339 Raistrick, A., *Quakers in Science and Industry*, The Bannisdale Press, London, 1950, p. 36
340 Lacock, R., 'Quakers in Gloucester: the first fifty years', *1655–1705*, *Bristol and Gloucestershire Archaeological Society*, 2007, pp. 268, 271
341 Raistrick, A., *Quakers in Science and Industry*, The Bannisdale Press, London, 1950, p. 33
342 'The Pease Family', *Quakers in the World* website, 2018
343 *Quakers in the World* website, 2018
344 *Barclays Bank* website, 2018
345 *Lloyds Banking Group* website, 2018
346 *Quakers in the World* website, 2018; *C & J Clark International's* website, 2018; and 'The Founding Fathers', *Huntley & Palmers'* website, 2018
347 *Shaftesbury Quakers'* website, 2018
348 *Rutter Family*, p. 19; and *Le Roter*, p. 44
349 Milligan, E.H., *Biographical Dictionary of British Quakers in Commerce & Industry 1775–1920*, William Sessions Limited, York, 2007, pp. 381–382
350 *Advices & Queries*, The Yearly Meeting of the Religious Society of Friends (Quakers) in Britain, 1995
351 Letter dated 27 April 1830. John Rutter MSS Miscellaneous Manuscripts 1829–1833, S&DHS, D.H.C., D-SHS/Box 41.3387
352 Thomas, A.B., *The Beaconite Controversy*, Bulletin of Friends' Historical Society, (Philadelphia) Volume IV, no. 2 (Third Month, 1912), retrieved from the

website of The Quaker Writings Home page, maintained by Peter Sippel

353 *Salisbury and Winchester Journal*, 29 September 1834 and 23 July 1838, The British Newspaper Archive; Notices by Clarence Rutter, facsimile copies, Gold Hill

354 Smith, J., *A Descriptive Catalogue of Friends' Books*, Volume II, 1867, p. 520

355 *Le Roter*, p. 44

356 Letter dated 19 April 1839 from Ann Elizabeth Rutter to her brother, Clarence

357 *Rutter Family*, p. 22

358 Minutes of the Monthly Meetings of Friends of Shaftesbury and Sherborne, Volume 60, October 1838 to December 1841

359 Ibid

360 *Rutter Family*, p. 25

361 *The Baptist Magazine*, December 1838, Volume 30, George Wightman, Paternoster Row, London, p.548

362 *The Inquirer*, Volume II, January 1839, by General Tract Depot, London, printed by John Wertheimer and Co, London, 1839, p. 43

363 *The Church Magazine*, Volume I, printed by Hayward & Moore, London, 1839, p. 384

364 *Salisbury and Winchester Journal*, 24 December 1838, The British Newspaper Archive

365 *Salisbury and Winchester Journal*, 29 September 1834, The British Newspaper Archive

366 *Independent Order of Rechabites, King Alfred Tent*, DC-SYB/I/3

367 *The Temperance Recorder*, Third Series, No 1, August 1842, p. 128

368 Ibid, p. 108

369 Rutter Scrapbooks, Mere Museum

370 *Sherborne Mercury*, 1 July 1843, The British Newspaper Archive

371 *Sherborne Mercury*, 13 July 1844, The British Newspaper Archive

372 *The Ipswich Journal*, 28 January 1837, The British Newspaper Archive

373 Notice dated 5 January 1837, Shaftesbury, printed by C. Rutter and Wallbridge

374 '*Temperance, Longevity, Insurance. A Tract for the Times*', Temperance and Life Assurance Company of North America, published by the *Canada Citizen*, Toronto, 1884

375 *Aviva Group* website, Our History, 2018 (Note: UKPI, as it was later named, was taken over by Friends Provident which is now part of the Aviva Group)

376 Ibid

377 *Vindicator*, 7 May 1842, The British Newspaper Archive

378 *Rutter Family*, p. 20; *Le Roter*, p. 44

379 *Journal of the American Temperance Union*, Volume X, 1 October 1846, New York, part of The James Black Collection, presented by the National Temperance Society to the New York Public Library, p. 156

380 Press cutting relating to the World Temperance Convention, V.58, Library, Society of Friends

381 *Bristol Mercury*, 27 May 1848, The British Newspaper Archive

382 Rutter Scrapbooks, Mere Museum

383 Hudson, T., Temperance Pioneers of the West, second edition, National Temperance Publication Depot, 1888, The Selwood Printing Works, Frome

and London, p. 181
384 *Quakers in the World* website, 2018
385 Carey, B., Plank, G., *Quakers & Abolition,* University of Illinois Press, 2004, p. 171
386 *Quakers in the World* website, 2018
387 Barlow, A., *He is our cousin, Cousin" - A Quaker Family's History from 1660 to the Present Day*, Quacks Books, York, 2015, chapter 8
388 Notice printed by C. Rutter and Wallbridge, March 1838, Mere Museum
389 Minute Book of the Council of the Borough of Shaftesbury in the County of Dorset, 1835 to 1857, p.84, DC/SYB/B/1/4
390 *The British and Foreign Anti-slavery Reporter,* 20 October 1841, The British and Foreign Anti-Slavery Society, p. 232
391 *Rutter Family,* p. 20; *Le Roter,* p. 44
392 The cream top hat is now in the possession of Simon Rutter, a descendant of John Rutter
393 *Bristol Times and Mirror,* 5 & 12 October, 1850, The British Newspaper Archive
394 *The International Committee of the Red Cross* website, October 2016
395 Milligan, E.H., *Biographical Dictionary of British Quakers in Commerce & Industry 1775–1920*, William Sessions Limited, York, 2007, pp. 381–382
396 Burial Notes of the Shaftesbury and Sherborne Monthly Meeting, Volume 50, 1838 to 1851
397 *Rutter Family,* p. 25
398 *Parliament History Shaftesbury, 1754–1790* website
399 Evans, E.J., *The Great Reform Act of 1832,* Routledge, London, 1994, p. 9
400 Parliament History Shaftesbury, 1754–1790 website
401 Ibid
402 Hutchins, J., *History and Antiquities of The County of Dorset*: Third Volume, John Bowyer Nichols and Sons, London, 1868; and The Shaftesbury Election or the Humours of Punch, Gold Hill
403 Parliament History Shaftesbury, 1754–1790 website
404 *Swyer versus Rutter,* p. 6
405 Handy, M., 'Shaftesbury: Pocket Borough', *Dorset Life Magazine,* July 2015, *Dorset Life* website; and MSS 12, John Rutter, Gold Hill
406 A capital burgess was akin to a modern day councillor
407 *Corruption and Reform,* p. 12
408 Ibid, p.9
409 Ibid, pp. 12 and 14
410 Ibid, p.14
411 Ibid, pp. 13 and 14
412 Ibid, p. 14
413 Ibid, p.15
414 Thomas, R., *An Evening with Shaftesbury's (almost) Forgotten Poet: Samuel Marsh Oram (1765–1791),* Swans Trust, p. 42
415 *Corruption and Reform,* p. 18
416 *Shaftesbury Borough,* D.H.C., DC-SYB/D/13/7
417 *Corruption and Reform,* p. 18
418 Ibid, pp. 20 and 24

419 Ibid, pp. 12 and 24
420 Ibid, p. 22; and Hopton 1830 Election, p. 24; and *Parliament History Shaftesbury, 1820–1832* website
421 *Corruption and Reform*, p. 27
422 Cockburn, E.O., *The Almshouses of Dorset*, The Friary Press, Dorchester, 1970, p. 41
423 Innes, B., *Shaftesbury, An Illustrated History*, The Dovecote Press, Wimborne, 1992, p. 72
424 *Corruption and Reform*, p. 4; and *Parliament History Shaftesbury, 1820–1832* website
425 This would have been the attorney John Jones of 2 New Square, Lincoln's Inn
426 *Le Roter*, p. 42
427 Handy, M., 'Shaftesbury: Pocket Borough', *Dorset Life Magazine*, July 2015, *Dorset Life* website; *Rutter 1830 Election*, p. 32; and *Hopton 1830 Election*, p. 25
428 *Corruption and Reform*, p. 28
429 Ibid, p. 28
430 *The Ballot Act, 1872*
431 *Parliament History Shaftesbury, 1820–1832* website
432 Ibid
433 *Swyer versus Rutter*, p. 7
434 Corruption and Reform, p. 29
435 Jervoise, E., *Notes on Shaftesbury Inns &c. from various sources*, from a facsimile copy, Shaftesbury Library, p. *iii*
436 *Corruption and Reform*, p. 29
437 *Salisbury and Winchester Journal*, 22 March 1824, The British Newspaper Archive
438 *Parliament History Shaftesbury, 1820–1832* website; and Bowles, C., *An Account of the Proceedings at Shaftesbury in consequence of the Resignation of the Recordership by Charles Bowles, with Explanatory Notes and Remarks*, Second Edition, February 1828, from a facsimile copy, Shaftesbury Library, Introduction, p. *vii*
439 *The Shastonian* No II, Shaftesbury, 10 October 1826, S&DHS, D.H.C., D-SHS/Box 40.3393, p. 32
440 *Swyer versus Rutter*, p. 10 and Appendix C; and *Defence of Rutter*, Appendix C
441 Jervoise, E., *Notes on Shaftesbury Inns &c. from various sources*, from a facsimile copy, Shaftesbury Library, p. *iii*
442 Innes, B., *Shaftesbury, An Illustrated History*, The Dovecote Press, Wimborne, 1992, p. 68
443 *Swyer versus Rutter*, p. 11 and Appendix B; and *Defence of Rutter*, Appendix B
444 Innes, B., *Shaftesbury, An Illustrated History*, The Dovecote Press, Wimborne, 1992, p. 68
445 *Corruption and Reform* p. 30
446 Swyer versus Rutter, p. 12; and *Defence of Rutter*, Appendix A
447 *The Times*, 16 August 1826, The British Newspaper Archive
448 *The Atlas*, 20 August 1826, The British Newspaper Archive
449 *Swyer versus Rutter*, p. 20; *and Defence of Rutter*, p. 20
450 Innes, B., *Shaftesbury, An Illustrated History*, The Dovecote Press, Wimborne, 1992, p. 68

451 *Defence of Rutter,* title page
452 Ibid, p. 12
453 *The Shastonian* No I, Shaftesbury, 2 October 1826, S&DHS, D.H.C., D-SHS/Box 40.3393, title page
454 Ibid, p. 14
455 Ibid, p. 15
456 Ibid, p. 16
457 *Swyer versus Rutter,* p. 20
458 Ibid, pp. 30, 31
459 Ibid, p. 40
460 Ibid, p. 52
461 *The Dorset County Chronicle,* 12 October 1826, The British Newspaper Archive
462 *The Dorset County Chronicle,* 16 October 1826, The British Newspaper Archive
463 *Swyer versus Rutter,* p. 65
464 Ibid, p. 73
465 *The Shastonian* No II, Shaftesbury, 10 October 1826, S&DHS, D.H.C., D-SHS/Box 40.3393, p. 38
466 Ibid, p. 34
467 The Shastonian No III, Shaftesbury, 1 November 1826, S&DHS, D.H.C., D-SHS/Box 40.3393, pp. 59–65
468 *Corruption and Reform,* p. 32
469 *Swyer versus Rutter,* p. 67
470 Ibid, p. 69
471 Ibid, p. 72
472 Ibid, p. 77
473 *Rutter Family,* p. 13
474 Acland, J., *John Rutter, Enemy of Corporate Despots, Memoirs and Correspondences of a Ghost,* 1827, licensed under a Creative Commons Attribution-Noncommercial - No Derivative Works 3.0 Unported License, 2010
475 Ibid
476 Letter dated 11 February 1829 from John Rutter to Philip Chitty. John Rutter MSS Miscellaneous Manuscripts 1829–1833, S&DHS, D.H.C., D-SHS/Box 41.3387
477 Letter dated 26 February 1829 from John Rutter to Edward Buckland. John Rutter MSS Miscellaneous Manuscripts 1829–1833, S&DHS, D.H.C., D-SHS/Box 41.3387
478 *Corruption and Reform,* p. 37
479 *Dorset County Chronicle,* 8 October 1829, The British Newspaper Archive; and *Parliament History Shaftesbury, 1820–1832* website
480 *Rutter 1830 Election,* p. 66
481 This could be a reference to either Charles Hannen or George Chitty who supported Rutter in his fight against the political clique
482 Anonymous letter annotated about May 1829 to John Rutter. John Rutter MSS Miscellaneous Manuscripts 1829–1833, S&DHS, D.H.C., D-SHS/Box 41.3387
483 *Rutter 1830 Election,* various mentions; and *Hopton 1830 Election,* pp. 24–27
484 *Dictionary of National Biography* Volume VII, 1972, p. 214
485 Letter dated 20 July 1830 from John Rutter to the Prime Minister, Rutter,

D.H.C., D-50/3
486 *Rutter 1830 Election*, p. 16
487 Ibid, p. 29
488 Ibid, p. 32
489 Ibid, p. 36
490 Ibid, p. 35
491 Ibid, p. 37
492 Ibid, p. 37
493 Ibid, p. 46
494 Ibid, p. 48
495 Ibid, p. 48
496 Ibid, pp. 70–74
497 Ibid, p. 74
498 *Rutter 1830 Election*, p. 74
499 Ibid, p. 141
500 Ibid, p. 143
501 *Rutter 1830 Election*, p. 76
502 Ibid p. 83; and *Hopton 1830 Election*, p. 26
503 *Evening Mail*, 9 August 1830, The British Newspaper Archive
504 *Rutter 1830 Election*, p. 142
505 Ibid, p. 148
506 Ibid, p. 83
507 *Dorset County Chronicle*, 30 September 1830, The British Newspaper Archive
508 *Rutter 1830 Election*, p. 159; and *Hopton 1830 Election*, p. 26
509 *Hopton 1830 Election*, p. 26; and *Salisbury and Winchester Journal*, 1 September 1831, The British Newspaper Archive
510 *Rutter 1830 Election*, p. 159
511 Ibid, p. 160
512 Ibid, p. 164
513 Lord Grosvenor, of course, but not spelled out
514 Reid, T.W., *Life of The Right Honourable William Edward Forster*, Volume I, Chapman and Hall, London, 1888. Taken from a digitised copy, made by Google, of an original third edition book held by Harvard University Library, pp. 44, 45
515 Ibid, p. 45
516 *Rutter 1830 Election*, Appendix entitled 'List of those who have received Notices to Quit the Earl Grosvenor's property, up to October 18th, 1830'
517 *Rutter 1830 Election*, Practical Reform in Parliament, p. 6
518 Ibid, p 5 519 Hobsbawm, E., and Rudé, G., *Captain Swing*, Verso,, 2014, p. 72
520 Kerr, B., *Bound to the Soil, A social history of Dorset, 1750–1918*, by John Baker, Pall Mall, London, 1968, p.100
521 Ibid, p. 100
522 Hobsbawm, E., and Rudé, G., *Captain Swing*, Verso,, 2014, pp. 260–262
523 Ibid, p. 215
524 *Rex versus Rutter*, p. 134
525 *Rutter 1830 Election*, Appendix entitled *Borough-Mongering Prosecutions at Shaftesbury, March Assizes, held at Dorchester, 1831*, p. 2

526 Ibid
527 *Hopton 1830 Election*, p. 28
528 *Dorset County Chronicle*, 1 April 1831, The British Newspaper Archive; and *Parliament History Shaftesbury, 1820–1832* website
529 *Dorset County Chronicle*, 1 April 1831, The British Newspaper Archive; and *Parliament History Shaftesbury, 1820–1832* website
530 *Parliament History Shaftesbury, 1820–1832* website
531 *Evening Mail*, 16 May 1841, The British Newspaper Archive
532 *Rutter Family*, p. 16
533 *Dorset County Chronicle*, 22 & 29 September 1831, *The Times*, 23 September & 1 October 1831, The British Newspaper Archive
534 Notices printed by Barnstable of Shaftesbury, Gold Hill
535 Evans, E.J., *The Great Reform Act of 1832*, Routledge, London, 1994, pp. 68, 69
536 Ibid, p. 63
537 Ibid, p. 2
538 Correspondence of John Rutter of Shaftesbury concerning Shaftesbury elections, 1830 to 1833, Rutter, D.H.C., D-50/3
539 Letter from John Rutter to the Marquess of Westminster, 26 June 1832, Grosvenor Estate Archives
540 *Parliament History Shaftesbury, 1820–1832* website
541 Notice of Election 1832 - *A Song for the Merry Men of Shaston. Old Voters, New Voters, Voters Altogether, signed 'QUIN'*, printed by Neave of Gillingham
542 *Parliament History Shaftesbury, 1820–1832* website
543 *Sherborne Mercury*, 14 March 1834, The British Newspaper Archive
544 Westminster, open letter dated 2 January 1835 to Electors of Shaftesbury, Thomas Shirley's Scrapbooks, S&DHS, D.H.C., D-SHS/Box 44.2646
545 Grosvenor, open letter dated 6 December 1834 to Electors of Shaftesbury, Thomas Shirley's Scrapbooks, S&DHS, D.H.C., D-SHS/Box 44.2646
546 *Rutter Family*, p. 16
547 *Corruption and Reform*, p. 3
548 *The Report of the Commissioners appointed to enquire into the Municipal Corporations in England and Wales*, March 1835, p. 1353
549 Ibid, p. 1356
550 *The Parliamentary Gazetteer of England and Wales*, Volume IV, A Fullarton & Co, 1851, Volume IV, p. 94
551 *Corruption and Reform*, p. 41
552 Ibid, p. 41
553 This was *Swyer versus Rutter*
554 *Le Roter*, p. 43
555 *An Account of the Sufferings of Friends of the Monthly Meetings of Shaftesbury and Sherborne*, Volume No 57, 1793 to 1836
556 *Tipperary Free Press*, 30 April 1842, The British Newspaper Archive
557 *Salisbury and Winchester Journal*, 16 March 1840, The British Newspaper Archive
558 Letter dated 2 February 1829 from John Rutter to The Prime Minister. John Rutter MSS Miscellaneous Manuscripts 1829–1833, S&DHS, D.H.C., D-SHS/ Box 41.3387. Note: New Holland was the historical name for Australia given by

the Dutch seafarer, Abel Tasman, in 1644

559 Letter dated 13 February 1829 from Downing Street to John Rutter. John Rutter MSS Miscellaneous Manuscripts 1829–1833, S&DHS, D.H.C., D-SHS/Box 41.3387

560 Minute Book of the Council of the Borough of Shaftesbury in the County of Dorset, 1835 to 1857, p. 2, D.H.C., DC/SYB/B/1/4

561 The Shaftesbury Gas Company Minutes, 1836–1890, Gold Hill

562 Minute Book of the Council of the Borough of Shaftesbury in the County of Dorset, 1835 to 1857, p. 93, D.H.C., DC/SYB/B/1/4

563 Ibid, p. 95

564 Ibid, pp. 7–134

565 Ibid, p. 127

566 Notice to the Owners of Property and Rate-Payers of the Parish of St Peter, Shaftesbury, dated 12 October 1835, printed by Clarence Rutter

567 MSS *Mems on proceedings of the Shaftesbury Board of Guardians of Shaftesbury Poor Law Union by Rutter, Vice-Chairman from Nov 1835 to March 1837*, Gold Hill, pp. 1–15; and letter dated 15 March 1837 from John Rutter to Fellow Parishioners in the Parish of St. Peter, Shaftesbury, Layton Cottage, printed by Bastable of Shaftesbury, Gold Hill

568 Innes, B., *Shaftesbury, An Illustrated History*, The Dovecote Press, Wimborne, 1992, p. 73

569 MSS *Mems on proceedings of the Shaftesbury Board of Guardians of Shaftesbury Poor Law Union by Rutter, Vice-Chairman from Nov 1835 to March 1837*, Gold Hill, pp. 1–15; and letter dated 15 March 1837 from John Rutter to Fellow Parishioners in the Parish of St. Peter, Shaftesbury, Layton Cottage, printed by Bastable of Shaftesbury, Gold Hill

570 Ibid

571 *Dorset County Chronicle*, 28 September 1837, The British Newspaper Archive

572 Aldrich, Professor R., *Joseph Lancaster and Improvements in Education*, an invited lecture on 22 May 1998 at the University of London Institute of Education, pp. 11, 12; and *British and Foreign School Society* website, 2018

573 Notice of formation of Shaftesbury Instructive Institution, dated 30 December 1825, and manuscript notes by John Rutter, S&DHS, D.H.C., D-SHS/Box 41.3421

574 MSS notes by John Rutter on The Shaftesbury Reading Society, S&DHS, D.H.C., D-SHS/Box 41.3421

575 An indenture for the lease of land, 1 January 1839, signed and sealed by the Marquis of Westminster and John Rutter, and an indenture for the release of the same land, 2 January 1839, also signed and sealed by Westminster and Rutter, Gold Hill, D28-7

576 Notice dated April 17th, 1839, printed by C. Rutter, S&DHS, D.H.C., D-SHS/Box 44.2719

577 *Salisbury and Winchester Journal*, 20 January 1840

578 *Le Roter*, p. 44

579 *Salisbury and Winchester Journal*, 4 October 1841

580 *The Third Annual Report of The Shaftesbury Infant School*, 11 August 1841, printed by C. Rutter, Shaftesbury, facsimile copy, Gold Hill

581 *John Bull*, taken from the *Dorset Chronicle*, 14 September 1840, The British Newspaper Archive
582 *Rutter Family*, p. 20
583 Ibid, p. 20
584 Conveyance of property in St James, 29 September 1894, to the Primitive Methodist Connexion (sic), Gold Hill
585 *Kelly's Directory of Shaftesbury*, 1895, p. 146; and Auction Sale particulars of The major portion of the Town of Shaftesbury, Dorsetshire, by Messrs. Fox & Sons of Properties for Sale in Shaftesbury, May 27th, 28th & 29th 1919
586 Long, F.C., *Tales of Old Shaftesbury*, F.C. Long, Shaftesbury, 1979, p. 43
587 *Ordnance Survey*, 25 inch, England and Wales, Dorset IV.14, 1901 and 1929
588 Long, F.C., *Tales of Old Shaftesbury*, F.C. Long, Shaftesbury, 1979, p. 43; and Colin Francis, former church warden of St James' Church
589 *Manchester Times*, 7 September 1850; and Manchester Libraries, Information and Archives – Courtesy of Manchester Libraries, Information and Archives, Manchester City Council
590 Rutter, J., *A Letter to the Commissioners of the Shaftesbury District of Turnpike Roads*, 1827, S&DHS, D.H.C., D-SHS/Box 44.3396, pp. 1–18
591 *Salisbury and Winchester Journal*, 5 November 1838, The British Newspaper Archive
592 Ibid
593 Ibid
594 *Bradshaw's Railway Gazette*, Volume II, No 31, 26 November 1845, p. 714
595 *Exeter & Plymouth Gazette*, 29 November 1845, The British Newspaper Archive
596 Ibid
597 Letter from John Rutter to John Farley Rutter, 19 February 1846, MS Portfolio of Joseph Rutter; *Railway Times*, Volume IX, No. 46, 14 November 1846
598 *Salisbury and Winchester Journal*, 2 January 1847, The British Newspaper Archive
599 *Exeter & Plymouth Gazette*, 24 April 1847, The British Newspaper Archive
600 *Salisbury and Winchester Journal*, 1 May 1847, The British Newspaper Archive; Letter from John Rutter to John Farley Rutter, 2 July 1847, MS Portfolio of Joseph Rutter
601 *Salisbury and Winchester Journal*, 5 February 1848, The British Newspaper Archive
602 *Sherborne Mercury*, 19 August 1848, The British Newspaper Archive
603 *Salisbury and Winchester Journal*, 29 April 1848, The British Newspaper Archive
604 Innes, B., 'Shaftesbury and the Grosvenors', *Dorset Life Magazine*, February 2007, *Dorset Life* website, 2018
605 Letter dated 15 December 1849 from John Rutter to The Most Honourable The (2nd) Marquess of Westminster, Rutter Archives, Gold Hill
606 Innes, B., 'Shaftesbury and the Grosvenors', *Dorset Life Magazine*, February 2007, *Dorset Life* website, 2018
607 *The Report of the Commissioners appointed to enquire into the Municipal Corporations in England and Wales*, March 1835, p. 1353
608 *Corruption and Reform*, p. 22
609 MSS 12, John Rutter, Gold Hill

610 Letter dated 26 January 1832 from John Rutter to John Wallbridge. John Rutter MSS Miscellaneous Manuscripts 1829–1833, S&DHS, D.H.C., D-SHS/Box 41.3387
611 Letter dated 21 August 1833 from John Rutter to Mr Mullens of Semley Union. John Rutter MSS Miscellaneous Manuscripts 1829–1833, S&DHS, D.H.C., D-SHS/Box 41.3387
612 *Rutter Family*, p. 17; and *Le Roter*, p. 43
613 Acland, J., *John Rutter, Enemy of Corporate Despots, Memoirs and Correspondences of a Ghost*, 2010, licensed under a Creative Commons Attribution-Noncommercial - No Derivative Works 3.0 Unported License
614 *Tolpuddle Martyrs'* website, 2018
615 *The Legal Observer, Or, Journal of Jurisprudence*, Volume XV, November 1837 to April 1838, Richards & Co, Fleet Street, London, 1838, p. 78
616 *Sherborne Mercury* of 6 February 1847 reported that Charles Hannen died on 31 January 1847
617 *Sherborne Mercury*, 27 March 1847
618 Letter dated 12 February 1847 from William Hannen to the Freeholders of the County of Dorset, *Sherborne Mercury*, 6 March 1847
619 Thomas Shirley's Scrapbooks, S&DHS, D.H.C., D-SHS/Box 44.2645
620 *Robson's Directory*, 1839, Gold Hill, p. 48
621 Letter dated 19 April 1839 from Ann Elizabeth Rutter to her brother, Clarence, MS Portfolio of Joseph Rutter
622 *Pigot & Co.*, Trade Directory for Shaftesbury & District, 1842, p. 22
623 *Salisbury and Winchester Journal*, 1 February 1845, The British Newspaper Archive
624 Tithe Apportionment for Shaftesbury, 1846
625 *Salisbury and Winchester Journal*, 24 May 1845, The British Newspaper Archive
626 *John Bull*, 9 October 1847, The British Newspaper Archive
627 *Post Office Directory of Dorsetshire, Wiltshire*, W Kelly and Co, Temple Bar, London, 1849, pp. 2696, 2698
628 *Prospectus of Property Protection Society*, Blackfriars, London, S&DHS, D.H.C., D-SHS/Box 44.2802, p. 2
629 Rutter, J., *Register of Subscribers and Payments, Property Protection Society*, S&DHS, D.H.C., D-SHS/Box 44.2802, pp. 1–42
630 *Hunt & Co.'s Directory of Dorsetshire, Hampshire, & Wiltshire*, 1851, p. 170
631 *Le Roter*, p. 46
632 *Le Roter*, p. 48
633 Interview with Peter Tregelles Rutter on 25 March 2018, then aged 94
634 Rutter, F.C., *Descendants of John Farley Rutter*, after Rutter, J.B., The Rutter Family at 1984, published privately, 2004

Appendix 8
Index

This is a selective index of people, places and subjects. Most subjects are grouped under headings for Quakers, John Rutter, and Shaftesbury.

About the Author

JOHN STUTTARD WAS educated at Shrewsbury School and Churchill College, Cambridge. After a year teaching English with VSO in Borneo, he qualified as a chartered accountant with Cooper Brothers & Co (now PwC) in London. During his fifty year career with the firm he worked in the UK and abroad, mainly Finland and the other Nordic countries. He had a spell of two years in the UK Cabinet Office and, later, five years as chairman of the firm in China. During his career he wrote many reports on companies, as well as editing in house magazines and external publications.

His first book, *The New Silk Road – Secrets of Business Success in China Today,* was published by John Wiley in 2000. Since then he has written five further books on very different subjects, *Whittington to World Financial Centre - The City of London and its Lord Mayor,* following his year as Lord Mayor of London in 2006/07, *Travels in a Lifetime; A History of British McCalls; The Worshipful Company of Chartered Accountants in England & Wales – The First Forty Years* and now the biography of John Rutter (1796–1851), *The Turbulent Quaker of Shaftesbury.* He has been a By-Fellow of Churchill College and served as a trustee of many charities. He was honoured in 2004 by the Finnish President as a Commander of the Lion of Finland and was knighted in 2008 by Her Majesty The Queen as a Knight Bachelor.

Lightning Source UK Ltd.
Milton Keynes UK
UKHW051104231120
373920UK00007B/586

9 781906 978631